"Crastnopol's book divides up the world in a whole new way. *Micro-trauma* is a convincing conceptualization of some of the most problematic happenings between people. But despite its novelty—and it is brand new—what Crastnopol describes will be immediately recognizable to any clinician. Add lucid and entertaining writing that is often actually gripping, and you have the makings of a book that will be read at all levels of the field, from students to seasoned analysts."

—**Donnel Stern**, Ph.D., William Alanson
White Institute and New York University
Postdoctoral Program in Psychotherapy
and Psychoanalysis

"Margaret Crastnopol's *Micro-trauma: A Psychoanalytic Understanding of Cumulative Psychic Injury* is an exceptional book in that it's a genuinely original contribution to understanding ourselves and others in our day in/day out, lifelong, prosaic, and most intimate interactions. Crastnopol draws on the full range of psychoanalytic thinking to articulate the many ways that we undermine the self-worth and well-being of one another and of ourselves. Reading this book will help therapists and others, all of us, to better understand and catch ourselves as we subtly and unconsciously invalidate, misrecognize, and are misattuned to ourselves and each other. Her creative and literary explications of such relational dynamics as 'unkind cutting back,' 'psychic airbrushing,' 'chronic entrenchment,' and 'uneasy intimacy,' among many other characterizations, are both immediately useful and unforgettable."

—**Lewis Aron**, Ph.D., Director, New York
University Postdoctoral Program in
Psychotherapy and Psychoanalysis

"In our contemporary 'in-your-face' culture, nuance and subtlety have all but disappeared. Yet these barely-registering phenomena live on in the sounds and silences of the psychoanalytic consulting room. Indeed they are the heart and soul of psychoanalytic discourse. In this superb new contribution, Margaret Crastnopol, an astute observer of those quotidian minutiae that fly under the radar, provides a comprehensive survey of micro-traumas that make up the fabric of our existence but may go unaddressed and unobserved in the hustle and bustle of our everyday lives. She deftly depicts the little murders, the withdrawals, the slights, and the stifled emotions that can wreak havoc on one's sense of well-being, and she shows how psychoanalysis is unique among the panoply of treatments in today's marketplace in its potential for ameliorating the effect of those painful experiences. I highly recommend this book to both beginning clinicians and experienced analysts."

—**Glen O. Gabbard**, MD, Author, *Love and
Hate in the Analytic Setting*

Micro-trauma

Micro-trauma: A Psychoanalytic Understanding of Cumulative Psychic Injury explores the "micro-traumatic" or small, subtle psychic hurts that build up to undermine a person's sense of self-worth, skewing his or her character and compromising his or her relatedness to others. These injuries amount to what has been previously called "cumulative" or "relational trauma". Until now, psychoanalysis has explained such negative influences in broad strokes, using general concepts such as psychosexual urges, narcissistic needs, and separation-individuation aims, among others. Taking a fresh approach, Margaret Crastnopol identifies certain specific patterns of injurious relating that cause damage in predictable ways; she shows how these destructive processes can be identified, stopped in their tracks, and replaced by a healthier way of functioning.

Seven different types of micro-trauma, all largely hidden in plain sight, are described in detail, and many others are discussed more briefly. Three of these micro-traumas— "psychic airbrushing and excessive niceness," "uneasy intimacy," and "connoisseurship gone awry"—have a predominantly positive emotional tone, while the other four—"unkind cutting back," "unbridled indignation," "chronic entrenchment," and "little murders"— have a distinctly negative one. Margaret Crastnopol shows how these toxic processes may take place within a dyadic relationship, a family group, or a social clique, thereby causing collateral psychic damage all around.

Using illustrations drawn from psychoanalytic treatment, literary fiction, and everyday life, *Micro-trauma* outlines how each micro-traumatic pattern develops and manifests itself, and how it wreaks its damage. The book shows how an awareness of these patterns can give us the therapeutic leverage needed to reshape them for the good. This publication will be an invaluable resource for psychoanalysts, psychologists, psychiatrists, mental health counselors, social workers, marriage and family therapists, and for trainees and graduate students in these fields and related disciplines.

Margaret Crastnopol (Peggy), Ph.D., is a faculty member of the Seattle Psychoanalytic Society and Institute, and a supervisor of psychotherapy at the William Alanson White Institute of Psychiatry, Psychoanalysis, and Psychology. She is also a training and supervising analyst at the Institute of Contemporary Psychoanalysis, Los Angeles. She writes and teaches nationally and internationally about the analyst's and patient's subjectivity; the vicissitudes of love, lust, and attachment drives; and varieties of micro-trauma. She is in private practice for the treatment of individuals and couples in Seattle, Washington.

PSYCHOANALYSIS IN A NEW KEY BOOK SERIES

DONNEL STERN

Series Editor

When music is played in a new key, the melody does not change, but the notes that make up the composition do: change in the context of continuity, continuity that perseveres through change. Psychoanalysis in a New Key publishes books that share the aims psychoanalysts have always had, but that approach them differently. The books in the series are not expected to advance any particular theoretical agenda, although to this date most have been written by analysts from the Interpersonal and Relational orientations.

The most important contribution of a psychoanalytic book is the communication of something that nudges the reader's grasp of clinical theory and practice in an unexpected direction. Psychoanalysis in a New Key creates a deliberate focus on innovative and unsettling clinical thinking. Because that kind of thinking is encouraged by exploration of the sometimes surprising contributions to psychoanalysis of ideas and findings from other fields, Psychoanalysis in a New Key particularly encourages interdisciplinary studies. Books in the series have married psychoanalysis with dissociation, trauma theory, sociology, and criminology. The series is open to the consideration of studies examining the relationship between psychoanalysis and any other field—for instance, biology, literary and art criticism, philosophy, systems theory, anthropology, and political theory.

But innovation also takes place within the boundaries of psychoanalysis, and Psychoanalysis in a New Key therefore also presents work that reformulates thought and practice without leaving the precincts of the field. Books in the series focus, for example, on the significance of personal values in psychoanalytic practice, on the complex interrelationship between the analyst's clinical work and personal life, on the consequences for the clinical situation when patient and analyst are from different cultures, and on the need for psychoanalysts to accept the degree to which they knowingly satisfy their own wishes during treatment hours, often to the patient's detriment.

Micro-trauma

A Psychoanalytic Understanding of Cumulative Psychic Injury

Margaret Crastnopol

Routledge
Taylor & Francis Group

NEW YORK AND LONDON

First published 2015
by Routledge
711 Third Avenue, New York, NY 10017

and by Routledge
27 Church Road, Hove, East Sussex, BN3 2FA

Routledge is an imprint of the Taylor & Francis Group, an informa business

Library of Congress Cataloging in Publication Data
Crastnopol, Margaret, author.
Micro-trauma: a psychoanalytic understanding of cumulative psychic injury/
authored by Margaret Crastnopol.
p. ; cm — (Psychoanalysis in a new key ; vol. 25)
I. Title. II. Series: Psychoanalysis in a new key book series ; v. 25.
[DNLM: 1. Stress, Psychological—etiology. 2. Psychoanalytic
Therapy—methods. WM 172.4]
RC506
616.89'17—dc23
2014030466

ISBN: 978-0-415-80035-8 (hbk)
ISBN: 978-0-415-80036-5 (pbk)
ISBN: 978-0-203-87889-7 (ebk)

Typeset in Times New Roman
by Swales & Willis Ltd, Exeter, Devon, UK

Printed and bound in the United States of America by
Edwards Brothers Malloy on sustainably sourced paper

For Charles, Zachary, Evan, and Julia Purcell

Contents

Acknowledgments

I am indebted to many special individuals for their contributions to my efforts to write this book. In the most fundamental way, my late parents Dr. Philip Crastnopol and Madeleine Lasko Crastnopol helped me believe enough in myself that I could concentrate on trying to grasp what needed to be known. Their unstinting love, generosity, and intelligence launched and helped shape me to become the person and the psychoanalyst that I am. My sister Joan Friedland accompanied me caringly as we weathered our respective challenges as our parents' children and our children's parents.

I am fortunate to have an extraordinarily supportive family—my husband Charles and my three children Evan, Zachary, and Julia Purcell. Their fresh, sterling insights about both the inner and outer world have greatly enriched my understanding, and the gracious sacrifices they made on my behalf as I buried myself in my study to write meant the world to me. Charles has been my mainstay in this as in every other venture I've undertaken throughout our life together. His brilliance, wittiness, equanimity, good humor, and love nourish me on a daily basis.

Raul Ludmer is a fount of intuition, wisdom, and foresight. His depth of understanding and attuned encouragement have been immeasurably important to me for many years. Dodi Goldman has been a major interlocutor, muse, model, and spur for me. A remarkable friend and colleague, his wise and incisive observations and prodigious scholarship enriched each chapter either directly or implicitly. I am thoroughly in his debt. Robin Shafran, my "psychoanalytic sibling," is the quintessential friend and co-traveler who has been by my side through thick and thin for more than 30 years. Keenly perceptive, sensitive, and thoughtful, Robin always went directly to the heart of the matter in helping me shape and refine my thinking. Graciously reading and listening to earlier iterations of my ideas, Ladson Hinton kept me focused on the larger philosophical aspects of psychic phenomena. Deborah

Ashin's creative, warm-hearted, and sensitive perceptions of human nature, as well as her great skill as a wordsmith and writer, added a special dimension to my own writing process. Daphne Tomchak, with her razor-sharp intellect and broad range of knowledge, challenged me to be even more direct and rigorous in formulating my arguments. As someone exceedingly wise in the ways of the world and of our field in particular, Karol Marshall has been a most generous guide and mentor to me over the years. Naomi Bach Yellen taught me much about scholarship, resilience, devotedness, and the uses of humor, for which I am extremely appreciative. It would have been next to impossible for me to have worked on, much less completed this book, without the devoted involvement of Maria Anderson and Denise Antoine, who watched over our hearth and home when I couldn't.

Years ago, the late Stephen Mitchell, a wellspring of penetrating and creative thought, gave me what felt like his imprimatur and encouragement to proceed with my own variant of contemporary psychoanalytic thinking. I was also fortunate enough to work during that formative period with the dynamic Philip Bromberg, whose influence on me was highly beneficial. I am profoundly grateful to them both, as well as to the many other gifted supervisors and faculty members I came to know at the William Alanson White Institute. Speaking of the institute's impact, I heartily thank Don Greif and Ruth Livingston, the current editors-in-chief extraordinaire of its journal, *Contemporary Psychoanalysis*, for their invaluable help with earlier versions of several chapters.

As the editor of the series of which this book is a part, Donnel Stern was a wonderful support and a crucial guiding light throughout the conceptualizing, researching, and writing process. I benefited greatly from the background influence of Lewis Aron, Judy Kantrowitz, Margaret Black Mitchell, and Stephen Seligman, all of whom spurred me onward through their encouraging words and, especially, their inspiring example. My thanks also to all the others who gave constructive input along the way to earlier drafts of this work.

A number of close friends and colleagues each added something unique to my life and therefore to the growth of this project. They are Alejandro Avila Espada, Richard Bradspies, Sandra Buechler, Anjali Dixit, Glen Gabbard, the late Emmanuel Ghent, Robin Greenstein, Laura Martin, Casey and Doug Rosenberg, Wendie Rosenberg, Dan Sadler, Gail Wittkin Sasso, and Susan Sodergren. Each of these individuals has my deep admiration and hearty thanks.

I am enormously grateful to the incomparable John Kerr, whose ministrations deepened and broadened my psychoanalytic scholarship, furthered my self-expression, and sharpened my writing capabilities. His wealth of knowledge of the field and his sensitivity to clinical currents as well as to the reader's experience of spending time with me were of inestimable value. Kristopher Spring's finely tuned copy-editing caught much that my eye missed. His editorial organizational skills are nonpareil, and he unflappably brought the manuscript home. I was most fortunate to have his help. The great expertise and gracious supportiveness of Kate Hawes, Senior Publisher at Routledge, made what seemed impossible, possible for me. Without her stalwart presence over the years, there would have been no book. Further thanks go to Kirsten Buchanan and Susan Wickenden, also at Routledge, whose savvy and patience helped turn manuscript files into final, publishable pages.

Finally, I am greatly appreciative of and beholden to the women and men in my psychoanalytic practice who allowed me to accompany them on their journey toward analytic self-understanding and growth. The real people who inspired the examples I offer in this book have, through their own travails, taught me a great deal of what I've come to know about accumulated hurts, including how to tolerate working on them and pursuing their repair. I humbly thank those who so graciously permitted me to write about aspects of their lives and their clinical work.

Credit Lines

Chapter 1

Cumulative Micro-trauma that's Hidden in Plain Sight

An Overview

"Oh, sweetheart," an elderly woman crooned to her grandson, a late adolescent now verging on manhood, "That jacket of your father's looks marvelous on you—so much better than it ever did on him!" Caught up short by the last phrase—"better than it ever did on him"—the young man inwardly puffed up and cringed at the same time. He couldn't help but note both the compliment and the sideways swipe at his father, who was in the next room and could easily have overheard the grandmother's words.

The inner confusion carried over into his psychoanalytic session the next day, when the young man tried to sort out his response to the unnerving comment. He was proud to have his masculinity savored, pleased at this minor Oedipal victory, and guilty over having been praised at his father's expense—and having enjoyed it. But further thoughts, some rather insidious, cropped up in his mind. If his grandmother could cast aspersions on her own son's (that is, his father's) appearance behind his back, what might she be saying about the grandson himself when he was out of earshot? Did his grandmother perhaps enjoy elevating him over his father, and if so, why? How much love was actually there, underneath her doting tone? This changing body of his was beginning to feel a bit like a lightning rod. Could he afford to relish its new features, or was that asking for trouble? Well, maybe he was just being hypersensitive, letting himself get drawn into a kind of introspective morass by that bothersome psychoanalyst of his.

A throwaway remark such as the elderly woman's double-edged flattery can easily be dismissed or go unnoticed entirely. Injurious relating on the grossly abusive end of the scale is the time-honored stuff of history, fiction, drama, and contemporary psychoanalytic theory. But negative interactions that are evanescent can ultimately also have a strong psychic impact. Like sharp rocks only vaguely if at all visible beneath the water at the shore, such potentially damaging moments may go largely unregistered. As a result, these subtler occurrences, especially in the aggregate, can create psychic bruises that are hard to notice and harder to minister to, with the consequence that they accumulate invisibly. Such injuries can distort a person's character, undermine his or her sense of self-worth, and compromise his or her relatedness to others.

I call such emotional strafing "micro-trauma" and will argue in this book that discerning the operation of micro-traumas is an important aspect of psychoanalytic work. As Heraclitus (*c.*500 BCE) observed: "What we saw and grasped, that we leave behind; but what we did not see and did not grasp, that we bring." Or, as Sigmund Freud (1909) put it, "A thing which has not been understood inevitably reappears; like an unlaid ghost, it cannot rest until the mystery has been solved and the spell broken" (p. 122). The noted psychoanalyst Hans Loewald (1980) also invoked ghosts: "In the daylight of analysis the ghosts of the unconscious are laid to rest as ancestors whose power is taken over and transformed into the new intensity of present life . . . " (p. 249). This book aims to facilitate the understanding of those ghosts, so that as known, neutralized influences rather than surreptitiously toxic ones, they can be integrated into the richness and complexity of one's contemporary psychic experience.

Many individuals in today's world chronically experience a sense of low-level depressiveness, anxiety, and malaise. They present themselves for psychoanalytic work—if they do indeed seek treatment—with the disoriented feeling that they shouldn't need help, as there was nothing especially traumatic about their upbringing or childhood experiences. They express shame at not being able to lay claim to a dramatic, discrete source that could account for their garden-variety yet deep and thoroughgoing unhappiness. In fact, such people may attest to having felt more or less well-loved within their original family circle; they may recognize their good fortune at having material security and personal success; they may insist that there is nothing really wrong in their lives. This makes them that much more ashamed and self-critical in relation to their unhappy internal state. These kinds of obscure complaints or self-mystified anxieties are, of course, not new in psychoanalysis. Indeed, much of the recent interchange between developmental research and analytic theorizing is based on trying to understand patients like these in terms of "insecure attachment" (see Beebe & Lachmann, 2014), "pathological accommodation" to insufficiently responsive caretakers (Brandchaft et al., 2010), or a similar early skewing of the self. Moreover, the current developmental focus is based on a long, preexisting tradition within psychoanalysis of emphasizing "cumulative trauma," "strain trauma," and the like, which are viewed as stemming from early childhood; the literature pertaining to these subjects will be reviewed shortly.

All of this seeks to connect our patients' current distress and their character issues with pronounced disruptions in their earlier psychic formation within the original relational matrix. While probing that early territory is essential, in this book I will take a somewhat different tack. I will suggest that to understand the kind of psychic trouble I've just described, we need to look also—and sometimes instead—at smaller scale, repetitive interactive events, and we need to pay attention to those that happen not only early on, but also *wherever* they've occurred in the life cycle. I will recommend that we focus on the residues these particular events leave and on their manifestation or recurrence in one's contemporary way of being. To be sure, exploring day-to-day relating in a minute way is scarcely new. It has long been one of the pillars of relational and interpersonalist thinking (see especially Aron, 1996; Levenson, 1991; Mitchell, 2000; Mitchell & Aron, 1999; Stern, 2010) as well as certain self-psychological and intersubjective positions (e.g., Stolorow & Atwood, 1992). These approaches have looked at generalized patterns occurring within an interpersonal or interpsychic matrix, wherein (under unfavorable conditions) a person's anxiety is heightened and self-esteem lowered as a function of the conscious and unconscious influence two individuals have on one another. In this book, however, I want to narrow the focus from generalized patterns to certain specific types of problematic relational experiences, a number of which I will describe in detail. These "micro-traumatic" situations—some operative previously in life, but most also present in an ongoing way—can be hidden in plain sight; since these injurious moments occur within relationships that are otherwise felt to be valuable, the individual may be motivated to ignore them in service of not rocking the relational boat. Yet, as we shall see, they can seriously compromise the individual's ability to get out of the relationship what he or she puts into it or what such a relationship should indeed offer. Whether we think of the benefits of adult relationships in terms of attachment, dependency, self–object needs, or some other dimension, if micro-traumas in relation to the other accumulate, the individual will be burdened by fraught, contradictory feelings about him- or herself in the world.

As I've said, in my experience, patients may not necessarily notice and complain about micro-traumatic moments; often, they do not register them

at all. Or if these individuals have some inkling as to what it is about interacting with the other that injures them emotionally, the moments of special
hurt seem too small, too off-hand to have been truly impactful. He or she
may say: "It's no one thing that bothers me, since after all, each one is so
trivial; it's all of them put together, one on top of the other, that just feels
like too much and gets to me—though probably they shouldn't!" So, for
example, the unsung factor in much adult depression may be precisely this
pattern of small insults or failures that amass to seemingly prove one is
inadequate, contemptible, or outright bad. These minor injuries may—but
then again, may not—trace back to deeper, more malignant ones; vulnerability to these hurts likewise may—but then again, may not—spring from
deeper wellsprings. Regardless, the result is a psychic bruising that builds
imperceptibly over time, little by little eroding a person's sense of self-
worth and well-being. This build-up can happen in the context of a childhood or current relationship with a parent or with another close loved one,
but it can also develop in a long-term educational or work setting, or in
other social contexts that constitute important parts of one's life.

Micro-traumatic experience is by definition something that is under-
played, and as such, its impact remains unarticulated, dissociated, or suppressed. Because one hasn't seen the cuff coming or registered its full
impact, one hasn't defended oneself adequately. One hasn't taken either
the reparative or protective steps that might ease the injury in its aftermath
or guard against reoccurrences. So the damage mounts, and the result is
a skewing in one's sense of goodness, efficacy, or cohesion. In considering the significance of such day-to-day bruises, the analytic imagination
turns readily—in fact, sometimes too readily—to early life. This tendency
was termed a "developmental tilt" by Stephen Mitchell (1988). Certainly,
being wounded or betrayed emotionally by one's earliest significant others
during infancy and childhood can create a sequestered doubt that poses a
formidable resistance to creating generative bonds later in life. And micro-
traumatic moments may be part of the texture of those early hurts—and,
of course, merit close investigation as such. But similar or even brand new
patterns can also occur in later years and present their own significant difficulties. Like the young man who wondered about that disquieting compliment—and also about his analyst's harping on it—a person can become
so accustomed to there being a subtle destructiveness in his or her relationships that he or she ends up becoming inoculated against fully trusting
others—one's psychotherapist or psychoanalyst included. In effect, the
person comes automatically to overlook or "selectively inattend to," in

Sullivan's (1953) terms, someone else's moderately injurious maltreatment in order to sustain a sense of being a good self loved by a good other. This habitual ignoring results in dissociated anxiety that undermines a coherent and valued sense of self as well as a trusting relatedness to others.

Trauma and Micro-trauma

From a psychoanalytic perspective, the concept of trauma has come to mean, in the words of Laplanche and Pontalis (1973), "an event in the subject's life defined by its intensity, by the subject's incapacity to respond adequately to it, and by the upheaval and long-lasting effects that it brings about in the psychical organization" (p. 465). Laplanche and Pontalis go on to situate the idea of trauma within a Freudian economic perspective, that is, in terms of "excessive excitation" or of an accumulation of smaller excitations, either of which exceeds the tolerance of the psychic apparatus. If that build-up cannot be discharged or worked out and integrated into one's overall psychic functioning, then it remains present to undermine one's psychical organization.

The idea of an accretion of smaller excitations described by Laplanche and Pontalis anticipates the sense of my term *micro*-trauma as a way to differentiate repeated, built-up, minor hurts from massive, more egregious ones. The micro version is less intense, less obvious or direct in its destructive quality, and therefore more plausibly (though just as incorrectly) deniable by oneself or the other. The hurtful quality may reside only in the tonal undercurrents or peripheral implications of the act rather than in its main message. The overall interpersonal setting is, of course, a crucial factor as well—in certain circumstances, a hostile or critical act could be troublesome without necessarily being traumatic at either the micro or macro level. Much depends on the ongoing characters of the individuals involved, the health of their relationship, and sundry other factors.

Many dedicated social scientists and psychodynamic theorists have worked to document the horrific psychic effects of personal and massive atrocities in the real world. Among these pioneering early figures are Henry Krystal (1968, 1971, 1985, 1991, 1994, 1997), Judith Lewis Herman (1992), and Bessel Van der Kolk (1987; Van der Kolk et al., 1996), along with such contemporary theorists as Onno Van der Hart (Van der Hart et al., 2006), Jody Messler Davies and Mary Gail Frawley (1992, 1994), Sue Grand (2002), Elizabeth Howell (2005), Ghislaine Boulanger (2007), and others. To these contributors it may seem oxymoronic—or seriously misguided—to speak of any sort of trauma that could be of micro proportions. My using the term micro-trauma might seem to them like a trivialization of something vastly more impactful—Trauma—whose effect should not be watered down. I would counter that micro-trauma, just like "capital T" trauma itself, is consequential in its own way. It is akin to massive real-world trauma in that it reflects events in the external world and is not merely a private experience involving unconscious impulses or fantasies. And just as in "capital T" trauma, these real occurrences are experienced and absorbed to shape the intrapsychic world in particular ways that have lasting negative consequences for one's sense of psychological well-being, safety, and security. Micro-traumas, like those on the macro scale, call forth defensive operations that themselves often further dampen or distort aspects of self-expression, thwart self-cohesion, and bleed into ongoing relationships as they develop onward into the future.

My nomenclature's allusion to trauma is in keeping with the Freudian view I just mentioned (Laplanche & Pontalis, 1973) that a series of smaller psychic excitations can accumulate to have a large distorting effect on the self. I suggest, moreover, that to the degree that the development and organization of the self has been previously undermined by lesser degrees of insult and injury (that is, what I'm calling micro-trauma), it will be that much more vulnerable to the corrosive effects of more intense psychic assaults (that is, severe trauma proper). I concur with Freud's idea that the overall *empfanglichkeit* or "predisposition" of the self influences how any new psychic shock is experienced. I also believe that this predisposition continues to be shaped in an ongoing way both by constitutional factors such as temperament and by the prior interactions—be they neutral, constructive, micro-traumatic, or obviously traumatic—that the individual has undergone since birth.

Consider a newly pregnant woman who, let's say, is someone prone by temperament to be easily made anxious. Let's say further that her husband responds to her worries and fears about becoming a mother by retreating to his email correspondence, playing an extra round of videogames, or spending longer hours at the office. In what I call "unkind cutting back," the man deprives the woman of the comfort that closer contact would likely provide, instead of taking steps that might counterbalance her habitual, now-magnified anxiety. The husband's avoidance of his wife and her issues may be no more than his own effort at psychic self-protection to avoid recognizing his own underlying concerns about parenthood. Yet she may read it as an implicit rejection of her, as if he viewed her as inadequate for having the worries to begin with, or looked down on her for her inability to quell them all by herself. Should the husband's withdrawal evolve into a more chronic pattern of cutting back on his wife, both physically and emotionally, it would likely erode over time the wife's belief in her own competence and worth. Feeling this way could reflexively undermine her mothering capabilities, thus actualizing the very same dreaded self-image of being inept that the husband's distancing held for his wife symbolically. Of course, the husband's withdrawal in any one moment probably wouldn't be enough to undermine the woman's psychic security for good, but as a steady drumbeat it might make a major incursion on it over time. I believe that, in just this fashion, small psychic abandonments, blows, and betrayals—even if not intended as such—can mount up and combine with one's underlying psychic tendencies to disrupt our emotional functioning in a profound way.

In the chapters that follow, I discuss seven different types of microtrauma in some detail, and then others more briefly. My catalog is an idiosyncratically selective—one could even say accidental—list that is necessarily more preliminary or suggestive than exhaustive. I have chosen these specific practices because each has in some way cried out to me to be articulated by virtue of the role it has played in the lives of patients, friends, or myself. The kind of interpersonal, interpsychic, or intrapsychic occurrence that delivers this small jolt to the self can take many guises, some seemingly rewarding and having a predominantly positive emotional tone, others more explicitly punitive and having a predominantly negative one. Among those that have an upbeat feel are what I will call "airbrushing and excessive niceness," or inflating oneself or the other by minimizing or covering over flaws; "uneasy intimacy," an intensified closeness that tends toward co-opting the other; and "connoisseurship gone awry," in which one person inculcates the habit of making fine distinctions in another in a way that ends up undercutting the other's equanimity and sense of self-worth.

Four versions of micro-trauma with a largely negative cast are "unkind cutting back" (illustrated briefly above), which is a seemingly arbitrary withdrawal from prior involvement, often motivated by unexpressed anxiety or anger; "unbridled indignation," a moralistic stance that can backfire, undermining one's own or the other's sense of well-being, efficacy, and moral goodness; "chronic entrenchment," being locked into either a self-diminishing or overly self-contented attitude in a way that generates collateral damage in others; and "little murders," which can range from simple slights to ample putdowns delivered in an off-hand manner.

Each type of micro-trauma is underwritten by its own admixture of narcissistic self-investment, hostility, envy, indifference, anxiety, or shame. But in each, the party inflicting the hurt maintains a semblance of being at least measured and neutral, if not well-meaning and benevolent. Some micro-traumatic relating is conscious and intentional and some unconscious or inadvertent. It may be registered as meanness by the injured party or may do its damage subliminally. It may occur within a dyadic relationship, a family group or clique, or a larger social system whose policies consistently injure in some fashion (see Sue, 2010, and below). An instigator's micro-traumatic relating hurts the other but often inadvertently also depletes him- or herself as well. Elusive and ephemeral as they sometimes are, the micro-traumatic processes I address—and other varieties yet to be formally articulated—beg for our closer attention.

Theoretical Considerations and Related Concepts

Khan's "Cumulative Trauma" and Kris' "Strain Trauma"

In the face of ongoing micro-traumatic experience, one could in principle always leave the relationship. Yet, this is precisely what tends not to happen. The reason micro-traumatic relating can mount up into a damaging pattern is that if there is anything good to be had from our significant others at all, we are prone to staying connected with them even after they've wounded us. The urgent need for ongoing connection is the prime motivator in human behavior, according to theorists of the Independent British object relations school (Kohon, 1986). To recognize inadequacy or outright badness in a mostly good other feels self-depleting, because it calls into question the health and viability of the attachment. In acknowledging the other's badness, we would thereby be sullying the good in them, as well as damning ourselves too by identificatory association.

D. W. Winnicott (1965) helped set the stage for an appreciation of the disruptive impact of chronic, steadily destructive relating when he observed, "Often, the environmental factor is not a single trauma but a pattern of distorting influences: the opposite, in fact, of the facilitating environment which allows of individual maturation" (p. 139). Masud Khan (1963, 1964) picked up on this theme in calling the accrual of discrete injurious moments "cumulative trauma." (I am, of course, standing on Khan's shoulders in my formulation of cumulative *micro*-trauma or psychic injury.) For Khan and Winnicott, such trauma was situated squarely in the early mother–child relationship, representing breaches in the mother's role as a protective shield . . . from infancy to adolescence—that is to say, in all those areas of experience where the child continues to need the mother as an auxiliary ego to support his immature and unstable ego functions.

(Khan, 1963, p. 290)

In other words, by virtue of her or his own needs and psychic makeup, the parent may inadvertently thwart the child's efforts to cope with the anxieties inherent in psychological development. This maladaptation of the parent to the child's dependency needs creates a chronic tension that doesn't inflict dramatic damage but instead gradually biases or undermines the child's psychic maturation.

With the idea of a chronic, cumulative tension that disrupts healthy development, Khan was also picking up on the earlier comments of Ernst Kris (1956), who distinguished the "shock trauma" entailed in a single horrific experience from "the effect of long-lasting situations, which may cause traumatic effects by the accumulation of frustrating tensions—the strain trauma" (p.72). Kris explains:

It is well known and has not long ago been emphasized by Anna Freud (1950) that what the analytic patient reports as an event which had taken place once appears in the life of the growing child as a more or less typical experience, which may have been repeated many times. Her suggestion, then, is that analysts tend to be misled by the telescopic character of memory. On the other hand, the single dramatic shock, e.g., seduction at an early age, appears not with sharp outline; the experience is overlaid with its aftermath, the guilt, terror and thrill elaborated in fantasy, and the defense against these fantasies. We are misled if we believe that we are, except in rare instances, able to find the "events" of the afternoon on the staircase when the seduction happened: we are dealing with the whole period in which the seduction played a role—and in some instances this period may be an extended one. The problem is further complicated by the fact that the further course of life seems to determine which experience may gain significance as a traumatic one.

(p. 72)

In identifying "strain trauma," Kris was thus pointing to the type of damage inflicted habitually by an *overall* psychic environment that could erode an individual's well-being and be equivalent to the infliction of a massive psychic assault. But he was also bringing attention to bear on an epistemic point—namely, that the victim or the interpreting analyst might well "tele-scope" multiple events and thereby create a possibly fictive single trauma. My own experience suggests that in the area of micro-trauma at least, tele-scoping betrays itself when the reaction to the event seems truly dispropor-tionate; under these circumstances, we often discover on further inquiry that the particular blow was only the latest in a series. Beyond this, I would aug-ment both of these theorists' views by suggesting that "impingements"— failures to shield, but also in my view, direct and active attacks of whatever intensity—can have profoundly biasing consequences in terms of emotional equilibrium even when they are first encountered only much later in adoles-cence or in adulthood—that is, past the point where one would ordinarily think the now almost-grown child would need parental benevolence. Also, parents are not the only ones whose infractions can be so destructive. Other significant family members, long-term friends, romantic partners, and even close adult associates can also wreak considerable damage.

In his writings about cumulative trauma, Khan goes on to argue that impingements are not necessarily recognizable as traumatic in the context wherein they occur, but may come to light only retrospectively and as they build up. He is careful to add that thinking about cumulative trauma as a recur rent "failure in environmental provisions" averts the potential damage that can be perpetrated by "incriminating reconstructions" that target a supposed bad, seducing mother or such "anthropomorphic part-object constructs as 'good' and 'bad' breast" (1963, pp. 291–292). These types of Kleinian-influenced object relations formulations, in his view, unfairly judge the female parent and muddy our understanding of the fuller parent–child relationship as it shapes the child's inner world. The implication is that "part object" formulations give too much weight to hypothesized unconscious fantasies and not enough weight to the actual interactions with the real, live, external parent.

Khan's perspective suggests that we should look at the whole spectrum of a formative relationship—I would add current relationship as well— with its varyingly favorable, not-so-good, and unfavorable aspects. In my view, micro-trauma is what it is—undramatic, hidden, cumulative—in part because it occurs in the context of seemingly "good-enough" relating. It's the presence of the good with the bad, the pleasure with the pain, that keeps the damaged one connected and coming back for more.

Fairbairn and Sullivan

My views on the "venial sins" of micro-traumatic relating have taken shape under the influence of particular Independent School object relations theorists, interpersonalists, and relational analytic writers. Especially compelling for me are the ideas of W. R. D. Fairbairn and Harry Stack Sullivan. According to Fairbairn's (1952) view, and in keeping with Ogden's (2010) exegesis of it, a person wants to preserve a view of the self as being healthily loved by a good other. But as others are imperfect and often frustrate one's needs and wishes, the child develops ambivalence toward the other that greatly complicates his or her psychic development. To the degree that the other is experienced as hostile or destructive, this "bad other" is controlled by being internalized into the self and split into an inner rejecting object and an inner exciting object. The exciting object is linked to an internalized "libidinal ego," the latter being the hopeful inner self that seeks to be loved by the object. (It seems to me that it is this attachment of a hopeful inner self to the internalized exciting object that inclines someone to stay close to the outer, not-so-good, "actual" other, a situation that underpins the perpetuation of certain types of micro-trauma—such as, for instance, connoisseurship gone awry.) At the same time, the inner rejecting object is linked to an internalized "anti-libidinal ego," also called quite evocatively the "internal saboteur." Fairbairn argues that this internal saboteur, the negative aspect of the self, is unremittingly aggressive toward the libidinal ego—that is, the love-seeking aspect of the self. (Here we may have a substrate for certain negatively-toned micro-trauma—including, for example, little murders.)

This psychic interplay clearly involves pursuing, while shaming oneself for pursuing, a connection with the inner exciting object, the latter of course being the internal representation of the tantalizing, actual other whose approval one can never definitively win. In the situations I consider, the inner exciting object is not egregiously bad or bad on a chronic basis; it is moderate in its destructiveness and seemingly arbitrary in its bestowal of approval and nurturance. So the inner "hopeful" self remains hopeful, if only tenuously so (see Fairbairn, 1952, pp. 114–115, 168–173). And this side of the self must endure the mistrust and self-shaming inflicted by the internal saboteur, not to mention the internal rejecting object. This makes fertile ground for self-disparagement and pessimism. Highly ambivalent inner relations that are so adhesive pave the way to interacting externally in recurrently micro-traumatic ways. In other words, variations of this scenario could represent the intrapsychic mechanisms generated by and underlying further external micro-traumatic functioning. To be clear, what makes the Fairbairnian inner dynamics and the bond with the external other so adhesive is the actual other's status as an often-enough good, often-enough loving other who in certain *particular* respects behaves hurtfully.[1]

Harry Stack Sullivan (1953) put anxiety and its interpersonal arousal at the center of his theorizing, unseating sexual and aggressive urges as prime motivators of psychological maturation. Sullivan believed that a modulated level of anxiety reflected a flexible, realistic self-system. The self-system originated, in the first instance, through the vagaries of anxiety and approval in the interaction with the mothering figure.

For Sullivan, the paradigmatic interaction was feeding, in which the mother might offer a "good," "bad," or "wrong nipple." The good nipple was satiating and therefore gratifying, the wrong one was "unusable" for appeasing hunger, and the bad nipple was one that communicated maternal anxiety and instilled it in the baby. Through experiences with these nipples (which come to stand for "aspects of the other"), the person develops a sense of what is "good-me," "bad-me," and "not-me." The self-system, as it develops, seeks to avoid experiences of being either the bad-me or the not-me. Sullivan (1953, p. 162) explains the bad-me in this way:

> *Bad-me* on the other hand, is the beginning personification which organizes experience in which increasing degrees of anxiety are associated with behavior involving the mothering one in its more or less clearly prehended interpersonal setting. That is to say, bad-me is based on this increasing gradient of anxiety and that, in turn, is dependent, at this stage of life, on the observation, if misinterpretation, of the infant's behavior by someone who can induce anxiety. The frequent coincidence of certain behavior on the part of the infant with increasing tenseness and increasingly evident forbidding on the part of the mother is the source of the type of experience which is organized as a rudimentary personification to which we may apply the term bad-me.

The bad-me is thus an image of oneself comprised of one's worst, most undesirable qualities, ones that garnered the most disapproval from significant others. To repeat, the self-system from the first seeks to avoid bad-me experiences if possible. The bad-me is the basis on which we hate or reject ourselves, whereas the not-me is so horrifyingly unacceptable that it is unthinkable. The mother shows what is objectionable to her and the wider society—and helps the child learn how to discriminate these features—through the unconscious or unformulated communication of her own wishes, needs, and values. (All of this is implicitly powered by her own anxiety and efforts to quell it.) She does this through the medium of "forbidding gestures":

This matter of the infant's refined discrimination of what we call forbidding gestures first applies to the mother and thereafter applies throughout life to practically all significant people—that is, those people who come to have an important place in his living, in other words, his interpersonal relationships. The discrimination of heard differences in the mother's vocalization and seen differences in the postural tensions of the mother's face, and perhaps later of differences in speed and rhythm of her gross bodily movements in coming toward the infant, presenting the bottle, changing the diapers, or what not— all these rather refined discriminations by the distance receptors of vision and hearing are organized as indices frequently associated with the unpleasant experience of anxiety, including the nipple of anxiety instead of the good nipple. As such indices, these discriminations, the organization of the data of these discriminations, become *signs of signs*—signs for other signs of avoidance, such as the nipple when the mother is anxious.

(Sullivan, 1953, pp. 86–87)

So the vulnerability of the self-system to anxiety, its need to ward off bad-me experiences, becomes the basis for educating the child. In other words, there are particular seeable and knowable expressions coming from the other that indicate that a given aspect of the child will invite disapproval, loss of emotional security, and a reduced sense of being loved and cherished. These are the forbidding gestures that come at first from the mothering one, but later from other important individuals in one's life. These gestures arouse one's anxiety in that they point to the bad-me—or, in extreme cases, the not-me.

Of course, for Sullivan, in contrast to Freudians or object relations theorists, the actual quotidian moment-by-moment interactions between self and other were key to understanding the development of psychic life. In fact, he spoke about the central component for understanding an individual's character or personality as being a *dynamism*, which he described as "the relatively enduring pattern of energy transformations which recurrently characterize the organism in its duration as a living organism" (1953, p. 103). So someone's individual psyche is not a function of a particular drive or drive derivatives, defensive structures, fixed attributes, or intrapsychic agencies. Instead, one's psyche is a much more fluid and contextualized thing, being a composite of the pattern of one's customary styles of relating to others (see Jones, 1995, p. 315). The self-system is one such dynamism:

The self-system thus is an organization of educative experience called into being by the necessity to avoid or minimize incidents of anxiety. The functional activity of the self-system—I am speaking of it from the general standpoint of a dynamism—is primarily directed to avoiding and minimizing this disjunctive tension of anxiety, and thus indirectly to protecting the infant from this evil eventuality in connection with the pursuit of satisfactions—the relief of general or of zonal tensions.

(Sullivan, 1953, pp. 165–166)

So the self-system is a necessary, generalized dynamism in all individuals. And, insofar as it closes off certain domains of experience in order to avoid anxiety, it is also potentially a source of unrealistic appraisals, of both self and other, in all individuals. This provides a ready explanation for why micro-traumatic relating can fly under the radar even though it is injurious—because examining it might raise more anxiety than the individual's self-system is prepared to deal with.

In Sullivan's nomenclature, the term *dynamism* also refers to certain specific patterns of behavior such as obsessionalism or selective inattention that a person may characteristically overuse in times of stress. Jones (1995, p. 316) explains it this way:

A mental disorder is said to exist when a dynamism is misused; that is, it interferes in its application with either the pursuit of the biologically necessary satisfactions or the maintenance of security. For instance, if a dynamism leads to a way of interacting with others that hinders the establishment of satisfactory interpersonal relations, it results in a loss of self-esteem and in accompanying anxiety. When either of these two problematic outcomes occurs, the dynamism may be considered to be a "dynamism of difficulty."

In other words, Sullivan sees mental disorder as simply a "misapplied dynamism," or a "pattern of inadequate or inappropriate action in the field of interpersonal relations" (Jones, 1995, p. 316). The behavior itself may be quite common as part of the human repertoire, but it is misdirected, overused, or employed in circumstances where it cannot possibly further the person's emotional goals.

Sullivan's view of misapplied dynamisms is excellent grounding for the specifics of micro-traumatic relating. It captures the idea that people have elaborate patterns of relating to others that are not necessarily always injurious, but that can *become* injurious when directed in certain problematic ways toward certain people, prompted by particularly fraught motives. That is to say, these patterns become toxic when the behavior is being employed in the service of responding to a real or imagined, consciously or unconsciously perceived threat to one's sense of security. We may then employ them to stave off the anxiety of stimulating a sense of bad-me (or possibly even not-me) and to preserve a sense of being good-me. Sullivan himself concentrates on certain collections of dynamisms as characteristic of a given type of diagnostic entity (obsessive, paranoid, hysteric, etc.), and in so doing, he emphasizes more extreme types of character pathology. In speaking about micro-traumas, I too am in a sense articulating dynamisms, but less serious, subtler versions that combine over time to alter one's self-image and eat away at one's emotional well-being, without *necessarily* creating full-blown characterological distortions (though these can also occur).

Sullivan and many interpersonalists after him tend to be resolutely focused on interpersonal relations as they happen in the world. On the subject of internal structures, they take a more or less agnostic approach. By definition, relational analysts see the internal and external worlds as co-creating one another inextricably and, as an object relations-oriented relationalist, I am more comfortable than Sullivan and many other interpersonalists with conceptualizing an inner psychic world replete with seeming "structures" (including so-called inner objects) that are metaphoric and analogical inner images of aspects of self and others. I see micro-traumatic dynamisms or habitual modes of relating as emanating from or received by an individual's "psychic center" (Wolstein, 1987). This is to say that micro-traumas are enacted by virtue of an individual's inner psychic self- and other-representations, even though they find habitual expression in the interaction with the inner psychic and outer interpersonal life of a specific significant other.

R. D. Laing and the Double Bind

Working within a framework congenial to Sullivan's, R. D. Laing ([1961] 1971) astutely discussed what I consider to be historically the first specific example of micro-trauma in his elaboration of Gregory Bateson et al.'s (1956) concept of the "double bind." Here, as the reader probably recalls, "[t]he 'victim' is caught in a tangle of paradoxical injunctions, or of attributions having the force of injunctions, in which he cannot do the right thing" (Laing, [1961] 1971, p. 144). Laing explains this more fully a few pages later:

One person conveys to the other that he should do something, and at the same time conveys on another level that he should not, or that he should do something else incompatible with it. The situation is sealed off for the "victim" by a further injunction forbidding him or her to get out of the situation, or to dissolve it by commenting on it. The "victim" is thus in an "untenable" position. He cannot make a move without catastrophe.

(pp. 145–146)

As a steady mode of interaction, the double bind naturally can lead to severe pathology and disordered attachment—schizophrenia in particular, according to Laing and others—but even at lesser levels it creates a potential for distortion of the self.

Let me mention here that in the same discussion, Laing expanded psychoanalysis' customary focus on the socializing influence of the parent on the child by noting a reverse influence as well. In the context of discussing the double bind, he comments:

One must remember that the child may put his parents into untenable positions. The baby cannot be satisfied. It cries "for" the breast. It cries when the breast is presented. It cries when the breast is withdrawn. Unable to "click with" or "get through," the mother becomes intensely anxious and feels hopeless. She withdraws from the baby in one sense, and becomes oversolicitous in another sense. Double binds can be two-way.

(p. 147)

Building on this point, we could say that children may put their parents in "untenable positions" that micro-traumatize them at various junctures throughout their shared life spans. Generational influence is not simply linear and unidirectional, with adults always helping or harming children; a psychic structuralizing influence swims back upstream as well. And undoubtedly micro-traumatic relating happens, and hurts, at the lateral, peer-to-peer level as well.

A Self Psychological View of Psychic Trauma

From the perspective of classical self psychology theory (Kohut & Wolf, 1978), the young child needs two things for the healthy development of the self: someone who provides the affirmation or mirroring of his or her "innate sense of vigor, greatness, and perfection," and someone with whom he or she can identify and merge with by virtue of the other's "calmness, infallibility, and omnipotence" (p. 414). In other words, the child must have available both a mirroring selfobject and an idealized parental imago. A firm self is constituted by "strivings for power and success," "basic idealized goals," and by the "tension arc" between these ambitions and ideals that makes use of the child's basic skills and capabilities. Psychic trauma inheres to the degree that the child's basic needs along these lines are not responded to effectively through the empathic ministrations of the parental selfobjects, with the result that the person emerges with a structurally damaged self. Such a self is lacking to a greater or lesser degree in cohesion, vitality, and functional harmony. Significant early developmental failures in the bond with early selfobject figures create "primary disturbances of the self." Among these disturbances, a subgroup highlighted by self psychology theorists is a type of narcissistic personality disorder, whose hallmarks are depression, lack of vitality, hypochondria, and a hypersensitivity to slights. All of these symptoms can be tied in one way or another to recurrent *narcissistic injury*, which is the central form of psychic trauma in which the vulnerable self deflates or fragments in response to perceived attacks on its worth. The emotional result is shame, hurt, and sometimes rage. Kohut and Wolf declare outright that it is more the personalities and psyches of the parents than specific child-rearing philosophies or techniques that ensure healthy maturation of the child's sense of self. They insist, recapitulating the positions of Khan and also Kris, that it is not so much "grossly traumatic events" but distortions in the familial psychological matrix that cause serious undermining of the self:

> [W]e have come to incline to the opinion that such traumatic events may be no more than clues that point to the truly pathogenic factors, the unwholesome atmosphere to which the child was exposed during the years when his self was established. Taken by themselves, in other words, these events leave fewer serious disturbances in their wake than the chronic ambience created by the deep-rooted attitudes of the selfobjects; since even the still vulnerable self, in the process of formation, can cope with serious traumata if it is embedded in a healthily supportive milieu. The essence of the healthy matrix for the growing self of the child is a mature, cohesive parental self that is in tune with the changing needs of the child . . . Some parents, however, aren't adequately sensitive to the needs of the child but will instead respond to the needs of their own insecurely established self.

(p. 417)

In pointing toward a problematic "chronic ambience," Kohut and Wolf are clearly articulating something akin to Khan's "cumulative trauma," in which there are repeated instances of damage that leave the child later vulnerable to moments of psychic (here, more specifically, narcissistic) injury. This has hints of Sullivan's view of the destructive impact of steady negative appraisals from the parent, with self psychology emphasizing shame as the operative affective factor rather than anxiety. In an updated position, Wolf (1995) redefines psychic trauma from a self psychology perspective as something that involves the interaction between the subject's self and his or her environment: "Thus, anything that threatens the continuity of the experience of the ongoing mutually reciprocal relationship between any pair of interacting psyches is a trauma for both, whether the pair be infant-mother, child-parent, spouse-spouse, analyst-analysand, or any other" (p. 219). It's a small step from this postulate to the view advanced here that psychic derailment may result from two individuals inflicting small degrees of damage on one another's sense of self in the context of—or by virtue of the "chronic ambience" created by—an ongoing relationship. Where the damage isn't symmetrical, it nonetheless does tend to have noteworthy consequences for the injuring one as well.

Dispositional Underpinnings of Micro-traumatic Experience

Propensities for inflicting or sustaining micro-traumatic damage are undergirded not only by psychic conflict, but also by one's temperament or disposition. To the degree that the person's dispositional tendencies influence his or her intrapsychic scenarios and defensive structure, he or she may be prone to engage in—or be wounded by—one or another sort of injurious relatedness. Looking at parent–child relating for the moment, the cheerful parent may blithely downplay or try to "jolly" her daughter out of her anxious distress in the face of team try-outs. The humorous parent may playfully tease a teenager for being overly precise in trying to make a good omelet for the first time. The introverted parent might minimize the importance of the outgoing daughter's large web of casual friendships. The sardonic, dour parent might pour cold water on a son's optimistic essay about changing the world.

Conversely, a given dispositional aspect of the child can be psychically injurious to the parent. A child born shy or melancholic may well grate on the nerves of a sunnier-natured parent or make his or her parenting efforts seem inadequate, leading to subtle feelings of rejection (see Chess & Thomas, 1987). Some children are born with a high degree of fascination with the mechanics of how a part relates to a whole, how inanimate things fit together.

At the same time, they may have relatively little interest or involvement in relationships among people. These individuals, many of whom later gravitate toward interests in math, computer sciences, technology, engineering, and so on, are described by Baron-Cohen (2003) as highly "systemized" and very low in "empathizing." In the extreme, this behavior can be alienating to a more emotional parent. The child who, by contrast, is quite high in empathizing can create considerable unease in a systemizing parent, who can feel mystified by the child's emotional needs and sensitivities and incompetent to deal with them. In short, a child's individual personality and temperament can at times fray the psyches of his or her parents (or, for that matter, other close relatives). This damage is compounded to the degree that the parents believe mistakenly that these psychic and interpersonal issues are attributable solely to themselves and their parenting and are therefore, in a sense, their own fault.

In some unfortunate families, parents and children micro-traumatize each other reflexively through a series of misattunements, some of which are pathologically motivated and some not. Chess and Thomas (1987, p. 64), exploring the "goodness of fit" between parent and child, give us an example of a child's unintentional micro-traumatization of the parents:

> Some parents with a temperamentally difficult child attempt to avoid stress and turmoil by appeasement, giving in quickly to the child's every demand. Such parents only create a child tyrant, who learns to dominate the family by throwing tantrums. In such a case, the parents will have to learn to endure the stress on themselves as well as on their child by saying "No" quietly but firmly when appropriate and sticking to it until the child's tantrum subsides. . . . Through this process, though she [the child] may go through periods of turmoil she achieves a good fit with the reasonable expectations of other people.

Having a child who chronically throws temper tantrums tends to generate stress under any circumstances, but Chess and Thomas underline the way in which having to exert authority over the child's emotional outbursts can be particularly taxing for parents whose personalities incline them toward placating and pacifying. In fact, the need to try to adopt a greatly modified parenting stance may clash with a parent's typical temperamental tendencies or prior sense of identity in a way that can be vastly unsettling to the parent's larger sense of self in the world. With luck, however, the dialectic between one's own tendencies and what's evoked by the child's unique personality becomes a stimulus for the parent's further psychic maturation (see Therese Benedek, 1959, on parenthood as an educative developmental influence).

Developmental or Relational Trauma

In more recent years, Philip Bromberg (2006) has invoked the terms "developmental" or "relational trauma" to explore the role of ongoing shaping influences in the individual's psychic evolution. He writes compellingly of this sort of trauma as a function of the "prolonged experience of nonrecognition" (p. 139) on the parents' part: "It embodies an act of nonrecognition that is as traumatizing as the pain caused by a parent who is actively abusive, and sometimes it is *more* debilitating" (p. 140). In Bromberg's view, this non-recognition eventually generates a dissociative structure in the child's character, one that plagues him or her in an ongoing way in adult life:

> I am speaking about the early failure of responsiveness by the mother or father to some genuine aspect of the child's self, not necessarily open disapproval or abusiveness (which communicates that this aspect of the child's self is "bad"), but a masked withdrawal from authentic contact that leaves the child experiencing part of herself as having no pleasurable value to a loved other and, thus, no relational existence as part of "me." Nonrecognition leads to a *structural* dissociation of a part of the self. If too broad a segment of the core self is encompassed, there will be impairment in the early attachment process and in the capacity for mutual regulation and "implicit relational knowing" (Stern et al., 1998).
>
> (p. 139)

Bromberg explains further that these situations occur when the parents themselves are emotionally damaged, which leads to some degree of shame within the parent that is itself dissociated, but that causes the parent to disavow qualities in the child that he or she finds intolerable in the self. The result is terrible in that the parent will distance from and fail to enjoy the child or the relationship, with a seriously stunting effect:

> If the other systematically disconfirms (Laing, 1962) a child's state of mind, particularly at moments of intense affective arousal, by behaving as though the self-meaning of the experience to the child is irrelevant, the child grows to mistrust the reality of her own experience. The child becomes correspondingly impaired in her ability to process cognitively her own emotionally charged mental states in an interpersonal context—to reflect on them, hold them as states of intrapsychic conflict, and thus own them as me. Dissociation, the disconnection of the mind from the psyche-soma, then becomes the

most adaptive solution to persevering selfhood. The child's own need for *loving* recognition becomes despised and shame ridden. The need becomes a dissociated "not-me" aspect of self that, when triggered, releases not only the unmet hunger for authentic responsiveness, but a flood of shame, the affect associated with failure in who one *is*, not failure in what one *does*. Failure in what one does leads to anxiety and lowered self-esteem or to guilt and depression, but failure in who one is leads to shame, the signal of impending self-destabilization, the shock of no longer being "me."

(p. 140)

To draw these threads together, Bromberg believes that the fear of being shamed causes various parts of the child's psyche to become split off into "a rigid multiplicity of adversarial self-states," each of which has its own "specific pattern of interpersonal engagement that gives it self-meaning" (p. 191). One small, also dissociated aspect of the person is always on the lookout for an experience that might cause him or her to become exposed to a self-state that might induce shame. And such shame must be averted at all costs, so the person attempts to hide the existence of those unacceptable parts of self from her- or himself and the other. The goal of psychotherapeutic work is to evade the "lookout" and provide opportunities for "surprises" about the self that are "safe but not too safe." That is, in the context of a trusted therapeutic relationship, the person can be brought to encounter the shame-saturated part of the self closely enough that it becomes possible to integrate it into the whole self. This permits the growth of a more harmonious, continuous, and coherent sense of "me-ness" that can be newly treasured.

Robert Stolorow (2008, p. 114), writing from an intersubjective perspective, echoes Bromberg's view:

[D]evelopmental trauma is viewed not as an instinctual flooding of an ill-equipped Cartesian container but as an experience of unbearable affect. Furthermore, the intolerability of affect states can be grasped only in terms of the relational systems in which they are felt. Developmental trauma originates within a formative intersubjective context whose central feature is malattunement of painful affect—a breakdown of the child-care-giver system of mutual regulation. This leads to the child's loss of affect-integrating capacity and thereby to an unbearable, overwhelmed, disorganized state. Painful or frightening affect becomes enduringly traumatic when the attunement that the child needs to assist in its tolerance, and integration is profoundly absent.

Relational and developmental trauma as described by Bromberg and others overlaps the territory covered by my own term, micro-trauma. Non-recognition, invalidation, and misattunement are viewed as key vehicles for this damage (as they are in the "microaggressions" of D. W. Sue, which I'll come to momentarily). I agree wholeheartedly with Bromberg's view of the role these features play in eroding psychic well-being. I also agree that these patterns persist in part because the individual tries to avoid the shame that would come with a clearer recognition of what is and was going on, and that the roots of all this may lie far back in development. But in this book, I am primarily interested in trying to articulate *specific instantiations* of the ways that one individual can undermine the self-worth and well-being of another—or indeed, how one may do it to oneself. It seems to me that by describing particular ways in which non-recognition, invalidation, and misattunements are enacted, we offer ourselves and our patients clearer cues as to the sorts of interactions for which they should be on the lookout. Identification of the "dance steps" takes us three-quarters of the way toward forestalling or correcting the troublesome dance. And as I have tried to make clear, I also think that these processes go on and leave their mark not only in the ongoing relation with one's early caregivers, but also in later stages of life and with other significant individuals such as one's spouse, children, intimate friends, and so on.

D. W. Sue's "Microaggressions" as a Psychosocial Version of Micro-trauma

I have been gratified to discover that theorists from the parallel universe of academic research psychology have also been attempting to identify specific mechanisms of chronic emotional assault. For these social scientists, however, the focus is not on damage sustained by the *individual* by virtue of his or her unique characteristics, but on the damage sustained by an entire *class* of individuals by virtue of that group's signature identity. Derald Wing Sue's (2010) book *Microaggressions in Everyday Life: Race, Gender, and Sexual Orientation* is a masterful and exhaustive study of these sorts of experiences and their effect on members of those marginalized groups. Sue offers the following definition: "Microaggressions are the brief and commonplace daily verbal, behavioral, and environmental indignities, whether intentional or unintentional, that communicate hostile, derogatory, or negative racial, gender, sexual-orientation, and religious slights and insults to the target person or group (Sue et al., 2007)" (Sue, 2010, p. 5).

Sue differentiates among three types of microaggression: microassaults, microinsults, and microinvalidations. All three may be conveyed either via interpersonal communication or through environmental cues. Microassaults are conscious, "deliberate," biased expressions that may be verbal or behavioral. The intent here is to hurt the victim through active derogation and discrimination or avoidant snubbing. Microinsults, often unconscious and subtle, diminish the other by virtue of his or her gender, race, or sexual orientation, these characteristics being devalued by the perpetrator. Microinvalidations are attitudes that "exclude, negate, or nullify the psychological thoughts, feelings, or experiential reality of certain groups, such as people of color, women, and LGBTs" (p. 37). Sue views these latter as especially damaging in that they invalidate the *subjective experience* of the individuals in these groups, thereby potentially having the most oppressive and annihilating effect of all. The writer emphasizes the ambiguous nature of microaggressions, noting that their meanings can be masked and must be carefully deconstructed in order to counter their ill effects. It is clear that much of his thinking would apply to the understanding and handling of the hostilities I term micro-traumatic, which are based on individual attributes and situations.

Another point of confluence between Sue's perspective and my own is that he too sees microaggression as a two-way, interactive process rather than a unidirectional one, in which not only the targeted person, but also the antagonist is damaged and suffers losses in the traumatic interchange. Here is Sue's clearheaded view of the impact of being a chronic "oppressor"—a version of microaggression involving social domination of a marginalized group:

> In essence, oppression inevitably means losing one's humanity for the sake of the power, wealth, and status attained from the subjugation of others. It means losing a spiritual connection with fellow human beings. It means a refusal to recognize the polarities of the democratic principles of equality and the inhuman and unequal treatment of the oppressed. . . . People who oppress must, at some level, become callous, cold, hard, and unfeeling toward the plight of the oppressed.
>
> (p. 132)

Drawing on his research, Sue offers the following generalized sequence for the unfolding of a potential microaggressive event. The process starts with a microaggressive incident, such as the "ascription of intellectual inferiority" (which I would call a "little murder") to a person of color or the "sexual objectification" of a woman. This can be via verbal, behavioral, or social channels, and is generally communicated via hidden and ambiguous messages. The next phase is the *perception* and subsequent *questioning* of the event by the target—was it really a biased statement by intent, or is the target being oversensitive? The third phase involves the target's *reaction*, which can include "healthy paranoia," a "sanity check," "empowering and validating the self," and "rescuing (or making excuses for) offenders." Next, there is the need to *interpret the meaning* of the experience. And finally, there are the *consequences and impact* on the aggressor's victim, including feelings of powerlessness, invisibility, forced compliance, and a loss of integrity, not to mention the perceived pressure to represent members of one's own group. Under optimal circumstances, the targeted person survives this experience psychically by displaying "strength through adversity," which is its own reward and yields further psychic fruits of keener interpersonal perception, enhanced supportive identification with one's peers (that is, those sharing the same devalued characteristics), greater attunement to contextual threats, and the capacity to see and identify with multiple cultural vantage points. In general, Sue seems to be drawing on the same sort of therapeutic perspective that informs psychoanalytic work. He believes that withstanding the pain and anxiety of covert mistreatment long enough to access a constructive coping mechanism will ultimately strengthen one's ability to counter microaggression. Bringing to bear reflective processes on the hurtful encounter will ultimately empower the target and grant the leverage needed to put an end to the traumatic effects of systematic covert harassment. All of this accords closely with a psychoanalytic approach to identifying and curtailing the type of micro-traumatic encounter described in this book, one that is based on a person's *individualized* attributes and psychodynamics.

Gaslighting

A form of micro-trauma that has been well-articulated already in the analytic literature and that also enjoys a certain popular notoriety is the mechanism of "gaslighting" (Calef & Weinshel, 1981; Dorpat, 1996; Rush, 2000). I describe this here because I think it gives a sense of how such interpsychic mechanisms give us a handle on capturing subtle unconscious phenomena that might otherwise remain below the radar of one's conscious interpersonal functioning. As Calef and Weinshel (1981) note, the term gaslighting was coined as an outgrowth of the popular movie *Gaslight*, in which shortly after marrying, a young woman is driven to think she is losing her mind by her evil-intentioned husband. The latter surreptitiously alters the gas lighting in their home, all the while denying it has been adjusted, in order to undermine his wife's trust in her sanity. The husband's purpose is to have her committed to an institution, which will leave him free to retrieve treasure hidden in their home, the booty being jewels previously owned by an old woman he had murdered years before. What appears to be the wife's mental instability is actually her psychic reaction to her husband's psychopathy and the machinations it generates.

From this specific scenario, Calef and Weinshel offer a generalized description of gaslighting as a commonplace two-person maneuver:

> It is, first of all, a piece of behavior in which one individual, with varying degrees of success, attempts to influence the judgment of a second individual by causing the latter to doubt the validity of his or her own judgment. The motivation may be conscious, although it is usually unconscious; and almost invariably the conscious motives are rationalizations and/or distortions of deeper, more complex, and less acceptable motives. The victim becomes uncertain and confused in regard to his or her assessment of internal or external perceptions and the integrity of his or her reality testing. Schematically, at least, gaslighting should be differentiated from those phenomena in which there may be comparable experiences of doubt and uncertainty about one's perceptions primarily because of intrapsychic difficulties . . . We say "schematically, at least" because in practice internal conflicts always play some part.
>
> (pp. 53–54)

The authors go on to suggest that "the basic motive for the gaslighting is to rid oneself of unacceptable mental content or functions, not by a random expulsion and externalization, but by 'transferring' that content to another individual" (p. 63). The victims, on their end, are

> invariably unsure of their own perceptions and motivations. That insecurity seems to arise originally from some biological given, bolstered by a childhood environment that shakes the child's faith in her/himself and the world about her/him. It appears that not all individuals will predictably react in the same fashion to a given gaslighting attempt or to the same gaslighter. If in the victim the gaslighting impinges on an area of internal conflict involving greed, guilt, or shame, the chances of that attempt being successful will be enhanced considerably.
>
> (p. 65)

Calef and Weinshel offer four compelling clinical examples. Two of these echo the original movie's scenario in that they involve the gaslighting of a relatively passive wife by her dominating, transgressing husband. The last two pertain to the analytic situation and are sketches of a female patient who feels trapped in a "catch-22" situation by her supposedly overly demanding analyst, and an analyst who feels disempowered and beleaguered by his compulsively chattering patient.

The possibility of gaslighting occurring in psychoanalytic psychotherapy is picked up on and elaborated by Theodore Dorpat (1996; see also Rush, 2000). This author emphasizes the covert control the psychotherapist may exert over the patient through the therapist's adherence to and insistence on certain theoretical articles of faith. Dorpat ardently decries gaslighting within psychoanalytic treatment, along with "brainwashing" and other efforts to colonize the patient's mind.

Addressing Cumulative Hurt

As we have seen, the idea that injurious modes of relating can sum to the point where they have a truly traumatic impact has a long tradition within psychoanalytic theory; indeed, variants of this view can be found in virtually all the dominant psychoanalytic schools. As we have also seen, in most of this literature the emphasis is placed squarely on the relationship with early attachment figures (whether attachment per se is theorized or not) and on the long-term consequences that can accrue for personality in general. In this book, I follow the foregoing traditions to the extent that I too argue that micro-traumatic experiences can mount up to the point of having a truly profound, if not "capital T" traumatic effect. I also readily concur that for both the target and the perpetrator, the attitudes and behaviors that constitute micro-traumatic interaction often draw on early psychic formations. But in what follows, I will not usually be attempting to trace these lines of development back to their infantile source, presuming that they have such roots. Rather, I will be content to document the kinds of micro-traumatic interchanges we encounter in adults or much older children. My analysis of the characterological sources and consequences of these interchanges will largely stay in the recent past or the present, as I think these experiences are more impactful as significant sources of enduring psychic harm than we've heretofore acknowledged.

In the upcoming pages, I describe certain modes of relating to another or even to oneself that I consider micro-traumatic. In my view, if one is subject to too many interactions along these lines, one's inner experience and overall self-regard become swayed in a negative direction. The person is likely to be subject to higher levels of chronic anxiety and depression than would otherwise be the case, as his or her efforts to defend against the distressing interaction generate strategies that only worsen the quality of the relatedness, damaging his or her psychosocial life structures. I will give some examples of micro-traumatic relating that are personal, but most will come from my practice, from the psychoanalytic literature, or from literary fiction and drama. Where the exemplars are from my clinical practice, I have disguised and, to some degree, fictionalized them to render the person's individual identity unknowable to anyone else— sometimes even to the person in question. The main thrust of the interaction is left intact, however, and the arc of its micro-traumatic effect is just as it originally was.

Let me mention that this book may contain a higher than average concentration of clinical interactions in which the psychoanalytic clinician and patient challenge or even wrangle with one other. Such moments are not representative of the overall treatment with that particular patient, but were culled from a fuller range of analytic interchanges—often quite harmonious and constructive in tone—to highlight how tricky, subtle, and painstaking the work with micro-trauma can be. In my experience, the process of identifying and working through a micro-traumatic patterning does not always have a linear trajectory, or one that seems immediately remediable. The psychoanalyst struggles to metabolize, process, and give words to what's going on, and the patient works to get past his or her defensive wish to ignore it. (Though unfortunately, at certain moments these positions are sometimes reversed!) The reader may feel dropped into the midst of a struggle that doesn't resolve quickly, cleanly, or definitively. It's as if the patient—and sometimes the psychoanalyst—has a wound that, in order to heal, must be gingerly examined and cleaned out; at the same time, though, the person injured would prefer that the wound not be touched at all. The unpacking of micro-traumatic experience involves steady patience and repetitive reexamination to catch the momentary elements that generate the toxic impact. As the psychoanalyst, one must continually ask oneself to what degree this difficult engagement is really expressing something problematic in the patient, and to what degree it is a countertransferential response coming from one's own area of insufficiently worked through micro-traumatic history. It will usually be some of both, but the tangle should obviously only become the focus of the analytic exchange if it is key to the patient's own psychic issues. (Otherwise, the underlying factors should as usual be worked on privately

by the clinician in an appropriate venue.) Work with micro-trauma is sometimes not the most fun or pleasurable part of doing psychoanalytic work.
Yet at the same time, it often ends up bringing both analyst and patient the
deep satisfaction of having plumbed a previously unreachable set of psychic
issues, whose resolution can bring the patient welcome relief from anxiety
and dysphoria, and can lead ultimately to the expansion of his or her psychic
freedom in the world.

Note

1 Fairbairn's conceptualizations of the split internalized bad object and the fate of the
"actual good" object are much contested and re-jiggered within the neo-Fairbairnian
literature (see Goldberg, 2007; Mitchell, 1988; Ogden, 2010; Sherby, 2007; Skolnick
& Scharff, 1998). As just one example, Goldberg (2007) suggests "repositioning" the
exciting object as "spanning both good and bad object realms." She goes on: "Fairbairn's
exciting-object concept is potentially broad enough to encompass good-enough as well
as bad repressed objects. The power of the concept of the exciting object is precisely in
its melding of good and bad, needed and promising as well as frustrating and betray-
ing" (p. 275). Goldberg argues for the value of the analyst's providing a benign exciting
object role in the therapeutic situation, as this, in her view, offers an enlivening hope that
presumably offsets its potentially disappointing elements.

Chapter 2

Unkind Cutting Back and Its Navigation

When we could no longer delay revamping our outdated kitchen, we naturally hired the contractor who had piloted us magnificently through a series of minor projects in years past. But this time, as soon as the bulk of the work was done (predictably, three months beyond the promised deadline), the contractor and his minions stopped showing up with any regularity. There was finishing work to be accomplished before the house could be set to rights. But no amount of delicate prodding or, eventually, impassioned begging could bring our contractor to return our calls, much less show up in person. Having seemingly lost interest, he would neither come and finish nor call it quits and fully leave. Had we done something to contribute to this standoff? Was there anything within our power that could be done to resolve it? Might the contractor's periodic profession of his *intent* to come mean he actually might complete everything one day? Sparks of hope would flicker in my mind only to be extinguished, as the continuing household upheaval eroded my peace of mind.

Our experience with the contractor is a quotidian but telling example of what I call "unkind cutting back." By this, I mean an unexpected, unilateral bid to attenuate a relationship in a way that engenders hurt, confusion, and frustration in the other. The decision to reduce contact in this situation occurs summarily and without a convincing explanation. By shortening or postponing contact, spreading it out, or minimizing its original importance, the one stepping back from contact inflicts micro-trauma by undercutting the other person psychologically. In the case of our kitchen remodeling, having the contractor fade from view was vexing in its own right, but what it implied for us going forward was even more troubling. After all, we had entrusted our house to this fellow for years. He was exceptionally competent in building maintenance, troubleshooting, and enhancement. Having shepherded it through many a domestic nightmare, he knew the house's quirks—and the solutions for addressing them—better than anyone else ever could. Now we could no longer count on him; we were hamstrung. It felt nearly impossible to think of retaining him, but foolish to think of letting him go either.

It is especially awful, of course, if the person cutting back on the emotional investment is not an employee hired for instrumental purposes but an intimate friend or family member—or for that matter, one's psychoanalyst (see Hirsch, 2008). This person might well know you inside out (as our contractor knew our house), such that his or her new scarcity causes you to feel less in touch with yourself, less whole, and less secure. You may feel deprived, but also devalued and even betrayed by the other's withdrawal. Often, the reasons for the reduction are ambiguous, allowing you to project all manner of painful meanings onto the withdrawal—are you being selectively ignored, given the cold shoulder? Nonverbal gestures often speak volumes, but their actual message is ambiguous, because they may be subtle and fleeting enough to mean—well, nothing at all. As the one still wanting connection, you are left hanging, not sure if you should ask point blank whether the other really *has* pulled back and thereby risk making it more real by naming it. Questioning things may make you sound hypersensitive if you're wrong, whiny and dependent if you're right. Seeming needy or weak could well drive the other even farther away.

A cutback's damage depends on a few things: how and in what way the two individuals were interdependent to begin with; the manner or tone with which the attenuation occurs; the intentionality or meaning behind the distancing; and the interpretive lens through which the action is viewed. A precipitous withdrawal is often an expression of conscious or unconscious anger manifest in a conscious or unconscious desire to exert unilateral power over the other. At other times, however, the withdrawal might be a byproduct of a profound sense of personal inadequacy or shame in the one retreating. Either way, backing away from contact, the person ends up "dropping" the one whose presence evokes the negative self-experience without giving a full accounting of what is amiss.

As it happens, the cutback in our renovation was symbolized graphically in the new "environmentally sound" faucet our contractor blithely installed in the kitchen sink. He mentioned in passing that it would yield a thinner stream with weaker water pressure than before—but no problem, we would get used to it. To the contrary, turning on the tap for months afterward made me frustrated, rueful, and nostalgic for the powerful spray arm that once turned its user into a cleaning dynamo. So, too, when a relationship thins to a trickle—though the reduction may be constructive in certain respects—the lost power and intensity literally leave much to be desired.

In speaking about cutting back as opposed to cutting off, I am suggesting that there is something particularly painful about being held onto while being held at arm's length. Because one is still "on the hook," the person who is the target of this treatment cannot employ the same defenses and adaptations, cannot shift the full psychic investment elsewhere to assuage the loss, and cannot do the emotional work of accepting and mourning someone who has faded but is not entirely gone (see Freud, 1917). Moreover, in an unkind cutback there is ambiguity in the motive, the meaning, and perhaps even in the planned duration of the absence. It is reminiscent of the still-face paradigm in the developmental literature (Mesman et al., 2009; Tronick & Beeghley, 2011), where a mother is asked to present an emotionally flattened face to her infant. This generally leads to such distress that the baby breaks into tears, his or her sense of security utterly disrupted by the mother's inexplicable inexpressiveness. For adults, remaining present while giving someone the cold shoulder is a notoriously hurtful act that signals—what exactly? It implies an attitude of disapproval or devaluation of the other, with the reasons for the negativity left unspoken. This ambiguity makes the affront especially distressing to the receiver of the slight and may preclude its being effectively addressed.

The still-face paradigm described above calls to mind moments in which an analyst's demeanor suddenly changes toward being quieter or more "neutral." Very often, the patient is befuddled by what seems like the analyst's emotional withdrawal. He or she has no way of knowing the source of or reason behind the altered stance and may experience it as some sort of emotional abandonment or cutback. It carries the potential implication that, perhaps due to one's own flaws or sins, one has forfeited the analyst's good will. This psychic disruption in my view is unnecessarily unsettling and therefore, in my terms, unkind, even if it can be turned into grist for the mill.

A cutback is sometimes used as the lesser of two evils, as the withdrawing one retreats to avoid the expression of a more serious degree of anger or disapproval that could be that much less bearable to the other. Hence, a cutback in which the person retreating is "being cruel to be kind" carries the menacing possibility that a sentiment even worse might lie underneath.

But whatever the circumstances, having someone cut down on contact with you, while still being potentially there, can be like dealing with a wraith. Consider this evocative stanza penned over a century ago by Hughes Mearns (McCord, 1955):

Yesterday, upon the stair,
I met a man who wasn't there
He wasn't there again today
I wish, I wish he'd go away . . . [1]

The poem is obviously talking about a supernatural event rather than a real one, but what a disconcerting specter it is! So it is also in unkind cutting back, where the receding one is like the ghostly man on the stair. The person withdrawing is scarcely present, but neither is he or she fully gone; his or her influence is felt, but not firmly enough either to engage with or to counter. Of course, cutting back may thwart some of the retreating person's needs while satisfying others, so frequently the instigator of the withdrawal is also hurt in the process.

In micro-traumatic relating generally, one stays in the grip of a pathogenic bond of whatever kind either because one has no choice, or because although it's not good, it's not quite bad enough to make one sever relations. The attachment per se, whatever its cast, is somehow unconsciously its own reinforcement. That is, the feeling of being attached has its own compelling rhythm and logic, and for that reason alone, we have cause to let a connection persist irrespective of how fraught it may be. With unkind cutting back, the tension between staying and going gets boiled down to its essentials: do we have a relationship or not?

Or looking at this from another angle, problematic relationships may be prone to *inviting* an eventual cutback. Micro-traumatic relationships are often used to bolster one's inner self-valuing. But receiving such potentially thorny support may at some point begin to feel less boistering and more stultifying, while (oddly enough) providing it also can become onerous. Either of these constraining situations can stimulate an instinctive pulling back from one of the parties involved. Or the rhythm of giving and receiving that had been established previously may simply become disrupted by the accident of changing life circumstances. When these shifts in availability (physical, psychological, or both) occur in ways that are non-synchronous, it is likely to cause a wrench in the other party. Whether responding to a life demand or just an inner unarticulated urge, the withdrawing one does damage in simply enacting the change rather than exploring or explaining the wish or need that generates it.

Mary had always felt insecure, disadvantaged, and different from her age-mates by virtue of the death of her mother when she was 12. Not only did she envy her peers for having mothers who were still alive, she also resented how involved the girls' mothers seemed to be in their daughters' daily lives. She yearned to feel as important and attended to in *her* family as her friends must have felt in *theirs*. Mary finished high school and college, and after an intensive and very involved courtship, she married an oncologist whose outstanding professional prospects enhanced her own feelings of self-worth. It was a very happy time. But as the demands on his professional time increased and he had to attend to patients, or teach, or be on call six days a week, Mary's loneliness returned. Now at home with a young son, she felt increasingly demoralized by her husband's unavailability and lack of involvement in domestic and childrearing matters. Mary's own role seemed far less valuable, which exposed her again to painful self-doubt and cravings for closeness to assuage the self-devaluation. Sunday, the one day a week that her husband could spare from his practice, became an idealized occasion of extreme celebration, but one that could be dashed at any moment by a pager calling him back to the hospital. Mary felt and largely *was* powerless to fend off these rupturing cutbacks. After an unexpected emergency page—and predictably, every Monday morning—she would be plunged back into a rut of mourning, frustration, and emptiness. Realizing it was "irrational," Mary nonetheless felt angry that she was no match for the severely ill patients who had an incontrovertible right to her husband's attention and ministrations. She felt insignificant, just someone to be left behind. She was again the little girl whose mother had died, leaving her without that loving involvement and sense of being prized.

To compound the problem, Mary's needy clinging and haranguing of her husband vis-à-vis his work demands caused him to distance himself further from her emotionally. This emotional remove on the husband's part worsened her sense of abject dependency and powerlessness, shame-ridden feelings that made her feel even less desirable. As Mary sensed her role in driving her husband farther away, these secondary emotional cutbacks became that much more painful to her. Unable to leave the marriage because she depended on and admired her husband, she couldn't get enough of what she needed to find a measure of self-gratification and joy in her life circumstances outside the home.

Not surprisingly, Mary's young son picked up on his mother's sense of depletion in relation to the father's departures. He too seemed to lose vitality and sink into a mini-depression on saying goodbye to his father—and to other close figures as well. In later life, he would steel himself from others' comings and goings as a defense against renewed painful loss. As a result, the son's own significant others in adulthood would feel the sting of his emotional detachment on parting. Here was an intergenerational transmission of micro-trauma, in which the mother's hypersensitive narcissistic injury—both at the father's unavoidable actual absences and then his affective cutbacks—generated anxieties in the son, in identification with his mother. The son then adopted the father's distancing pattern as a defense against his highly charged and conflicted dependency needs.

Apropos of such distancing, let me emphasize that cutting back often occurs primarily at an emotional rather than pragmatic level. A person may be disappointed, disillusioned, or simply disaffected from the other and yet be loath to attenuate the relationship for all sorts of reasons. So the rhythm of overt contact remains the same, while the emotional juiciness has leeched out. The person withdraws only psychically, sharing fewer intimate thoughts or feelings or sequestering large slices of his or her subjective world. Some degree of oscillation in emotional closeness is normal in relationships, but a deepening withdrawal over time is undoubtedly corrosive.

Cutbacks differ from outright abandonment in that, just like the ghostly man on the stair, the other isn't entirely gone. He or she has not fully vacated the space, making room for a more suitable or more fully engaged other to step in. The frustration, anger, and aggression have nowhere to go and further block the ability of the person cut back on to seek satisfaction elsewhere. Tantalized, the person remains trapped by the possibility of repair.

Cutbacks loom large as a psychic defense during instances of significant psychosocial transition, and often they are quite scarring. The self-help media describe how divorcing individuals are not infrequently wounded to discover some of their erstwhile friends siding with the other partner rather than with them. It is particularly painful when, rather than addressing the issues directly, these former friends simply make themselves scarce to the one they deem the offending party. People making lifestyle choices that run contrary to that of the local social milieu may be shunned without explanation, leaving them isolated and bereft.

A poignant instance of cutting back was described by a woman whose aging mother was dying from emphysema. There had been increasing friction between the two in the mother's last decade, as the mother's grandiose self-absorption and sense of righteousness had increased exponentially. The daughter traveled cross-country to the mother's nursing home on hearing of a steep decline in her health. One of the few ways left to express her love was by offering to rub the mother's feet. At first, the mother indicated that this would be fine, but shortly afterward jerked her feet away with a sharp "That'll do." The daughter ruminated about that moment for weeks afterward. Was the jerking away an intentional cut, an extension of the mother's habitually haughty disapproval and anger? Or was it simply an instinctive withdrawal from sensation, made worse by chronic pain? Her mother was certainly no longer quite herself by virtue of beginning dementia and physical decline—or was she? The daughter would never know how her mother truly felt about her at the time of her death, as the mother's organic decline made the meaning of her cutback inscrutable—a situation ripe for engendering troubling projections of the darkest kind.

Maternal Cutting Back and Its Reverberations in the Therapeutic Relationship

A law student in her twenties, Sylvia described the relationship, conducted largely by text messaging, that she has with her parents who live in another state. She tries to tell them about the new decisions or advances in her life, and they send back a brisk text to say "So what?" or "Why did you do *that*?" in reply. In order to be connected on any level, she must tolerate these bursts of incomprehension, dismissal, or disapproval. Sylvia associates to an iconic moment at about the age of 5, when she anticipated the treat of her mother reading to her before bed. This particular night her mother was delayed, so to stave off boredom in the meantime, Sylvia decided to listen to the story being read by their father to her younger sister. When the mother finally came in, it was only to announce bedtime. Young Sylvia was shocked. No, she protested urgently, it was time to be read to. No, the mother responded, it was too late, it was now bedtime. No, the little girl countered with mounting desperation, it's time for reading. No, the mother insisted, it's gotten too late, you were already read to with your sister. Sylvia burst into tears and was inconsolable for perhaps an hour. Her mother tried to reason with her but was apparently at a loss as to what was happening. The ritual of her mother reading to her was hugely important to the 5-year-old Sylvia because, being highly precocious, she was chronically famished for stimulation. She believes this is why she cried so hard over something her family thought trivial.

What seems significant to me about this painful memory is that being read to in the evenings was the only time Sylvia could count on any contact with her mother, whose tendencies to be inward and detached made her a shadowy, removed figure in her daughter's life. So being shortchanged in reading time was a cutback that could have registered unconsciously in Sylvia as being tantamount—if only temporarily—to being unloved.

When the thread is thin to begin with, cutting it down further may be unbearable.

That said, I would mention that Sylvia herself disputes my view of the impact of her mother's unavailability. In her conscious view, at least, the father's hands-on involvement was enough for two parents. But that leaves hanging the question of why this is a memory involving her mother rather than someone else, and why there is so much frustration expressed currently at the mother's paltry, unattuned reactions to Sylvia's life events. We may have the kind of telescoping of multiple childhood events into a single remembered moment that Kris (1956) warned about. But what kinds of events may have led up to this scene have not so far emerged, and the matter remains unclear.

Be that as it may, Sylvia enacts cutbacks now with me in her therapy. She seems engrossed in our work. Yet, when a scheduling conflict arises for her, she will unthinkingly delete our session from her smartphone without remembering to tell me. When she fails to come, I'm left high and dry, wondering where she is. What does this absence mean, if anything? Probing its significance once she returns without generating a rattling feeling of anxious guilt in her is no easy task. At those times, Sylvia is momentarily guilty of something she herself suffered, deleting or cutting back on our work and on me, and I continue to suspect that this recapitulates incidents not yet uncovered from her early years. Knowing that in her family the pragmatic handling of logistical matters trumped emotional expression, I also believe that she assumes that she is fungible for me—as perhaps I am for her. It's as if people were not distinctive, idiosyncratic individuals with particular hearts and minds and deepening attachments to one another based on those specificities. It's no wonder that one of Sylvia's favorite morals is Facebook executive Sheryl Sandberg's advice not to leave a job before you've really left it—meaning not to cut back on your emotional investment in the work until your employment there actually ends. This self-reminder is helpful because Sylvia does abruptly drop people and things; she does so defensively, out of a fear of being held back by prior involvements, as she champs at the bit to take the next step in life. When Sylvia drops me, I believe that she unconsciously needs me to register the disheartened feeling of my seeming insignificance for her, even as I grow—almost despite myself—increasingly fond of and attached to her. She needs me to protest her absence, just as she once protested her mother's. And I do, gently hoping one day we'll be able to articulate these feelings and their sources more fully together.

Emotional Paralysis as the Legacy of Repeated Familial Cutting Back

There are families in which cutting back is close to the only means for dealing with ambivalence. A 75-year-old, mild-mannered architect, Eric, came into therapy to talk about his difficulty dealing with his female life partner's worsening arthritic hips, which for various reasons were inoperable. The woman, whom he dearly loved, was becoming increasingly needful of his support, both physical and psychological. He was in principle more than happy to offer it—consciously—but he too often found himself unable to rise to the occasion when she would become especially distressed and seek his steadying influence. Paralyzed, he was largely unable to speak to her at those moments, not knowing what he could offer his partner that would be useful to her. In the face of his silence, and terrified of her disability's progressive pace, she would become frustrated and attack him for not being sufficiently attuned, assertive, and "take charge" in his response. The situation escalated her anxiety at the possibility of her becoming increasingly hampered and immobile over time.

We puzzled over Eric's situation, one in which he invariably—and seemingly involuntarily—cut back emotionally on his woman friend. We realized that this unbidden silence was part of a broader and deeper swath of passivity in his personality that would come out in times of strain. We were gradually able to link it to a longing for his phlegmatic mother's approval and a reluctance to do anything that would threaten obtaining and keeping it. (There was nothing to gain from turning to his father, in the face of the latter's harsh, detached, judgmental manner.) Even more importantly, as a child, the closest person to Eric had been his older brother, some eight years his senior, who on reaching the age of 18 simply disappeared and was never heard from again. The other family members speculated that he had grown tired of the father's harshness and the mother's detachment, but there was no way of knowing if this were the truth or simply a projection. Eric had struggled for years to deal with the cruelty of this loss, sometimes wondering what he himself had meant to the brother, given that the latter was so willing to give up their relationship completely and with no explanation.

As it happened, just a few years prior to the therapy's initiation, there had been a fresh instance of cutting back on the part of a member of Eric's family. His sister had been living in Seattle for some years when she began encouraging Eric to relocate from Boise to join her there. Yet, six months or so after Eric and his mate had indeed re-settled nearby the sister in Seattle, they discovered inadvertently that the sister had secretly and inexplicably begun making plans to move to California. When he confronted her as to whether this was so, she just shrugged her shoulders, as if to say, "Too bad, that's just how it is." The sister felt like moving and that was that. She excused her decision by complaining that Eric hadn't been free enough from other involvements to spend time with her, a charge both Eric and his life partner thought patently untrue. Eric was hurt, aggravated, and once again blind-sided by the loss, but there was no way to work it through with the sister.

In short, Eric came from a family in which conflict was unsupportable and disagreement unthinkable. The undigested loss of the older brother served as a warning that one could incite a lifelong abandonment at any moment. It was best to hold still, squelch one's emotions, and try to be satisfied with whatever thin thread of attachment still existed. But this stance led to a situation in which Eric himself could only respond to a health crisis by cutting back from his life partner; saying the wrong thing carried too great a risk, and being angry with or objecting to aspects of her growing needfulness was too great a danger. The result was a reenactment in miniature of some of the very things that had plagued him in his own attachment history, with Eric now the perpetrator. At the same time, in cutting back on his life partner, he risked arousing her own urge to cut back on him.

Eric and I had initially agreed on a time-limited, once-weekly therapeutic contact for two months. When he reached the agreed-upon termination date, he told me that, indeed, the therapy had been of great use and he was ready to stop as planned. As part of that final session, I asked Eric to read the above account, and he told me that it hit the nail on the head in all respects but one: I'd failed to mention (and, in fact, he hadn't yet made this entirely clear to me) that understanding the role of cutting back in his life had given him the handle he'd needed to refind his voice with his life partner. He was now much better able to share his full reactions to her situation. This in turn relieved and gratified her, as what she'd wanted all along from him was an open responsiveness, not a magic wand for her arthritic condition or the anxieties it engendered. In addition, there had been a welcome change in Eric's attitude toward his architectural activities. At the start of treatment, he'd felt disconnected from his projects, probably because he'd been recoiling (cutting back) unconsciously from certain criticism they had garnered. By the time we'd wound to a close, Eric had become newly re-engaged and excited by the projects, and was delightedly putting more and more time into them.

Unkind Cutbacks during Periods of Separation-Individuation

It can sometimes be injurious to oneself to be the person instigating distance, even if doing so is in the pursuit of one's own well-being. Marta, a woman in her mid-thirties, comes into my office with a tear-stained face, warning apologetically that she's likely to cry further during the session. She's recently received word that the 63-year-old mother of a childhood friend had finally succumbed to a long illness. Marta starts the session reviewing her connection with the deceased woman and with her daughter. She describes the nature of her high school friendship with the daughter and the trials and tribulations this family had experienced in dealing with the mother's long illness. Marta and I make the link between all this and its implications for her own parents' mortality. Eventually, though, it emerges that the depth of her current grieving is not so much about the actual death of this woman or even of her own parents' inevitable demise. She is actually mourning the loss of the community she'd left behind, a loss that hearing this news now drives home to her. Marta had moved to the Pacific Northwest from New England, nursing the hope of finding a vibrant cultural mix of people and a sophisticated professional world that would have some of the specialness of her own region but be free of some of its downsides for her. She had to distance herself both from her high school friends and her own family members, many of whom were unusually needy, in order to avoid falling into the miasma of taking care of them. Their expectation that she would salve their anxieties and mediate their differences had come to weigh too heavily on her, even while she had to keep their insecurities and aggressive tendencies at bay. But in the cutting back of her relocation, Marta deprived herself of a closeness that, despite its draining aspects, had also been gratifying. As is so often true in separation-individuation processes, though the move was in the service of her own development, it hurt her at the same time. Leaving her familiar environment, Marta diminished the likelihood of being able to work through and resolve the interpersonal friction she felt with those she'd left behind. Poignantly reminded of them upon hearing of this death, Marta now keenly felt the sacrifice associated with her geographic—and psychological—withdrawal.

Late adolescents moving into young adulthood may engage in unkind cutbacks when they're at the point of leaving home. Should they lack the requisite skills to traverse this stage of separation-individuation effectively while still staying in touch with their parents, these teenagers may blame this on the parents themselves; they may punish their parents for their supposed faults by going to extremes, such as hiding important details of their lives or even disappearing for extended periods of time. These acts may be intended as gestures of self-assertion and self-preservation, with the distance from the parents being imposed as part of the adolescent striving to develop the capacity for self-direction (see Skolnick & Scharff, 1998). But when not dictated by normative developmental needs, when abrupt, severe, and unexplained, this withholding or disappearance can indeed be an act of hostility and dismissal, resulting in the one left behind feeling psychically slapped in the face. In Fairbairn's terms, unkind cutting back fortifies the internal rejecting object in the psyche of the one being left, with predictably painful consequences for his or her sense of security and worth.

The conflicting pressures of other life stages can also figure into unkind cutting back. The middle-aged adult, perhaps nursing earlier resentment, may only sporadically visit the elderly parent newly placed in a geriatric facility. And sometimes the cutting back can be even more conscious and pointed. In folk-rock singer Harry Chapin's 1974 song "Cat's in the Cradle," a grown-up son, insisting he's much too busy himself now, fends off his father's pleas for contact, just as the father once promised and failed to find time for the son. The son placatingly assures his father that they'll have a good visit—someday. It's a chilling reversal—perhaps in unconscious revenge—of the original micro-traumatic effect the father's absence had had years ago. A self-removal of this kind precludes an effort to understand its psychic underpinnings; it sabotages the further evolution of the relationship into a new, more mature phase.

Occasionally, it happens that a parent not only makes him- or herself inaccessible, but also withdraws in a much fuller way and for no good apparent reason. The interdependent pattern of attachment is abruptly and more thoroughly violated, and the child is left bereft and powerless. There is nothing to be done but grin and bear it, and carry on. In an autobiographical play called *Humor Abuse*, Lorenzo Pisoni, the son of a founder of a family circus, links this dynamic with the origins of the traditional theatrical motif of the inner sadness of the clown figure. The play, performed by Mr. Pisoni and written by him with the help of co-author Erica Schmidt (Isherwood, 2009; Miller, 2011), describes the harrowing process of a boy's learning the clown trade from his father. The father's perfectionistic efforts to be the sharpest, most creative entertainer he could be generated a micro-traumatic "connoisseurship" dynamic (a concept explained more fully in the next chapter) with his son, as if the latter were no more than a younger colleague being trained for the trade. The son doggedly works to perfect his physical stunts to his father's satisfaction. The boy is often awash in shame when he can't achieve the necessary finesse in a given trick or skit. But what hurts the boy even more than the connoisseurship demand is the father's emotional detachment—the paucity of paternal tenderness, intimacy, or nurturance. That detachment is crowned by the day when their tour as a shared clowning act ends. The depressive, obsessive father bids him goodbye, with a casual "see you down the road." Simply put, his father is leaving town and withdrawing from the relationship. After months of at least a good *working* relationship with his father, the pre-adolescent son is left hanging. He returns to live with his mother, now divorced from the father, and his future is unclear. Perhaps he will pursue more show-business efforts on his own—and if he does, this solo enterprise would be all that is left of his partnership with his dad. In this moment of great pathos, the audience senses the birth of a terrible sadness in the boy, his father's cutback generating a hurtful loss from which he will never quite recover—hence the ironic reference to abuse in the title of a play that is supposedly about generating humor and the lifelong honing of a clown's skills. We are clearly in the realm of trauma here, but the art of the play, and of the clown's role, makes us see how such hurts can be hidden behind a smile and a theatrical energy that is meant to divert more than communicate. And such grin-and-bear-it measures are the means by which micro-traumatic moments on a smaller scale are so often parried in the moment, when parrying the hurt is all that's possible to do.

And yet later, it may be possible to do one thing more—that is, to sublimate the hurt into a work of art that communicates as much or more than it diverts. According to the *Humor Abuse* playbill (Miller, 2011), later in their lives, Lorenzo and his father began work on repairing their rift. In fact, one gets the sense from the playbill that the son's having created and performed this play might have brought them closer to one another than ever before. As is often the case in the life of an artist, here the son's creative self-expression may have worked therapeutically to assuage and transform his prior micro-traumatic experience—and perhaps to transform the contemporary father–son relationship as well.

Cutbacks in Psychoanalytic Sessions' Length and Frequency

Just as a cutback can be disturbing in and of itself, so too can the process of negotiating one. Cutting back has, of course, a specialized meaning in the psychoanalytic field, referring to the reduction of therapeutic contact over the course of the week. In treatment, one person's venturing of the idea and the other's response can be the occasion for mutual misrecognition, misattunement, and the bruising of one another's sense of self. Dreading the ache of a weakened connection, the one threatened by the other's cutback may be unconsciously primed to wound the other in return as the decision is worked through.

A more circumscribed cutback occurs when the patient arrives late for the session. A middle-aged patient, Ryan, charges into my office, apologizing profusely for being 10 minutes late for his once-weekly, 90-minute double session—as if his lateness weren't habitual. He goes on to say that he wants to update me about how hard he's worked to make use of our last session. But first, he wants me to know that he's considering dropping down to a single shorter session each week. It might help him get to the sessions not just on time, but early; he'll become better organized and focused about the issues left to resolve. I try not to react precipitously, but clearly fail nonverbally, as Ryan interrupts himself: "Wait a minute—you always *do* this when I talk about cutting down on our time. You look at me like I'm crazy or something! What? Am I that defective and screwed up? I can't manage without two sessions? You must think I'll never learn!" A chuckle escapes me as I respond: "Is that what you think I'm thinking? That you need to be here this much because I think you're so screwed up? Come on!" (Far from being defective, Ryan now functions pretty well in many spheres and is justifiably happy with his life.) Ryan again: "Ok, Ok, I know, you're reacting because I'm so damn defensive. Massively so. Here and in all my relationships. I tidy things up and pull my punches, and it screws me up. And that's why you think I should keep the double."

Ryan knows full well it takes a good initial chunk of our double session for him to let his guard down and present things as they really are. His lateness shaves time off the deepening process and telescopes the session's denouement—already a cutback in itself. It's frustrating to know what he could get from this process—and from me—if he'd only give it enough time to taste those possibilities himself. But he gives the process short shrift or hurries it along. So, therefore, yes, in self-fulfilling fashion, the analytic work will do less for him than he wants and needs, just as he fears. How do I sustain my belief in our work and convey this to him as nondefensively as possible, in order to forestall further cutting back? With Ryan, I feel that establishing such a baseline of belief and commitment on my part is necessary as an anchor before I venture into the murkier waters of sharing my countertransferential exasperation at his moves to cut back and what feel like his insipid justifications for doing so.

Another patient, Rhea, a businesswoman in her early forties, comes to her once-weekly session seven or eight minutes late with some regularity. She is always gracefully upbeat and friendly as she overlooks the late start. She reports a phone conversation with an ex-boyfriend, one who had left her but still "wants to be friends." He now uses Rhea to help him think through his work options, as if she were no more than a career counselor. After an hour of her supporting him through what feels like an erasure of herself as a person, he lobs one final thoughtless remark, and she hangs up on him. I think about how Rhea has masked her hurt and fury from him during the phone call, and wonder if that could be playing out in the transference as well. I suggest to Rhea that she may withhold parts of herself from me that she fears I won't approve of. To hold onto this ingratiating stance with me, she may need to come late to sessions to reduce the amount of time she's having to play the "good patient" with me. But coming late does deprive me of time with her, which simultaneously punishes me and weakens my power and influence over her, even while it seemingly protects me from more fully encountering her negative aspects. So Rhea's customary seven-minute cutback both offers protection to us and damages us in that it constrains the effectiveness of our shared therapeutic efforts. Rhea is at first uncomfortable, but then ultimately relieved to have this dynamic called out. As the session winds down to its conclusion, I urge her to avoid forcing herself to arrive on time just to comply with what she thinks I want. She needn't judge the lateness negatively herself or fear that I will do so; instead, we will try to listen for its meaning and function further, so that if she wishes to give the action words instead, she can eventually do so. Notwithstanding my advice, Rhea begins showing up on time more often and seems to express attitudes and feelings that are more unvarnished than before as well. As in other micro-traumatic situations, a cutback such as Rhea's lateness conveys a mixed message that both withholds negative feeling and expresses it at the same time; then again, it also honors a potentially hopeful view of the relationship by not being a total or dramatic rupture.

The type of cutback that is generally most salient for psychoanalytic work is one that involves the frequency of sessions rather than their length. Perhaps because it is so very common, we find little explicit focus on this moment in the analytic literature (at least, judging from what is available on the PEP-Web, the online psychoanalytic literature archive). A bid for cutting back is often presented as necessitated by pragmatic considerations, and frequently those realistic factors do loom large and have validity. But, of course, psychosocial motives often mask underlying anxieties, disappointments, and criticism, not to mention, on the favorable side of the ledger, the beginnings of an adaptive independence from the process. The patient may have difficulty articulating these more emotionally fraught issues—even improvement—in the face of the shared implicit expectation that the therapeutic relationship continue just as before. So he or she simply pulls back. The complex tangle of conscious and unconscious issues in a cutback is often difficult to tease apart.

However, Lena Theodorou Ehrlich (2010) attempts to do just that in an unusually thoughtful article on the analyst's ambivalence about deepening the work. The patient is Ms. A., a middle-aged, married lawyer, dissatisfied with her marriage and insecure about her professional abilities. Ms. A. had experienced significant childhood neglect, abandonment, and abuse. Unsurprisingly, trust and dependency issues plagued the analytic relationship from the start. Ms. A. initially turned down but eventually agreed to come four times weekly until a financial setback caused her to broach the idea of cutting back to three times per week.

Ehrlich reports feeling terribly conflicted about how to handle the request. She is partially swayed by Ms. A.'s economic concerns and inclined to go ahead and permit the cutback. She also weighs the idea of just reducing her fee so the frequency can remain the same. But on reflection, she decides that either of these steps would be a mistake, motivated by her own countertransference. Thinking about matters further, Ehrlich comes to feel that the patient has failed to take ownership for preserving the analysis, and that this may be an indicator of underlying resistance. She comments to the patient that "she claimed she wanted to continue the analysis but did nothing to solve the problem and make that happen" (p. 524). I want to flag this intervention, which I'll return to momentarily. The analytic couple goes on to identify Ms. A.'s inclination to cut back as being attributable to her traumatic childhood bonds with abusive others.

Although Ehrlich seemingly takes her patient to task, she also chastises herself for her initial inclination to assent to the cutback. She wonders whether, in even toying with the idea of going along with Ms. A.'s request, she had let herself be "taken in" by its supposedly external causation, when instead she should have more fully questioned its defensive motives. Perhaps, she thinks, she herself had a countertransferential need to withdraw from the analytic intensity and allowed this need to trump her ordinary inclination to take a more probing stance. Ehrlich sensitively and responsibly asks herself: "Did *I* want to see her less frequently? What might *I* be trying to avoid?" (p. 524). And in this context, she experiences herself, among other things, as "greedy and exploitative," which she soon comes to see as a projective identification with the patient's earlier destructive objects.

Now back to Ehrlich's comment about the patient's "[doing] nothing to solve the problem." As readers, we can readily concur with Ehrlich's point that it is essential for the clinician to examine the overall context of the patient's request; certainly, it can be counterproductive to simply give in to a patient's request without reflecting on its meaning. But it can also be problematic—and generate its own form of enactment—if the patient feels unduly pressured by the analyst to continue coming at a particular frequency. Moreover, it can be emotionally disruptive if the patient feels put down by a suggestion that she or he is evading responsibility for finding a way to afford as much frequency as the analyst deems optimal. The patient may hear the analyst as saying: "You claimed you wanted intensive work, but in fact you're not up to the challenge." Such an interpretive tack could feel demanding and judgmental, thereby recreating, micro-traumatically, hurtful interpersonal dynamics from the patient's earlier history. As I hear it, Erhlich's comment ought to have been—and in the long run seems to have become—the beginning of a renegotiation of the initial analytic contract.

Speaking of which, this initial contract as to the frequency of meetings—in Ehrlich's instance as in all such treatments—tends to be arrived at on the basis of fairly scanty information about the patient's needs and the analytic relationship-to-be, since these have yet to truly unfold. That is, because they were new to each other at the start of their relationship, the analyst was from the get-go probably more swayed by analytic principles per se, and the patient more influenced by his or her own ongoing character issues or acute need, than they would be later on, once they better knew each other and their shared analytic fit. For this reason, if for no other, it makes sense that the patient may want to revisit and rethink, together with the analyst later in the analysis, the rationale behind the originally established frequency. The patient is now in a better position to weigh in on the decision, armed as he or she is at this point with a felt experience of that frequency's advantages and disadvantages.

Analytic clinicians of *any* stripe—and with the best of intentions—may err in the direction of skipping this reconsideration and negotiation. We tend toward reductionism, which can verge on being exploitative, when we imply to the patient that a cutback request can only *really* be about a deep fear of relational intimacy or resistance to change. For that matter, it seems to me that we err when we view concerns about deepened intimacy as only neurotic and not reality-based. (In relation to this point, Ryan's complaint about my nonverbal protest was fair play!) If the patient needs to defend against too great an intimacy or investment in a relationship slated for extinction—after all, the analysis will presumably terminate at some point—this "defense" has its own existential validity.

In discounting conscious reasons as mere "rationalizations," we also risk overlooking important clues to other areas of psychic vulnerability.

In Ehrlich's case, just for the sake of argument, the patient might have been attempting to convey something about her actual confusion and inadequacy in dealing with personal budgetary issues. This would have indicated an area of developmental arrest or immaturity, perhaps an outgrowth of the deficient parenting Ms. A. had received in childhood. If so, then her wish to cut back was not just a defense against owning "deeper" relatedness conflicts, but carried its own direct, substantive psychic meaning. In general, we do well to consider the full range of a patient's motives, both conscious and unconscious, rather than too quickly minimizing a patient's subjective reasons for cutting back.

I think that our handling of a patient's urge to reduce therapeutic contact is too often affected by the insistent pull of the underlying analytic credo that a greater frequency equals deeper and, therefore, better work. As I (Crastnopol, 1999) and others have argued elsewhere, the analyst's professional identity can at times act as a silent competitor for the analyst's investment and loyalty, which can be problematic irrespective of the analyst's particular theoretical alignment. In moments like this, the pull of values inherent in his or her chosen orientation can channel the analyst's interpretive stance into only one "right" direction.

In short, a cutback exploration can be counterproductive and even hurtful to the degree that it is weighted toward averting it at all costs, or if it seeks the "truest" unconscious meaning, rather than fully considering other relevant possibilities. The patient can feel unheard, as if the analyst were more wedded to his or her theory and technique than to the patient's own particular psychic needs. This adds insult to what may already be the injury of a soon-to-be thinned out attachment.

The upshot in this particular case was that Ms. A. remained in four-times-weekly analysis, and the analysis appears to have proceeded favorably. But naturally, as in any such case illustration, we have no way of knowing for sure how much it was the avoidance of the cutback, or Ehrlich's astute and thorough way of engaging the relevant therapeutic issues, that ensured the patient's progress.

Sometimes a cutback itself is a matter of course and "just a cigar," and ancillary matters such as associated fee adjustments instead become the focus. Even then, it's not simply the fact of a change in arrangements, but the psychic meanings that matter. Stephen Mitchell (1993) recounts a frequency negotiation with an architectural student, Roger. Mitchell starts treating Roger twice per week but is soon asked for an increase to three times, which he facilitates through a slight fee reduction. Now, six years into the treatment, the patient wants to make a costly business investment. He and his analyst decide to reduce the economic strain of this move by cutting down to only two sessions temporarily. Roger then reports a dream that actually seems to imply an unconscious balking at Mitchell's continued fee concession, as if the analyst were being dangerously over-solicitous like Roger's engulfing father. In this instance, perhaps counter-intuitively, Mitchell's *support* of the patient's need for frequency reduction—to the point of himself making an economic sacrifice for it—is thus experienced as injurious by the patient. This case illustrates that it is what the analytic couple comes to understand about the decision, and how they come to understand it, that makes exploring a cutback micro-traumatic or constructive. It is striking how evenhanded Mitchell is in exploring with Roger a range of pertinent psychic meanings for their unfolding process, rather than his leaning toward there being one right view—or, for that matter, one right outcome. While side-stepping that Scylla, Mitchell at the same time avoids the Charybdis of leaving open so many possibilities that no one formulation feels particular and persuasive enough and therefore useful.

The Analyst's Cutbacks in Frequency: Kind or Unkind?

Though the tables would seem to be turned, the issue of potential micro-traumatic injury to one or both parties exists yet again when it's the analyst rather than the patient who advocates cutting back. Not long ago, I myself lobbied for a cutback from four to three sessions per week in one patient's long-term analysis. The patient in question was Sophia, a 50-year-old woman who, as the heiress to a large family fortune, had emigrated to the United States from Belgium some 20 years ago. After nine years of analytic treatment, Sophia still remained relatively schizoid and detached, though she could tentatively acknowledge missing greater intimacy with others. Avoiding most pursuits that would engage her outside her sizable home and grounds, she shirked involvement with anyone besides employees or others providing a service to her. She depended on an older and a younger sister also now living in the US—and her analyst—for most of her human camaraderie and stimulation. An avid gardener, Sophia fought tooth and nail to convince me that she was getting more than enough from tending her flowers and shrubs, although she seemed to me lonely, isolated, and understimulated. Her perfectionism in designing her garden and any other endeavor was extreme, and her criticism of others thinly masked a constant, if unarticulated and unconscious self-derogation. You might say that she was in a chronic state of being partially cut back from external circumstances and external resources, possibly on the basis of a fear that they would upend her precarious sense of self-esteem.

During the first five years or so of the analysis, we nonetheless success-fully leaped a number of emotional hurdles. But then the work reached a plateau in which Sophia seemed to have precious little to talk about, other than railing about various historic disappointments or misfortunes. She seemed to have little intention of rethinking this posture, but wanted me there to witness her misery as she expressed her disappointment in all and sundry. Efforts to interpret this defensive "enclave" (O'Shaughnessy, 1992) led to protests: "Can't you see how scared I am to grow or change? Don't you understand that analysis is a slow process and requires patience?" True enough, but I wasn't sure how much was fear of change and how much was a willful insistence on and rationalization for using our analytic connection as a substitute for pursuing real-life ones.

Eventually, given the dearth of material Sophia actually wanted to explore, and with the disquieting feeling that we were just killing time together, I raised the question of our cutting back on the number of weekly sessions. I urged her strongly to consider the plan, but of course I didn't insist on implementing it. I knew that I was taking a risk, because it was likely that Sophia would interpret my suggestion through the lens of her own projected feelings when she herself cut back pointedly on those whom she felt had slighted *her*. In fact, though she had since renounced this approach, it had happened often in the early years of our work that a particularly probing session would cause Sophia to skip three or four succeeding ones—each session cancelled just prior to its starting time in a kind of extended delicate torture for me. Each time Sophia would claim that it was only a general feeling of ennui rather than an explicit objection to our work that precluded her driving in to meet with me that day. A week or two later, though, she would admit that by cancelling, she was actu-ally avoiding expressing her underlying fury at me for being insufficiently accepting of her in the precipitating exchange. Thus, it was easy to imag-ine that she might experience my current suggestion to cut back as a with-holding of connection, possibly my passive–aggressive way of expressing disapproval of her. Such an interpretation on her part was especially likely given that indirect aggression was still her own modus operandi in related situations.

As expected, Sophia's response to my cutback suggestion was at first righteously indignant. As the patient, didn't she have a right to reserve the time with me whether or not she used our time for analytic processing? What if she herself felt that each session was beneficial (irrespective of *my* opinion), even if she only vented her upsets? Was I insulting her for not hav-ing worked hard enough or being clever enough to change? Was I punishing her for not being "a good girl," or for not making me look like a "successful analyst" in my own eyes? Shouldn't her analysis be one place where her progress wasn't judged, where she could evolve and develop just as she needed and wished to? This last thought certainly gave me pause.

But gradually, Sophia became more reflective and better able to absorb my explanations vis-à-vis the proposed cutback. Entertaining a contrary perspective, she conjectured that perhaps I was indirectly telling her that she had, in a sense, won the right to cut down on sessions because her analytic work had succeeded. And she *had* indeed met some significant psychic benchmarks she had set. Perhaps I was re-empowering her to chart her own goals, however ambitious or modest those might be, which might mean she *could* rather than *must* come less. She mused that my recommendation for cutting back could then be considered an affirmation rather than a critique or rejection of her.

There was considerable truth in these more positive views, even granted that they were still framed in terms of what I wanted from her. But none of this relieved me of the obligation to consider the countertransferential meanings of my wish to reduce the extent of our weekly time together. In part, I was sparing myself the frustration of her remaining in and even buttressing her defensive cocoon. I knew Sophia was anxious, lonely, and possibly bored (whether consciously so or not), and I knew these feelings fueled her episodic hostilities toward others, including me. I recognized that in trying so desperately to reach her, I was reenacting certain proverbial longings in relation to my own early objects, who had been as armored as Sophia. But it felt to me that only by curtailing our contact would I have the necessary buffer to avoid getting unduly demoralized, aggravated, or bored by her resistive state. Her earliest traumatic relationships now well-explored, and our understandings of these put to good use, I now felt occupied (that is, "reserved for service") but unused and relatively useless. Without our shared immersion in promoting her psychic growth, I felt that Sophia had already rather severely cut back on me. But—and here's the rub—this was her choice to make.

I therefore reasoned that by recalibrating my own investment in our process, it was more likely that I could retain the energy to continue to give wholeheartedly whatever Sophia was still willing to take from me. Through a sparing of contact, I was hoping for an "affect sparing" (Stein, 1998) that could help me remain as constructively engaged as possible for her. By affect sparing, I mean a containment of feelings or the avoidance of triggering an outflow of emotion—here from either analyst or patient—that might be too intense to process at a given point in time or might be otherwise counterproductive. (Here I think of Winnicott's momentary cutback on Margaret Little (1985)—that is, his withdrawal from the treatment room to collect himself so as not to burden her with his upset after she broke his vase.)

With all this in mind, I worked to distinguish the significance the cutting back had for *me* from what it had for *her*. I sought to explore any insulted or ashamed feelings Sophia might have had in response to my recommendation. I told her point blank that she needed a larger vacuum in her life that would pull her to fill it with extra-therapeutic involvements. This in turn could be fodder for further analytic work. I tried to keep in play all the diverse meanings of "failure" and "success" of the cutback, and I was able to tell her quite truthfully that I would miss her were it to go forward. The reduction eventually did occur and, to our joint relief, actually began yielding some of the benefits I'd hoped for. She seemed to want to make more intensive use of the time we continued to have together, and it helped that she knew the decision was reversible and that I would be responsive to any signals that it should be reconsidered.

Of course, a cutback of this kind does have reverberations for which we must continue to listen. Five months later, Sophia herself suggested a further reduction to coming only twice per week. I wasn't entirely surprised, as she had begun hinting at some disquiet around the time when I'd mentioned an annual fee increase. Now, she told me that she was feeling much stronger and somewhat more connected to others than she'd felt before, and she referenced an example of having withstood an experience that had heretofore been more trying for her. I viewed this particular instance as a rather faint achievement, and yet I agreed that overall she seemed happier and more relaxed than in the past. At the same time, it struck me that she was viewing a further cutback as a reward for improvement—and nothing more. She was not factoring in the vexed question of her overall analytic goals and where she stood in meeting them. I felt we needed to get more clarity as to whether she should strive further to broaden and deepen her engagement with the world (admittedly, my own view of what she would need in order to feel more self-valuing and greater joy in life), or whether her goals had become more circumscribed, a healthy and apt development. If the latter, a cutback was just what the doctor—Sophia's own internalized doctor—ordered.

Sophia, however, wasn't interested in addressing this question directly. "You're forgetting how immature I can be!" she said both seriously and teasingly. "Can't you tell that in some ways this is tit for tat?" And adopting the taunting tone of a 7-year-old, she added: "You cut back on *me* before, so now I'll cut back on *you!*" With that honest admission, we were thrown back into a consideration of authentically ambivalent motives. And in a puzzling reversal of my initial posture, I now found myself yearning to hold onto Sophia for three sessions per week long enough for us to make what I felt would be more solid gains. We agreed to leave the decision open and let the matter ripen over another few months' worth of exploration.

An unkind cutback in psychoanalytic work is one that is precipitous and insufficiently understood. It is especially challenging because in such a withdrawal, as in the situation with my errant contractor, the retreating person's continued partial presence evokes the "memory and desire" of all we wished to be able to do together, whereas his or her cutting back reduces the means—the time and traction—available for doing so. When it is the patient's impetus to cut back, signaling a reduced investment in the analytic process, the clinician must of course contain any nostalgic or narcissistic dismay, so she or he can continue to take full advantage of however much connection remains. By the same token, a patient who is cutting back may incorrectly believe that the analyst lacks strong personal feelings for him or her or strong investment in the therapeutic relationship. The cutback is assumed to be of little consequence to the analyst. In such cases, it can be helpful for the analyst to express rather than contain whatever feelings of sadness, loss, or regret the cutback engenders. This establishes the analyst's actual level of concern for and connection with the patient. It should be done in a way that reassures the patient as to the analyst's continued investment irrespective of the patient's decision, rather than binding the patient to the former frequency—though, of course, being apprised of the analyst's involvement may reduce the patient's wish to cut back (Don Greif, personal communication, 2013). Whatever the situation, the analyst must continue to mine the therapeutic bond—strong or weak as it may be—for all it's worth.

Broader Considerations Regarding Cutbacks in Everyday Life

Our culture is, as a rule, highly ambivalent or even contradictory in its messages about attachment and dependency. We prize self-sufficiency and independence, placing them among our highest desiderata. We romanticize close bonding in early parent–child and adult love relationships, but we're quick to question its healthiness or utility in most other stages of life and most other relational configurations. Pursuing a cutback, for better or worse, jibes with this overall attitude. It implicitly queries how permissible it is to want and to get emotional sustenance from another, whether it is more admirable to do with less, and what the cost of doing with less might be.

Part of what makes a cutback so difficult is that it may put implicit pressure on one or both individuals to give as much and as well as he or she could when there was more contact. Or having felt slighted, rejected, or simply restricted by the cutback, we may feel the need to try to reestablish our worth to the other. These self-expectations can be a false antidote to the pain of loss. The self-imposed task to provide concentrated "goodness" is daunting, which in turn can burden the closeness that's still intact. But on the favorable side, a cutting back of interpersonal contact can lead to a crystallization of the heretofore more plentiful moments of involvement. It offers the chance to test the hardiness of the internalizations of the relationship's constructive influence.

That said, there can be great value in being able—with one's eyes open—to wait out a cutback, pending further understanding of its meaning and implications for the future. One might need to give the rift in rhythm time to settle, to permit oneself to either learn more about it, or at least let the pain and frustration over it fade. Letting the cutback be may in turn open up possibilities for constructive repair down the line. We did just that with our contractor, who did, in his own time, finish up the kitchen construction most ably. There never was an explanation of his unavailable periods, nor did he show any openness to viewing our complaint about it as valid or seem willing to discuss it with us in a forthright way. We did learn that apparently this in-and-out pattern extended to his work with other clients as well, which took some of the narcissistic sting out of the matter. We had to come to terms with the idea that if we wanted him as our go-to house wizard, we needed to learn to accept his comings and goings with some degree of equanimity. Our power lay in being able to choose when we did have the patience and emotional bandwidth for dealing with his approach, and when we did not. An existentialist attitude is often the most productive one for salving life's micro-traumatic situations!

Note

1 This is but one of various versions of this century-old verse, which according to Kahn (1939) had already "achieved a kind of folklore status" by 1939. The variant cited above can be found in McCord's (1955) version. The quatrain's multiple revisions over the years capture a cutback's uncanny staying power amidst all revisions of our understanding of it.

Chapter 3

Connoisseurship Gone Awry

The connoisseur's mindset involves a preoccupation with seeking ever greater refinement in his or her knowledge, mastery, or level of appreciation. This mindset is often a blessing, but it can also be a curse. Although there is much to celebrate in connoisseurship, in what follows, I concentrate on articulating its potential for micro-traumatic impact. I explore a sub-optimal form of connoisseurship shared by two individuals, examining its operation in a variety of configurations—between mentor and protégé, parent and child, analytic supervisor and supervisee, and analyst and patient.

A connoisseur, according to Merriam-Webster, is an expert who comprehends the "details, technique, or principles of an art and is competent to act as a critical judge." In addition, it refers to a discriminating individual whose enjoyment hinges on an appreciation of subtleties. "Connoisseur" is derived from the Latin word *cognoscere*, meaning "to know," which implicitly raises the question of what it means to know or to know something better than the next fellow. What competency or power does highly refined knowledge grant us? What status does it confer? How does being "in the know" play out in one's relationships?

I suggest that the connoisseur's perspective often ends up structuring a form of relatedness wherein the "savvy" person—for better or worse—inducts another person into the intricacies of a given subject matter, field of endeavor, or way of being. The aim may be a circumscribed one—that is, to alter a specific sector of the other's personality or lifestyle. Or the one "in the know" may take on the bigger mission of attempting to make over the other person hook, line, and sinker. Whatever the extent of the influence, I call this type of interplay "imparted connoisseurship." Usually, the influence of imparted connoisseurship is unidirectional from patron to protégé; other times, it is bidirectional, a shared or mutual connoisseurship between peers in which the two alternate between influencing and being influenced.

The paradigmatic version of *healthy* imparted connoisseurship is exemplified by a parent educating the child in such a way that the child is drawn into ever greater engagement with the world, both receptively and expressively. The child is invited to experience something more deeply, to appreciate this experience's fine points more fully, or to perform some action more expertly. Most teacher–student, master–disciple, and other relationships based on a training function involve some degree of healthy connoisseurship. But when the coaxing turns into a sort of coercion, when the guiding person's motive is more narcissistic than generative, or when it occurs compulsively as a replacement for more benevolent guidance, the influence depletes the one being taught. This form of imparted connoisseurship typically involves having a hyper-discriminating person trumpet his or her special knowledge of excellence to another person. In so doing, the "knowing one" implicitly or explicitly offers to share his or her greater sophistication with the other. The mentor's tone may be snooty and self-satisfied or even self-congratulatory. There is a continual rating of exemplars in a targeted area and a frequent comparison of those ratings. The connoisseur is the arbiter of what is better, and sharing this perspective confers special status on the protégé as well. Where once the protégé was "lost," he or she now is "found." Acquiring this higher level of cultivation may generate an elation akin to a high, as one heightens one's sensitivity to the gradations in an outer object or improves one's own skills or attributes. But the addictiveness can blind one to when the connoisseurship-based relating goes awry.

There are plenty of good reasons for not being sure as to how, when, or why the relationship has indeed become problematic. The expansion of finesse through imparted connoisseurship may redound to one's credit and lead to higher social or professional status. It invariably offers a narcissistic boost, not least because upgrading one's competence, little by little, truly does increase one's sense of mastery in the world. Thus, pursuing connoisseurship can be a defense that is adaptive, while also being an adaptation that is defensive. Being on the receiving end of imparted connoisseurship can reduce the anxiety and shame of feeling insufficiently cultivated. However, it can instead, or even simultaneously, generate further anxiety and shame by drawing attention to how much more there might be to learn. And in an information age such as ours, there is always lots more to learn.

That connoisseurship can at the same time heighten self-esteem *and* anxiety, particularly social anxiety, is highlighted by *New York Times* writer and editor J. Peder Zane (2013) in an article entitled, "In pursuit of taste, en masse." Zane argues that our society is shaped by the consumerist focus in today's world. We may not be wealthy, but we can prove how hip we are by having up-to-date ideas, by showing that we know what there is to know. And that in turn is advertised by what products we buy and how we are seen using them. To reference Zane's example, drinking the latest imported artisanal craft ale in a crowded bar, we broadcast our status as connoisseurs. And ironically enough, sometimes what we choose to consume or use is a product designed to seem simpler rather than more "gourmet." That is, current-day connoisseurship looks for products that seem authentic and original in order to demonstrate the absolute "most knowing" sensibility. Zane cites the cultural critic Thomas Frank, who noted that all this ends up being mostly in the service of boosting one's self-image in one's own eyes; it really doesn't prize the highest quality product, but the one that stands to make one seem most special. In the end, it all amounts to little more than snobbery.

Pursuing hipness is a means of binding the social anxiety to which we're all subject. At the same time, demonstrating the requisite kind of rarefied taste is a moving target. What makes us feel socially confident and "in" one moment can easily be seen as passé and "out" the next. And more fundamentally, the idea that being savvy is a measure of deeper worth is obviously bankrupt. Here's where connoisseurship runs aground—and the same can often be said of the interpersonal process of imparting a connoisseur-like sensibility to someone else.

Relating through imparted connoisseurship has two intertwined components: the subject matter of shared interest, and the emotional tie that develops between the two people as a result. The quality of that emotional tie can be cooperative or competitive, generous or withholding, genuine or false. Sometimes, the supposedly shared interest is just an excuse for two persons to be intimate (when there are healthy motives) or to "glom on" to one another (in the presence of unhealthy ones). In other words, relating via a shared immersion in connoisseurship can unfortunately become a "look-alike" for true emotional closeness (Ghent, 1990). The very real knowledge involved is put to wayward use, becoming something like what Khan (1966, 1979) called a "technique of intimacy" that substitutes for the real thing.

One has to get inside any particular connoisseur-based relationship to see how it functions. Sometimes there is such a rich mutual fascination with the subject matter that promoting its understanding is really the main event; other times, however, the artificial role-play of attempting to enhance or be enhanced by the other is what's most important, rather than the object of shared interest itself. In other words, when we point out a particular constellation to someone else on a starry night, we sometimes do it solely out of awe for the magnificence of outer space. But at other times, we do it because we want to garner admiration for how smart we are, astronomically speaking, and this also gets us off the hook for establishing our worth and reducing our anxieties in some other, potentially more solid, way.

Apart from the interpersonal manifestations of imparted connoisseurship, the same patterning also can occur within the microcosm of one's own internal world. We relate in a teaching, refining mode not only toward others but also, at times, toward ourselves. We urge ourselves onward to greater appreciation, attunement, and skill. In so doing, we may lift ourselves by our bootstraps—or drag ourselves down. Having internalized past connoisseurship bonds with significant others, we teach ourselves as our mentors taught us. We then re-project our internal self-relating onto new mentorship relationships in recursive fashion. Of course, we may be either supportive or contemptuous toward ourselves, with either constructive or denigrating consequences for our psychic well-being and, down the line, for the well-being of others we presume to influence in turn.

Being made aware of a higher degree of refinement in someone else vis-à-vis some dimension that matters to us can readily become a spur to envy. If one can glimpse but not attain that higher, better, deeper level, one can come to feel diminished and devalued. Of course, there are always those who are less sophisticated still. Becoming sensitized to more exacting standards can call forth "envy upward" and "scorn downward," to borrow the terms used by Fiske (2010) in her research about the impact of comparisons between individuals in higher or lower social brackets. In deleterious cases, the one "in the know" may identify projectively with the "novice" in relation to the latter's lack. The knower defends against his or her own unconscious sense of inadequacy by proxy, through an overbearing coaxing of the protégé in the direction of increased sophistication. In other words, the aim within the knower may be to quell his or her own shame and anxiety at any perceived insufficiency by overcorrecting for it in the other. In addition, there may be an unconscious agenda to spoil another's good inner feeling as a means of self-elevation. In intensive treatment, the latter dynamic can sometimes be more deeply explored as an expression of Kleinian envy and even Bionian attacks on linking

As part of a destructive connoisseurship dynamic, an intimate bubble may be established that elevates the two parties above the hoi polloi. The disciple implicitly feels elevated by the master, while people with blunter sensibilities are jointly disdained. This mechanism heightens the potential for feeling inferior down the road, should the disciple deviate from the standards set by the "one who knows." Even if the learner recognizes the lesson's arbitrariness, he or she feels graced. The other's finickiness is accepted as a finesse that seems all to the good. It becomes hard for the protégé to think differently from the patron or to leave room for the views of others, much less to pay adequate emotional attention to other sectors of life besides the one targeted for connoisseurship. So in the process of immersing oneself in the area of shared fascination, the protégé's life experience can paradoxically suffer a degree of impoverishment. His or her circle of constructive interpersonal connections may shrink as well.

The "Stars" Game

A highly anxious young woman, Charlotte, began therapy reveling in an odd but very intense and compelling connoisseurship relationship with Sam, her former boyfriend. Early in our work, Charlotte began a session in a blaze of excited insight. "You know what?" she exclaimed, "I realized just after I left last time what the issue is. It didn't make sense at first, but now I get it!" She proceeded to explain that the reason she was still obsessively tied to Sam was that he was the only one in her constellation of family and friends who "got" her. He, unlike anyone else, understood that her relentless drive to achieve did not enslave her, but rather was something she thrived on. Charlotte needed to go from success to success, to keep busy, to do as well as possible at everything she touched. By the age of 24, this engaging young woman had garnered top honors from an elite university in California that served the best and the brightest biochemistry students. And so had Sam.

Sam and Charlotte were still "partners in crime" despite the cessation of their romantic involvement. Each encouraged but also goaded the other onward to the next height. Sam was the only one who could and would go that far, that compulsively, with her. Though in some senses the connoisseurship was shared, it appeared that Sam was on the higher pedestal and suffered much less shame and self-doubt in the process. Sam was prone to preening about his own achievements while minimizing Charlotte's. She, on the other hand, not only refrained from minimizing his successes, but also quietly berated herself for any way in which he seemed to surpass her.

Charlotte experienced Sam as both alter ego and, in her words, "nemesis." They had kept daily—and sometimes hourly—tabs on each other's progress throughout their high school, college, and early professional years. If he got a prestigious internship in one location, she had to get one that was more special in another. If she received an honor he did not get, he minimized her success as being only due to reverse gender discrimination. (Charlotte insisted that this explanation did not offend her, it merely spurred her on to prove its fallacy.) Their shared drive fed an intellectual hunger that kept Charlotte feeling challenged and on task. She was so bound up in this dynamic with Sam that she ended up specializing in the particular areas that he himself thought important, rather than following her own inclinations. She could excel at both, she thought, so it "didn't really matter." It was fun proving to him she could do well in whatever he found valuable. In the background, readers of a certain age can probably hear the line from the old Irving Berlin duet in the musical *Annie Get Your Gun*—"anything you can do, I can do better." Sung by a male and female singer, each determined to top the other, the song captures perfectly the competitiveness (turned to comedy) that fueled Charlotte and Sam.

Sam played the "stars" game with her. In this game, Charlotte awarded herself stars if she performed well in the various spheres of her life (e.g., work, socializing, an artistic outlet, physical self-care). Not only was it critical that the total number of stars be high enough, but also they had to be balanced: it would be great to have a "5" in her professional life, but better still if all the other realms were at least a "4." Sam was less concerned about balance, more concerned that his total number of stars exceeded hers.

Charlotte expressed her own understanding of the reasons behind her thirst for high ratings—and recognition from Sam as competitor—in terms of her family:

> In my home, they all knew I could do whatever I tried to do, so my achievements never seemed to impress them much—they just took it in stride. They meant well when they said, "You're fine as you are, calm down, you don't have to push yourself." But it was so frustrating! They didn't seem to recognize that I *like* pushing myself! And, we were a polite family, so small tasks you did for the family got huge, out-of-proportion praise. Make a meal—"great job!" Load the dishwasher—"that's fantastic!" It felt silly, beside the point,

not what I needed. I ended up expecting congratulations for all the inconsequential things I did. At the same time, I got no real attention for the amazing ones. I couldn't tell what made my actions worthy or how they stacked up against anyone else's. Sam's approval, on the other hand, is completely conditional—which makes it much more satisfying for me. So now, it's very, very hard to give that up, even though I don't actually want to be his girlfriend anymore.

Why had Charlotte ended their boyfriend–girlfriend status? It was not that their mutual competitiveness had gone too far—there was no such thing as too far. Rather, it had started to bother her that Sam was always more critical of her than she was of him. Even more important, she had come to grasp that his emotional range for other facets of life was severely constricted. He was unable, for example, to join and support her in mourning a mutual friend's death, which they both suspected was by suicide. After trying her best to help Sam understand and sympathize, if not empathize, with her own despair at the time, Charlotte recognized that Sam would not be able to be there for her through life's emotional twists and turns in even the most rudimentary way. So she changed their romantic status—but not the constant contact and mutual contests. It was addictive. She was hooked on the continual challenge of scaling new heights together, however anxiety-provoking this might be at times.

In time Charlotte came to understand, not just theoretically but also viscerally, what the bond meant for her: it was a formulaic effort to provide exciting standards that could direct her growth in the absence of properly attuned attention from her parents. She realized that making Sam the designated arbiter of her worth, although in some ways satisfying, tended to swell rather than diminish the underlying current of anxiety that permeated her daily life. Perhaps, she mused, she could tolerate a longer stretch between their heretofore daily phone calls or texts. But then where would the support, direction, and camaraderie come from? Who would nourish her imaginings as to what to accomplish next and spur their actualization? During this period in the work, Charlotte was at times almost manically active. Some of this was constructive energy, and some was extreme anxiety as to whether she was doing well enough in her life strivings. With Sam fading from the picture, she did not know how to discern what her own actual desires and needs were within the sea of potentially accessible goals, all of which were likely to be reachable, given her extreme giftedness.

I began forming a picture of how this young woman might have developed such a strong craving for a connoisseurship bond. Charlotte's early childhood was moderately happy, but family life was conducted with some odd, rather depriving arrangements that could not be challenged. The parents, for example, did not cook regular dinners at home but instead ate haphazardly throughout the week. On weekends, they convened for a meal at her aunt's house. Charlotte's mother, also quite intelligent, had been abused in some unspecified way growing up. She had married multiple times (a fact that was unknown to Charlotte until later childhood) before marrying Charlotte's father, and during Charlotte's childhood, she had suffered from some form of heart disease that the mother herself and the family minimized.

In a nutshell, Charlotte's mother was so preoccupied with her own professional life and also her health that she was uninvolved with her daughter's life from childhood onward. It was taken for granted that Charlotte was responsible enough, even as a preschooler, to choose creative, constructive activities for herself. Charlotte was somewhat closer to her father, whose thought process and work interests were more like her own. He was responsive to her overt needs and, if asked, would offer opinions about her life direction—in a detached, disinterested sort of way—but he largely let her forge her own path.

Charlotte's parents' psychic limitations disrupted their ability to address her feeling states and undermined their capacity to respond sensitively to Charlotte as a specific individual. In Khan's (1963) terms, there was an early "premature and selective ego development" spurred by her precocity and the "impingement" of her parents' relative absence and suppression of information and feelings. Charlotte was left too much to her own devices. Though she tried to recast this in her mind as an expression of her parents' faith in her maturity, it was actually an abandonment.

The one bright spot was Charlotte's father's availability as a role model, albeit one limited by a degree of emotional remove. His high standards shaped her own. The connoisseurship-style following of her highly admired father was a replacement for a more thoroughgoing emotional involvement with both parents. Because it could not suffice, especially in late adolescence, Charlotte needed someone like Sam to come along and offer a more minute involvement in her efforts to raise herself during the all-important years of early adulthood. An addictive but ultimately shallow identificatory oneness—a state of mutually imparted connoisseurship—was established with Sam to stand in for the fuller emotional engagement that did not occur in the familial nexus of her childhood.

In contrast to a healthier sort of relatedness around aspirations, the emphasis in micro-traumatic connoisseurship is often on excessively nuanced degrees of refinement and matters of style over substance. The degrees of learning appear to involve overfastidiousness and sometimes a "misplaced precision." The upgrading can seem arbitrary and may not enhance the skill or attribute in any meaningful way. The emphasis is on boosting the prestige and cachet of the mentor, rather than on the growth of the one being mentored or on the domain of shared interest itself. Being part of an "in" crowd often involves a healthy dose of this kind of overfastidiousness.

Letting Slip One's Judgmentalism

Sometimes one individual in a dyad has unusually high standards for him- or herself, whereas the other does not. The first one's connoisseurship may spread to his or her evaluation of the other, with painful and divisive consequences. A male patient was obsessed with further hardening his already taut musculature. He recognized that this obsession went "a little overboard" but largely viewed it as a good thing. One day, smiling ruefully, he told me that his girlfriend had asked him about his perception of her body, specifically her weight fluctuations, over the course of their two-year relationship. Though usually careful to express only praise for her gorgeous figure, he let something slip: "I can remember you at times being *somewhat* less thin than you are now." His effort to temper the wording was to no avail. She shot back: "Ah, you're saying I was fat!" Indeed, all along he *had* been evaluating her body with a connoisseur's eye, just as he was always evaluating himself. Her initial question was probably far from innocent but, for better or worse, she'd now registered his exacting side. The man's judgmentalism strained their relationship, just as it had already taken an intrapsychic toll on the man's inner relationship with himself. His "slip" highlighted an aspect of his love that involved appreciating the girlfriend as a narcissistic extension. He had hoped to mask his own hypercritical, narcissistic connoisseurship, but his unconscious willed out. To judge from his report, after this interchange, the young woman became increasingly active in challenging the man's critical tendencies as an indicator of his own insecurity and rigidity, something she expected him to work on "with your therapist." This he proceeded to do. It is fun to lift weights, and fun, too, to do it before a mirror in a gym. But when the search for greater and greater "definition" goes too far, and is foisted on the other, the perfectionism becomes excessive.

The Full-Scale Connoisseurship Effect

An extreme version of imparted connoisseurship occurs when one individual tries to remake the other "whole cloth" in his or her own image. One of the earliest representations of this relationship is the Greek myth of Pygmalion described by Ovid. Pygmalion of Cyprus is a sculptor who falls in love with an ivory statue of his own creation. He prays to Venus, who answers his prayers by allowing his kiss of the statue to make it come alive, creating the young woman whom Jean-Jacques Rousseau subsequently christened Galatea.

Most readers are acquainted with the familiar elaboration of this myth in George Bernard Shaw's very successful 1912 play, *Pygmalion*, later popularized further in a movie of the same name and then yet once more in the hit Broadway musical *My Fair Lady* (Lerner & Loewe, 1956). The continued favor audiences have shown to this work should alert us that connoisseurship as a dynamic core of a relationship is somehow intrinsically fascinating.

Shaw's play tells the story of phonetics professor Henry Higgins, who enters into a bet with a friend that he can transform a simple flower girl, Eliza Doolittle, into a lady so refined that she can pass as a duchess. Higgins succeeds at this by teaching her the superficial gifts of proper speech and manners. Falling in love with Eliza in the process, he continues nonetheless to treat her with condescension and disdain. Now possessed of an impeccable style that simulates lifelong high breeding, Eliza no longer feels obligated to submit to the professor's dominating haughtiness. At the same time, her underlying goodness, integrity, and sheer spunk remain uncontaminated by her newly acquired refinement. In Shaw's play, Eliza struggles with her attachment to her "Pygmalion" Higgins but eventually breaks free and rejects him. She vows to go forth into the world and make her own way, teaching the phonetics she learned from him. In *My Fair Lady*, the ending is somewhat more ambiguous and the audience is left with the possibility that they will reconcile and stay together.

It is noteworthy that Eliza's participation in the connoisseurship relationship with Higgins, despite its having been wounding and restrictive, has also apparently strengthened her trust in her innate gifts and in her capacity to learn and grow. She has been enlivened by being the object of intensive instruction from a more sophisticated elder, notwithstanding the narcissistic and self-serving motives that initially fuel his investment in her.

Shaw's play, like most of his work, had a social-political bent. His point was that matters of style, and especially speech, served as badges of class and thus also as impenetrable barriers to upward mobility. The absurdity of this is what Eliza's transformation is meant to underscore. But for our purposes, and for most subsequent audiences, the moral is a personal one—namely, that it is wrong to overwhelm another with the elements of one's own presumably more desirable upbringing, taste, expertise, or what have you, as this enslaves the spirit of the other under the guise of elevating the person or conferring greater advantage. The gains in self-worth and prestige for the junior partner will ultimately have to be discounted by some degree of psychic injury. And yet what makes Shaw's play so compelling is that we are all complicit in Professor Higgins' wayward scheme: we root for him to achieve his goal, root for Eliza to pass herself off as a duchess, and are delighted when the ruse works. As an audience, we also want a happy ending. The consequence over the years was that producers and actors lobbied long and hard with Shaw to change the ending and have Eliza and the Professor end up together. There is something in us that wants to believe that this kind of relationship can work, that it can lead to deeper things. Shaw was having none of it. His resolve in this matter shows not only his understanding of stagecraft—the tension should not be broken—but also, I think, a deeper psychological understanding of the connoisseurship relationship itself and of psychological functioning in general.

One of the ways in which a person's unconsciously imposed expectations have a marked effect on another has been enshrined in the concept, the "Pygmalion effect," which was identified and explored almost 50 years ago by psychologist Robert Rosenthal and Lenore Jacobson in their book *Pygmalion in the Classroom* (1968; see also revised edition, 1992). Utilizing a California grade school, Rosenthal first administered a surreptitious IQ test to students in all six grades. At the end of the study, a retest showed all children scoring higher in raw scores. But he also "identified" at random a subset of children in each class who were primed, he told teachers, to make a big "spurt" in the coming year. And those children, who were known to the teachers, did in fact show even greater increases on the retest, at least in the first two grades. It has proved difficult to replicate the experiment for various reasons, including widespread knowledge of the phenomenon, but the Pygmalion effect stands as a shining example of how expectations can shape behavior and, more importantly for our purposes, achievement. It should be noted that the children did not know of their purported rating, nor did the teachers discuss it with them. The entire thing happened nonverbally, with the teacher's expectations triggering a measurable response in the child, though to be sure the effect was only statistically significant at the younger ages. Interestingly, Rosenthal (2014) began life as a clinician before switching to social psychology, and his own summary of his research interests speaks to that background:

> For nearly half a century I have been fascinated by the psychology of interpersonal expectations; the idea that one person's expectation for the behavior of another can come to serve as self-fulfilling prophecy. Our experiments have been conducted in laboratories and in the field, and we have learned that when teachers have been led to expect better intellectual performance from their students they tend to get it. When coaches are led to expect better athletic performance from their athletes they tend to get it. When behavioral researchers are led to expect certain responses from their research participants they tend to get those responses. For almost as long as I've been interested in interpersonal expectations I've also been interested in various processes of nonverbal communication. In part, this interest developed when it became clear that the mediating mechanisms of interpersonal expectancy effects were to a large extent nonverbal. That is, when people expect more of those with whom they come in contact, they treat them differently nonverbally.

The key comes in that last sentence: "when people expect more . . . they treat them differently nonverbally." This speaks to one of the genuine advantages of a relationship based on connoisseurship—more is indeed expected. But it is interesting that the effect should be carried through nonverbal channels as Rosenthal insists. In this case, the unconscious or subconscious fantasy of the teacher or mentor about the protégé sways the direction of influence upward as in imparted connoisseurship. There can also be a negative version of the same process, "stigmatization," where the teacher's diminished expectations, which can be based on criteria such as race, gender, or even, as was shown in one study, eye color, can foster diminished performance. Here the direction of influence is downward. Should we speak, then, of "imparted philistinism"? Actually, there are such relationships wherein people encourage others to outdo one other in how low they can sink. We see this in fraternities, sororities, and elsewhere, but it was perhaps never so brilliantly depicted as in the eighteenth-century French novel, *Les Liaisons Dangereuses* (Choderlos de Laclos [1782] 2008), a work that has led in recent times to not one but multiple movie versions, including a very apt version for the young, *Cruel Intentions*, which came out originally in 1999. In both the 1988 film version *Dangerous Liaisons*, and in *Cruel Intentions*, the mixture of great sophistication and utter moral depravity couched together within a shared malevolent connoisseurship is appalling and yet fascinating.

Jane Austen's novel *Emma* ([1815] 1971) is another masterwork that investigates a Pygmalion–Galatea dynamic. Early in this gentle and genteel work, the character Emma is heard denigrating the "coarse" people with whom her malleable friend Harriet wishes to associate. She decides to take Harriet's fate into her own hands:

> *She* would notice her; she would improve her; she would detach her from bad acquaintance, and introduce her into good society; she would form her opinions and her manners. It would be an interesting, and certainly a very kind undertaking; highly becoming her own situation in life, her leisure, and powers.
>
> (Austen, 1971, p. 20)

Emma acts as a connoisseur not only of Harriet's aesthetic choices, lifestyle, achievements, and so forth, but also disturbingly enough, of what sort of match she should make for herself. As part of Emma's campaign to raise Harriet's status to become a gentlewoman, for example, she dissuades her from pursuing a tie with Mr. Martin (for whom she has genuine feelings) because he is merely a farmer. Instead, she encourages Harriet to set her cap for Mr. Elton, the village vicar, who Emma feels would make a more seemly husband. Harriet does shift her interest to Elton, but the latter is angling instead for Emma and ends up feeling insulted when Emma rejects him. He finds another woman altogether to marry, leaving Harriet high and dry. Emma has vastly misjudged the situation and narrowly escapes steering Harriet toward grave disappointment. It is only through the good offices of the aptly named Mr. Knightley, someone older, considerably wiser, and much less snobbish than Emma herself, that Emma is eventually able to realize her wrong-headedness in the matchmaking role and much else. In Austen's rendering, the realization is charming. First comes shame, then exploration and reappraisal, followed by relapse, and so on, in a continued struggle to resist those meddling impulses. Here it all is, in Emma's thoughts:

It was foolish, it was wrong, to take so active a part in bringing any two people together. It was adventuring too far, assuming too much, making light of what ought to be serious, a trick of what ought to be simple. She was quite concerned and ashamed, and resolved to do such things no more.

"Here have I," said she, "actually talked poor Harriet into being very much attached to this man. She might never have thought of him but for me; and certainly never would have thought of him with hope, if I had not assured her of his attachment, for she is as modest and humble as I used to think him. Oh! that I had been satisfied with persuading her not to accept young Martin. There I was quite right. That was well done of me; but there I should have stopped, and left the rest to time and chance. I was introducing her into good company, and giving her the opportunity of pleasing some one worth having; I ought not to have attempted more. But now, poor girl, her peace is cut up for some time. I have been but half a friend to her; and if she were *not* to feel this disappointment so very much, I am sure I have not an idea of anybody else who would be at all desirable for her;—William Coxe— Oh! no, I could not endure William Coxe—a pert young lawyer."

She stopt to blush and laugh at her own relapse, and then resumed a more serious, more dispiriting cogitation upon what had been, and might be, and must be.

(p. 124)

The trope of elitism's toxicity is a commonplace in the arts. *Pygmalion* and *Emma* are just two of many works that elucidate the destructive dynamic of imposing successive refinements on someone else in the guise of enhancing his or her well-being. These two works also show how connoisseurship often goes hand-in-hand with the assumption that a manner or taste associated with an upper social class is necessarily a better form of human existence per se. Connoisseurship vis-à-vis improving one's *persona* as opposed to one's *person* has long been a recognized feature of embracing class distinctions too readily.

Connoisseurship between Parents and Children

Imparted connoisseurship plays out frequently across the generations, as members of one age group try to instill a greater sense of discernment in the other. It's a common tendency for parents to try to expose their children to higher degrees of refinement in appreciating life's various dimensions. But sometimes this can lead to narcissistic or even competitive tensions between parent and child. It is easy for a child and his or her mother, who were literally part of one another during the nine-month gestation, to experience the other as no more than a physical and emotional extension of the self. The child can readily become the container of the mother's own projected feelings (positive or negative) in the self-advancement process, rather than the child being experienced as someone more fully separate, whose success or failure is his or her own and not the parent's. When the parent (in his or her teaching function) is insecure or otherwise narcissistically challenged, a motive that appears salutary easily becomes poisonous. The parent with a connoisseur-like attitude may consciously intend to stimulate growth and improvement, but may instead end up being internalized as an exacting identificatory figure whose standards cannot be met.

Here I think of conversations I've had over the years with a childhood friend of mine, whose mother could be decidedly overzealous in teaching her daughter the social graces. One lesson my friend remembers was how to write a proper thank-you note for a gift. After her mother rejected each of her drafts for one flaw or another, she came to despair of ever being able to strike the right tone of gratefulness with just the right degree of panache. As my friend recalls, she became especially aware that her mother had taken up residence inside her as an exacting presence when she was confronted with the task of writing college-application essays. The very thought of tackling those essays generated dread and self-doubt. If she couldn't manage a thank-you note, how was she ever going to manage the far more elusive task of presenting herself as good college material? Someone who couldn't write a good thank-you note the first time round wasn't going to get in anywhere. No matter how much my friend struggled with those essays, though, she certainly wasn't going to get her *mother* involved, that was for sure. Eventually, she got over her fears well enough to write an adequate, if not superb set of admissions essays. And she did get into a fine college. But, she told me, she doesn't write her own thank-you notes to this day. She's found a website that sends very gracious, animated e-cards, and she lets it go at that.

Speaking of the writing process in adulthood, connoisseurship dynamics can occur in spades in the writer/reviewer/editor interface. It can be no mere coincidence that some of these very issues arose in the process of my drafting the article on which this chapter is based. One journal editor (whom I thank for generously encouraging my sharing of the following interchange) complained upon reading an early draft that I used too many words that were excessively formal ("redound"? "anlage"?). Some of those words seemed to her too obscure, while others seemed inapt or imprecise vis-à-vis my intended meaning. I was dismayed—here I stood, being accused of being grandiose, pedantic, and stilted—and foolishly off-base at that! I double-checked the words in my own dictionary. We had a further polite exchange, each of us attempting to be open to the other's view. With my anxiety sufficiently lowered, it now dawned on me that we were enacting the very subject matter of my article. I mentioned this to her, and she wrote back saying that underneath her critical tone, she had also felt embarrassed at not having previously known some of the words whose use she had challenged. Ultimately, we were able to clear up most, if not all, of my "over-the-top" language, while not depriving me of too much of my "fun with words." It helped that we each realized that we could be fallible *and open about our fallibility* without feeling that doing so discredited our basic competency in the roles we were occupying. This, I believe, is an important key to preventing connoisseurship from becoming cumulatively micro-traumatic.

In general, a child may have the necessary tools for a good, even sophisticated, effort in some arena, while at the same time he or she consistently envisions falling short of high standards that were inculcated and became internalized over time. In some instances, both between parents and children and between adults, the hyperacute awareness of one's own insufficiency under the gaze of the other can create an even stronger dependency on the other's "special" tutelage toward making the mark. Verbally and nonverbally, the parent thus confirms his or her position as the superior arbiter vis-à-vis the child. This would be an instance of Winnicottian impingement. Some parents will experience the child as a narcissistic extension rather than a separate object. Projecting her own weakness into the child, a self-disparaging mother, for instance, may seek to "cure" herself by over-critiquing her child. In Khan's parlance, she fails as a protective shield and may in fact undermine whatever preexisting shield (that is, protected and protective sense of self-worth) the child already has.

Imparted connoisseurship thus often trumps an attunement to the uniqueness of the individual. This occurs from parent to child typically, but it can and does happen in reverse too, as older children and young adults foist ever newer technology on their less tech-savvy parents. I can say from experience that the parent may not be at all immune to the shame this can induce.

In a grandparent's connoisseurship vis-à-vis the grandchildren, the attempt to instill good values—aesthetic or otherwise—can elevate or disparage the grandchild, while simultaneously "settling old scores" with the parent sandwiched in between the older and younger generations. Fondness and aggressive intent join forces, the very stuff of a perfect alliance. Why do grandparents and grandchildren get on so well? In part because, as the saying goes, the enemy of my enemy is my friend.

Moreover, the parent and grandparent may get into struggles to determine whose childrearing attitudes are optimal or the most *au courant*. These views may shift over the years, which further complicates matters. Grandparent and parent may vie with each other as to who should have the upper hand in deciding such values on the children's behalf. The proper hierarchy of power can be confusingly hard to establish. Which one is to be the imparter of wisdom, the connoisseur of childrearing? Whose views should hold sway? Connoisseurship in childrearing is a tempting trap for family members to fall into, but it's easier to resist if one remembers that one's worth doesn't rest on being in the right, and that ultimately there is no one best way to raise a child.

Connoisseurship within the Psychoanalytic Profession

In psychoanalytic circles as well, we may fall prey to the narcissistic gratification of fostering connoisseurship too intently and insensitively vis-à-vis our students and supervisees. We feel called on to hone their formulations just a little more precisely, with just a little more nuance or supposed depth. And we communicate in various nonverbal ways that the revised formulation is really the way to go. What Freud called "the narcissism of small differences" is a pitfall within our field that has been decried for decades (e.g., Levy, 2004) without going away. The effect is too often that of diminishing and demoralizing the other. Poland (2009), in a keynote address at a meeting of the International Psychoanalytic Association, noted the dialectic in our field between "self-aimed forces of narcissism and outward-aimed forces of curiosity." As Poland observes (pp. 253–254):

> The air of superiority spreads broadly. It is evident in collegial consultations when a supervisory tone replaces mutual respect (Gabbard, personal communication), and it appears in our literature when a writer's own thinking, presented in its greatest strength, is contrasted with contrary views presented in their weakest light.

The training process itself—by definition a tutelary situation—is, of course, ripe for playing out perilous forms of connoisseurship. Ever refining one's clinical armamentarium, attuning one's capacity for reflection even more closely, is the gratifying benefit of receiving feedback as a candidate. But the risk of having one's self-doubts activated beyond a constructive level goes hand-in-hand with this gratification. We may be explicitly treated in a shame-inducing way and, once shamed, we may develop shame about our shame, as Buechler (2008, p. 363) spells out:

> Clearly, then, in training all the ingredients needed to induce shame are present. The candidate intensely examines her self as she is being evaluated by people whose opinion of her deeply matters. But yet another pressure is often added. The candidate is frequently aware of an expectation that not only should he be able to reveal himself while being evaluated, but he should be able to do so relatively comfortably. To put it briefly, the candidate is expected to open himself to an unusual degree of personal scrutiny, and still maintain enough equanimity to function in his new professional roles. Since he often incorporates these expectations, he also expects himself to be comfortably self-revealing. At the same time, he is involved in a personal treatment process that facilitates less reliance on accustomed defenses, and therefore he is confronting anxiety his defenses previously kept at bay. He is learning a new, highly ambiguous task, absorbing complicated theoretical material, making new friendships, and attempting to integrate this new life with his previous responsibilities and relationships. And, often, any discomfort with this process is seen as problematic by the candidate himself, as well as others.

There is a paradoxical double jeopardy in the connoisseurship of clinical training—we purposively highlight candidates' weaknesses with the conscious intention of refining their work. Then we criticize them as insufficiently solid should they become distressed at having their deficits noted. Self-disappointment is perhaps a healthy and inevitable response, but what of shame? Need there be some stimulation of "optimal shame" in analytic training for learning to occur? Does a candidate's sense of shame imply she or he has insufficient self-esteem or is actually underskilled? Undoubtedly, much of this shaming is an unfortunate artifact of supervisors being narcissistically insensitive or too exacting to use tact or to curb their own misdirected connoisseurship.

Lawrence Josephs, in an emailed reaction (January 15, 2013) to an earlier version of this chapter, commented that destructive connoisseurship plays out as well in the branch of academic psychology devoted to testing psychoanalytic assumptions. "Holier than thou" tensions crop up among different researchers and between the researchers and theorists. Josephs comments:

> On the one hand, empirical research in psychology is more down-to-earth in the effort to operationalize concepts in things that are observable and measurable. Thus the theory is a bit more empirically grounded in something concrete and doesn't get lost in as much elitist esoteric and philosophical abstraction as does psychoanalytic theory. But on the other hand, there is connoisseurship in terms of research methodology and statistics so you can reject almost any empirical finding you don't like on the basis of some subtle design flaw or misguided statistical analysis that the researcher was too unsophisticated to appreciate. So you have empirical researchers trying to make clinicians feel stupid for not understanding the intricacies of research design that controls for various biases and psychoanalysts trying to make researchers feel lamely superficial for not appreciating the deep, profound, and ineffable psychological qualities that are beyond quantification and measurement.

In any field, the struggle to refine one's knowledge can well lead to psychological insecurity, which can set the stage for later competitiveness or insensitivity vis-à-vis others. Goldman (2007) suggests that learning is in a sense inherently "violent," a view he draws from the writings of Castoriadis, Laplanche, and Levinas. It is violent, Goldman explains, in the sense that learning confronts us with "otherness" per se, and that which is alien is almost always deeply jarring. But even more importantly, learning creates the demand that we alter the self, become something "other than what we were" (Goldman, personal communication, 2011). One must sacrifice one's customary way of knowing in order to sense or do something truly different.

Consider, for example, the teaching technique of master pastry chef Jordi Butron. In speaking to Adam Gopnik (2011) about instilling a connoisseur's sensibility in his apprentices, he explains that a pastry chef needs to develop an extensive palate of tastes and smells, and that this must be done through systematic repetition, just as one would in building physical prowess and strength. Butron recommends that the would-be patissier focus not on the appearance of a dessert, but on its flavor and how that flavor is experienced through all the other senses besides sight. The teaching technique he uses to isolate that exquisite oral experience is to blindfold his apprentices. Gopnik is taken aback—wait, *blindfold* them? He wonders if he has misunderstood, but the chef confirms that, yes, it should be done blindfolded, to help the student concentrate on the taste, mouth-feel, texture, smell, and so forth; a student works sightlessly for much of the time under his tutelage.

Butron is trying to break through his apprentices' aesthetic prejudices in order to foster creativity, and this requires breaking down old linkages and understandings that might hamper a fuller apprehension of tastes. The chef's quirky technique has an admirable seriousness of purpose and may well generate novel apperception in his students. But some might take issue with his extensive use of a blindfold and the somewhat haughty attitude that seems to accompany it. To rob another—even temporarily—of his or her sight is in fact to handicap him or her, and while this might indeed heighten the other senses, it could well also disrupt the apprentice's sense of basic competency and exaggerate the power differential between student and master. I guess training in psychoanalysis is not alone in falling prey to such potential pitfalls.

There is always something implicitly self-subjugating—or at least, humbling—in a training process. All the more reason that, whether making a pastry chef or a psychoanalyst, it behooves the trainer to consider whether the advantages of a given teaching approach truly outweigh its disadvantages. Fortunately, there are external referents—imperfect, but viable—that can be used in our field to gauge whether the material being taught is well-absorbed and productively used. An honest evaluation of the therapeutic process—its progress or the lack thereof—should have a grounding effect on whether we are learning simply in order to play with niceties or to truly enhance our clinical helpfulness.

Once, as a young candidate, I remember struggling to implement the time-honored abstinent communication style urged on me by my supervisor, whom I myself greatly admired, and who was highly regarded in the analytic community at large. I was to refrain at all costs from being the one to start the session, even if the patient in question seemed to have undue trouble beginning himself. I was also not to coax the patient's narrative along when he lapsed into silence. Neither one of these was in itself an unusual direction coming from an analytic supervisor; what was hard was that I was enjoined to stick to this tack even if the patient fell completely silent for long stretches or protested vociferously. The supervisor felt strongly that adherence to this stance was imperative. Otherwise, I would be rescuing the patient in a way that could collude to mask his anxieties about communications from deeper parts of himself.

With one patient in particular, it ended up proving impossible for me to follow these technical recommendations. In examining why, my supervisor seemed to conclude that it was either my own countertransference or a general weakness of will that precluded my weathering the patient's resistant stance. In the end, however, the patient shot down my approach entirely, making it clear that he would *not* be treated in such a "removed" fashion. I could have ended up with a successful analytic process but no patient to treat. It seemed best to forgo the supervisor's advice in this case and reserve it for a patient more willing to trust that the benefits of greater analytic formality would outweigh its drawbacks. In retrospect, I understood that the patient in question experienced me as engaging in a power play with him and was narcissistically injured by (what seemed to him) my insistence on winning it. The analytic work could proceed only after I released myself from that shared connoisseurship with my supervisor, whom I nonetheless continue to admire and with whom I largely agree, even about the usage of abstinence. I needed to let my patient's affective response in the moment speak louder than my own need for the supervisor's approval—and louder than the discipline's expectations as well.

It is increasingly customary and of course salutary that clinicians in advanced training feel empowered to evaluate their training institution and faculty in return, rather than simply being the subject of the institution's evaluation. However, a defensive clinician-in-training may take the stance that the supervisor's offerings—even when in keeping with current practice and standards—reflect only minor stylistic differences, are arbitrary, or are insufficiently persuasive to be worth trying. In making only a half-hearted effort at implementation, the trainee will inadvertently confirm his or her own doubts as to the value of psychoanalysis. The potentially constructive aspects of imparted connoisseurship are subverted as the learner gets the secondary gratification of trumping the teacher, teachings, and the field itself. We could describe such a candidate as acting with injurious connoisseurship toward the training process.

Many candidates enter analytic training for the credentialing prestige it confers—the status-boosting aspect of connoisseurship. These candidates seek out connoisseurship relationships so they can profit from having powerful supporters at the institute. This can end up being deleterious, in that their "mutual admiration society" makes them subservient to and uncritical of their superiors, undercutting the opportunity to hone their skills and develop their own identity as an analyst.

Destructive connoisseurship within the therapeutic relationship itself is of special concern. It is noteworthy that Sullivan (1954) views being a connoisseur as inherently negative and, as he uses the term, it is rather the *antithesis* of being a true "expert" in psychic life and relating, which the clinician should be. He groups the connoisseur with the "collector" and "fancier," who use their skill to further their personal interests. Sullivan further cautions that the psychoanalytic expert must be "keenly aware" of the power inherent in having expert knowledge of interpersonal relations and personality problems. The clinician is "estopped by the cultural attitude from using his expert knowledge to get himself personal satisfaction, or to obviously enhance his prestige or reputation at the expense of the patient" (p. 13).

The analyst, in my view, should be a connoisseur in the *constructive* sense vis-à-vis psychic life and interpersonal relating. He or she strives to heighten the patient's capacity for self-attunement, mentalization, self-interpreting, insight, and the ability to free associate, among many other things. We can be connoisseurs in this way while avoiding being over-exacting. We need to be conscious of how generative we really are or are not in our efforts to impart self-attunement and a capacity for self-reflection. How is our patient registering our interventions within the rapid-fire crosscurrents of transference and countertransference? Are we unconsciously fine-tuning the patients' self-understanding too closely, thereby arousing performance anxieties in them? Or might they at times project a destructive connoisseurship onto us, which we may fail to recognize due to countertransferential blind spots?

I have a patient who routinely censors her dreams, discarding rather than revealing those she considers "garbage" and reporting only those that meet her standards for creativity. She projects her own inner connoisseurship onto me partly to forestall my potential disapprobation. No amount of interpretive reassurance can persuade her to relax her standards. This woman's self-disparaging judgment is itself micro-traumatic; it is also a defense against the possibility, should she accept her own dream life, of discovering more profoundly troubling qualities in herself. This is unfortunate, as getting in touch with and coming to terms with those same qualities could ultimately be the most therapeutic thing of all.

Injurious Connoisseurship from Ogden's Fairbairnian Perspective

In an imaginative rendering of Fairbairn's (1952) thinking, Ogden (2010) revisits the intrapsychic bonds between the libidinal ego and exciting object and between the rejected ego and rejecting object. His recasting of the relationship between the paired internal images of an excited or tantalized self with an exciting object would seem a good analogy for imparted connoisseurship. This intrapsychic bond forms the basis for mutual projective identifications that are enacted in the actual patron–protégé relationship. The excited libidinal ego (or self) is gratified by the instructional attention of the tantalizing, exciting object that is "in the know." The excited learner absorbs the imparted fine points and is grateful to the expert object for its enrichment of the self. As Ogden notes, there is an addictive quality to the love between the libidinal ego and the exciting object. It creates a kind of mutually dependent bondage that can characterize imparted connoisseurship gone awry.

The mutual dependency can be problematic in and of itself, but the feeling of being addicted to the powerful other can become even more troublesome where it activates the negative tie between the rejected (self-sabotaging) ego and the rejecting object. As Ogden suggests, the mutual resentment between the rejected ego and rejecting object causes them to feel contempt for the seeming "love affair" between the excited self and exciting object. What this looks like in effect is that one begins to disdain oneself for delighting in one's own connoisseurship. Sharpening one's apperception often implicitly points to it having been relatively duller beforehand, which activates one's self-disdain (stemming from the hostile, spoiling alliance of rejected ego and rejecting object). Seeing the flaws in one's former level of sophistication can generate a feeling of inadequacy, as one realizes that a more advanced "other" would deem one underdeveloped. The excitement of the addictive tutelage may thereby be undermined, as the achievement comes to feel hollow or insubstantial. And all the while, the libidinal ego is dogged by concerns of never satisfying the exciting object or of never getting enough approval from the object to confirm one's worth. These intrapsychic elements and the scenario itself are projected and externalized onto outer relations with a real other who invites the "exciting object" role. The intrapsychic dynamics are then played out interpersonally with all the attendant desires, anxieties, and frustrations.

Applying this scheme to my earlier case example, we can think of Charlotte as having internalized split-off aspects of her unsatisfying parental figures, with her "exciting inner object" representing her ambivalently loved parents' potential regard for her. She projected this exciting inner object onto Sam, who readily introjected it and played it out with her as they incited each other to new heights of professional development and accomplishment. But the darker side involves Sam as "nemesis," judgmentally playing out the internalized rejecting object that is a distillation of Charlotte's parents' dismissive, detached side. Hence the addictive connoisseurship bond of "excited self, exciting object" easily activates a "rejected self, rejecting object" state. Here, discernment shades into the harsher state of disdainful judgment—the painful side of shared connoisseurship. Charlotte had let herself be drafted into an exclusive addictive relationship that substituted for a more benign, richer set of influences and a more fluid internal growth process.

Ogden's (2010, pp. 116–117) conclusion is an appropriate desideratum for Charlotte and others trapped in a problematic shared connoisseurship:

> Self-acceptance is a state of mind that marks the (never fully achieved) relinquishment of the life-consuming effort to transform unsatisfactory internal object relationships into satisfactory (i.e. loving and accepting) ones ... In order to take part in experience in a world populated by people whom one has not invented, and from whom one may learn, the individual must first loosen the unconscious bonds of resentment, addictive love, contempt and disillusionment that confine him to a life lived principally in his mind.

The implication is that in a relationship structured around the teaching of discernment, both individuals need to accept and tolerate inadequacies and imperfections in themselves and in each other while working to alter these. They must beware of overblown excitement on either side and guard against mistaking such excitement as promising a vindication of the imperfect self, because the human self is inherently a "work in progress," for which one need not apologize.

Harmful Connoisseurship from a Kohutian Perspective

Kohut and Wolf (1978) proposed that a firm sense of self is comprised of a "tension arc" between one's "basic strivings for power and success" (that is, one's ambitions) and one's "idealized goals." An intermediate area of talents and capacities gets "activated" by the two poles of ambition and goals. The developing individual needs consistent interactions with two kinds of selfobjects: those who provide mirroring of the person's basic capacities, and those who act as idealizable models for the direction of his or her ambitions and ideals. Perhaps the seed of a connoisseurship mode of relating develops—healthfully or not—in situations where the idealizable authority figure both implicitly sets goals and also offers admiration for reaching them. Moreover, the attitudes may be divided up within a relationship such that the young protégé looks for that which is idealizable in the older mentor, while the mentor looks for an admiring attitude in the protégé. Kohut and Wolf are quick to clarify that such narcissistic tendencies are not necessarily pathologic. However, when they *are* pathologic and don't resolve into a more even-handed connection of some kind, the result may be a problematic, compulsive search for connoisseurship-based relating that ends up being deleterious. This is the case for the "ideal-hungry" narcissistic personality type:

> *Ideal-hungry personalities* are forever in search of others whom they can admire for their prestige, power, beauty, intelligence, or moral stature. They can experience themselves as worthwhile only so long as they can relate to selfobjects to whom they can look up. Again, in some instances, such relationships last a long time and are genuinely sustaining to both individuals involved. In most cases, however, the inner void cannot forever be filled by these means. The ideal-hungry feels the persistence of the structural defect and, as a consequence of this awareness, he begins to look for—and, of course, he inevitably finds—some realistic defects in his God. The search for new idealizable selfobjects is then continued, always with the hope that the next great figure to whom the ideal-hungry attaches himself will not disappoint him.
>
> (p. 421)

When parental selfobjects are too attached to their own prized gifts, they may embrace ideals that are not suited to or viable for their offspring. This may occur if the child does not possess the innate attributes necessary to embody those ambitions and goals. Here, connoisseurship can become injurious, and the child may become severely disheartened as a result.

A poignant and concrete instance of this involved a female patient of mine who grew up in an upper-class Swiss home where physical charm and refinement, not to mention straight blonde hair and fair skin, were a particularly valued part of the feminine role. During her childhood, this woman's hair was remarkably curly, which—in the eyes of their community—made her unappealing. The mother, in particular, was horrified by the unruliness of her daughter's hair and lost no opportunity to lament it, arousing terrible self-consciousness in the girl. As part of a toxic intimate mother–daughter connoisseurship, the girl developed complicated rituals for styling her hair, but these efforts always fell short of controlling it sufficiently to silence her mother's criticism. This was just one arena among many that characterized the mother's demanding induction of her daughter into the "ways of the world."

The impact of her mother's intensive, hypercritical connoisseurship vis-à-vis the daughter carried forward into the patient's adulthood. She was now enormously proud of her capacity to discriminate but was simultaneously hampered by her own exactingness, by the large range of considerations that had to be honored when making decisions. She obsessed endlessly over possibilities for a personal career path, the optimal sink design for her remodeled kitchen, or a good math tutor for her child. In the end, she was often stuck in the "research" phase, unable to make a choice for fear of its being faulty or of there being a slightly more sophisticated or advanced version to be found that was not *yet* within her grasp. The preoccupation was not only with the end goal or in its being some ideal of perfection, but also more in the process itself of learning about refinements and of engaging others in extensive exploration of the possibilities.

This sometimes led to friction within the therapeutic relationship. When asking for my recommendation of a medical practitioner, for example, she once became enraged and insulted because I did not give a minute analysis of the relative strengths and weaknesses of the various individuals I suggested. She was in a sense demanding that I be the "imparting connoisseur" with her, whether or not I had the capability—or the inclination—to make such exact distinctions in the matter. The patient's resulting aggravation with me led to an acrimonious berating that felt micro-traumatic to me, as someone trying to be as helpful as possible. It is painful to be on the downside of such a demanding judgment, and it gave me a new understanding of what it had been like for her growing up. Moreover, I did not share the view that this is the sort of input the analyst should be obligated to provide; in fact, I could be taken to task for having done my part in the enactment in the first place by going along with her requests for such recommendations. Thus, in a double sense, the patient was now acting as the connoisseur of our treatment relationship, setting up a standard for my performance and finding it wanting, while triggering in me doubts as to what I had done.

Connoisseurship as a destructive element in Milanese society is elaborated in the film, *I am Love* (Guadagnino, 2009). As the story develops, the female protagonist is transformed from a gorgeous mannequin-like person, inhabiting a constricted role, into a living, breathing, complex woman. We watch as the woman emerges out of her rarefied wealthy milieu of style and art into the real world of full sensuality. It is interesting that the things that draw her out of the sterile connoisseurship of Milanese society are her passion for an ethnic-based, lower-class cuisine and also her illicit sexual passion for the master chef behind that cuisine—a life-affirming connoisseurship, par excellence!

Loewald and the Developmental Underpinnings of Connoisseurship

Loewald's (1980) thinking suggests a developmental trajectory that might undergird a connoisseurship mode of relating. He reminds us that Freud postulated a successive progression during early childhood: from an ideal ego to an ego-ideal to the superego. The ideal ego is a pre-Oedipal state representing "a recapturing of the original primary-narcissistic, omnipotent perfection of the child by a primitive identification with the omnipotent parental figures" (p. 46). This identification has a "hallucinatory wish fulfillment" quality, as the nursery-aged child savors a fantasied, magical, undifferentiated merger with the powerful other.

Over time, the ideal ego evolves into a more differentiated and elaborated form: the ego-ideal. Through participation with the parents' perfection and omnipotence, the child now moves out of the present to envision, however vaguely, a more evolved future for him- or herself. Loewald explains: "No stable internal structure representative of the ego's self-transcending exists as yet; the self-transcending is dependent on a magical communication with an ideal authority and model taking an intermediate position between external and internal" (p. 47). I see in this the early anlage of embracing the other as connoisseur.

However, once the magical relationship with the parents has been partially relinquished and internalized, the superego of the Oedipal period takes shape. More structuralized (in Loewald's view) than the ideal ego or the ego-ideal, the superego holds within it explicit aspects of authority figures whose values and virtues the child admires (though perhaps some vestigial sense of magic remains from the proto-superego stages). At this Oedipal juncture and beyond, fine distinctions might crystallize along a spectrum of "good/better/better yet/best/ultimate." These are based first on what has been internalized of the parents' ideals and values. Later, they come to be influenced by extrafamilial sources from whom the child may learn self-refinement and growth. I posit that this is how a connoisseurship attitude proper arises during the late childhood and preteen years, when having things be "just so" begins to preoccupy the child and teenage idols loom large to offer their implicit connoisseurship-based connection. The child copies his or her idols in ways large and small and, from that process, begins to believe in his or her ability to become admirable to others as well. This strengthens his or her sense of security in the world.

This psychic progression of early childhood seems an apt metaphor for the unfolding of connoisseurship. The ideal ego captures a person's magical absorption in the "wonderfulness" of the older and wiser figure, the connoisseur. The protégé in effect takes the position: "I feel strong and excited—life is marvelous—when I am absorbed in this new field of endeavor with this charismatic guide. We are both part of one great thing."

In the course of childhood development, the ideal ego evolves into a blurrily separate ego-ideal. This again has both developmental and metaphoric significance for connoisseurship as the protégé is in some sense incompletely differentiated from the authority. Eventually, however, just as the superego crystallizes in childhood, the learner wants to become something of a connoisseur him- or herself. One holds oneself accountable for embodying those knowing characteristics and no longer necessarily depends on an external authority for refining oneself. But one may nevertheless voluntarily seek other idealizable models outside the family orbit to firm up or enhance one's capacity for connoisseurship.

Destructive forms of connoisseurship in later life might well reflect a childhood experience of cumulatively traumatic relations with overly demanding, excessively insensitive parental figures. If those figures were too flawed, overbearing, or too needy for admiration, the child might be left with a lingering hunger for a healthy version of dependent tutelage. In other words, the child might not have absorbed enough strength and knowledge from those figures to be able to internalize unambivalently the figures' attitudes and values and transform these so they become more fully his or her own. Therefore, in adulthood the child may court those kinds of connections that are compelling enough to replace the missing internalization of authorities.

Lena's Struggles with Connoisseurship

Lena is a 65-year-old woman whose family had moved from the Midwest to New York City when she was 12 years old so that her father could join a high-level law firm. The parents had eagerly embraced the upper-crust New York social scene and, as they became increasingly wealthy, they immersed themselves in all the cultural activities the city had to offer, focusing especially on the art world. The parents entertained frequently and lavishly and took regular trips to Europe, leaving the children in the care of a sequence of nannies. When they were home, her parents presided over the household and the children's lives with a sort of benign neglect, as they concentrated on climbing their own social ladders. Though well taken care of in relation to the external things of life—school, extracurricular activities, and so forth—Lena was left relatively alone and on her own at the emotional level. She felt backward and unsophisticated relative to her age-mates in school and would try to adopt their habits and attitudes, only to feel that she never quite got it.

Like her parents, Lena had an acute intuitive sense of what was good, better, and best in various spheres of life. And, like her parents, she could be swept away in cultivating herself in the direction of "the best," in part as a way of compensating for not having felt accepted and acceptable just as she was to begin with—either by the New York City kids or, more fundamentally, by her self-preoccupied parents. In any event, Lena got through some rather troublesome high school and college years and eventually followed in her father's footsteps to become a lawyer herself. After only a few years of legal practice, she could see which aspects of her firm's legal approach were underdeveloped, under-theorized, or inefficiently pursued. She would note and then point out what was lacking in the previous approaches her project group had taken before she came on board. She would lobby the group continually to try to get them to see the issues with more nuance. This branded her as an independent thinker—which was good—but along the way, she often managed to insult or offend her co-workers by challenging their reasoning. Once the project ended, Lena would be left feeling that others had found her critiques, along with her drive itself, to be too much. And if they hadn't been persuaded by her perspective, or if they'd resisted her efforts to sharpen things up just a bit more, Lena ended up feeling dismissed.

In her mid-twenties, Lena had married someone very accomplished, sensitive, and appreciative of her strengths. By her mid-thirties, feeling disenchanted and unrecognized as a lawyer and yet also suspecting it was something about the difficult "fit" between herself and her fellow attorneys, Lena had let go her law practice and had decided to devote herself to raising the couple's two children, an older daughter and a younger son. She would be the best, most attuned and nurturant mother and, in that way, she would help the children avoid all of her own mistakes. They would find true fulfillment in areas she herself had had to retreat from. This went well in many areas, especially in the children's early years, but it became very difficult for her when it became clear that her eldest child, Chloe, was not the kind of person she best understood or resonated with. Lena had raised Chloe to be attentive to the world's expectations of her, to fit in to the upper-middle-class lifestyle they had, and to socialize with other interesting and stimulating (though hopefully still conventional) kids. If she got a B on her homework, Lena would tutor her to be sure it was a B+ next time and an A soon after. She nudged her to apply her critical thinking to pre-law subject matter and, at first, Chloe complied. But the teenage and then young adult Chloe was a free spirit, and she ended up finding her calling in making complex, experimental computer artwork. Though it was a new genre, Chloe was determined to make a living at it. Lena had always tried to help her daughter be a "new and improved" version of herself, who (unlike Lena herself) would make a go of whatever she did. So Lena gamely tried to apply her discriminating efforts to helping Chloe in this field as well. She would hear what Chloe was doing to develop herself and further her artistic process, and she would tweak it a few steps further—and then a few steps beyond that.

Chloe would seem interested and open at first, but their conversations would devolve into Chloe feeling inadequate to the task and worried that her mother would always be disappointed in her. Lena in part knew that she was foisting her own strivings onto the daughter and that this was making the daughter feel increasingly incompetent rather than the opposite, but she couldn't help herself. It felt too risky to let Chloe put out a product that was subpar or make a career move that might not yield the optimal result. Lena ended up hugely conflicted and very self-deprecating, as she recognized she was having a negative effect on her daughter's growth and sense of self-worth—while having a positive effect had been the very thing she'd counted on to resurrect her own self-esteem after her sense of pride in her professional identity fizzled.

I got a taste of Lena's ongoing striving for improvement early in the treatment: at the start of each session, before lying down, she would first straighten and plump the couch pillows and pick off any lint they had acquired earlier that day. (They always did look better afterward.) She had trouble starting her hour, as she silently sifted through the various strands of her inner experience to find the potentially most productive one to begin with and got bogged down in the process. Also Lena often had difficulty accepting my interpretive offerings as they stood. It would often be, "Well no, that's not my point," and then she'd restate it with a slightly different twist, but still (from what I could tell) having the same gist. And toward the session's end she would frequently arise from the couch frustrated with herself that she hadn't been able to say the very most important thing. There was probably a better way to be an analytic patient and deeper depths to probe, but she hadn't found it. All this preoccupation with fine-tuning our process and herself seemed to lock me out of the interchange and Lena out of the analytic process itself. We are still working on these things. What is most striking is Lena's earnest wish to bring her discriminating intelligence to bear on whatever she's involved in, as if her life—or one of her children's—depended on it. She must pursue this even when doing so also generates shame and a sense of alienation in herself or in the other. I think this is a hallmark of how micro-traumatic Lena's early life—so full of small slights and abandonments—actually was for her.

Relishing the Good while Remedying the Ills of Connoisseurship

So how are we to get the most benefit—and escape the harm—from imparted connoisseurship? Because benefits there are. Adam Gopnik (2011), whose reportage on the subject I drew from earlier, asked the White House pastry chef Bill Yosses to help him recreate the soufflé he remembered from childhood. The blissful side of connoisseurship is reflected in the exquisite moment when the soufflés emerged from the oven—indeed, they were transcendent. Each element of the soufflé was just as it should have been—the apricot flavor strong, the whole concoction airy and hot. Gopnik exults in the way many small, correctly executed movements, done according to the rule, became a true skill, and that then all the skills he'd learned from Yosses metamorphosed into an artistic creation. Gopnik was thrilled by Yosses' expert influence and the remarkably essential results student and master were able to achieve.

Now this is connoisseurship at its best! Such is the paradox of imparted connoisseurship: it can enrich or impoverish. As psychoanalytic clinicians, it is up to us to become sensitized to indicators of the sort of oppressive, aggressively tinged, master–apprentice dynamic that actually depletes the psyche of the learner. But we must also remember that many people apprentice themselves in one way or another, and many others accept the mentor role, and sometimes the outcome is indeed improved performance, whatever the accumulated injuries along the way. My prose may still stray too often into the deep end of the dictionary, but an apricot soufflé . . . well, the proof is in the pudding. As always, it is up to the patient to say whether it was worth it.

Chapter 4

Uneasy Intimacy

A Siren's Call

When a state of intimacy exists between two people, it generally means that they each know something important about the other's internal world. Each registers many central facets of how the other thinks, feels, and reacts to things. They are aware of one another's strengths and vulnerabilities, their preferences and idiosyncrasies. There is an expectation that each will aim to be responsive to the other's needs, safeguarding his or her well-being to whatever extent possible. Intimacy often brings a feeling of shared emotional intensity, along with the sense that the mutual closeness is something relatively private between the two and potentially exclusive of others.

"*Uneasy* intimacy," in contrast, is the problematic stepchild of intimacy proper. I use the term to refer to a micro-traumatic maneuver involving the subconscious or unconscious use of one's capacity for psychic resonance to co-opt the other into an emotional embrace that is less than truly nourishing and that in fact tends to be injurious. I stop short of calling uneasy intimacy "emotional seduction"—though an element of seduction may be present—to avoid the implication of its necessarily being planned out or intentionally undermining of the other—though this too may sometimes happen.

Uneasy intimacy is a kind of insecure closeness that can feel thrillingly engaging, but also unsettling. There is a cocoon of supposed mutual rapport and a feeling of specialness in being (again, supposedly) simpatico with that other person. You do resonate with that person—but only to a point. And you don't know exactly where that point is. You may keep thinking to yourself that maybe your unease will resolve itself, that your anxious discomfort is meaningless, that it's just your own "craziness"—an outcropping of your own sense of inferiority, self-doubt, or some other inner quirk. Like a "siren's call," this form of intimacy is an alluring but confusing bond that ends up thwarting more than helping you, undermining your belief in your own judgment, and weakening your trust in others. Because (like the call of the siren) it feels both compelling and rewarding at the outset, uneasy intimacy can be hard or impossible to extricate oneself from on one's own.

Sometimes the relationship with the other feels just fine for an extended period of time, until something happens that makes you wonder about it. Perhaps the other person, who initially had seemed to "get" and approve of you overall, lets slip a gratuitous criticism of you and then tries to downplay or sweeten it. And then the same thing happens again. Soon this sort of thing retroactively calls into question the prior sense of safety and security you'd had beforehand in the relationship. You may then feel like a fool, not having realized that you'd viewed the relationship as more positive and more special than it was for the other person.

Another manifestation of uneasy intimacy occurs when two people each feel alone and lonely in a setting they share—say, a work group where problematic values hold sway—and they gravitate to one another on the basis of a shared alienation from that situation. They're so relieved to find another person who seems to share their attitude that they over-generalize the similarity and assume that the two of them are "in sync" overall, and, on that basis, they begin to build greater closeness on a broader scale. But at some point, one of the two begins to perceive an area of discord or difference, which makes him or her feel uneasy about the expectations of mutual agreement and support that have been built up between them. He or she may want to cover over the uneasiness in order to sustain the illusion that they're still "in this together," but the feeling of solidarity starts to ring hollow.

Uneasy intimacy often begins and evolves differently than healthier intimacy does, in that the two individuals become privy to each other's inner world to an excessive degree and at an unduly heightened rate. The closeness is often patently premature. This intensity of degree and rate often fails to take into account other features of the two individuals' roles vis-à-vis each other. These are the features such as age discrepancy, role asymmetry, conflicting ties, value differences, and so forth, which under other circumstances would have modulated their closeness. While one person is usually the primary driver, both of the intimates can get carried away in their involvement, almost without being aware of it.

That said, strange circumstances can sometimes make "strange bedfellows," without the connection being necessarily uneasy. In her book *Bel Canto* (2002), about a fictionalized Latin American embassy takeover, the novelist Ann Patchett offers an example of how emergency situations can result in precipitous or unlikely intimacies that are actually not in bad faith or otherwise disingenuous. Patchett depicts captives and captors developing personal bonds not only among themselves, but also across their adversarial divide. It all rings true, however. For, as Sullivan maintained many years ago, emergency situations allow people to act outside of the self-system, with its manifold protective and distorting maneuvers, and engage in direct, unbiased, truly straightforward communication (John Kerr, personal communication, April 13, 2014).

In uneasy intimacy, by contrast, the communication is anything but straightforward. That doesn't keep it from being oddly inviting, however. Consider this delightfully unrepentant poem from William Carlos Williams (1968):

This Is Just to Say

I have eaten
the plums
that were in
the icebox

and which
you were probably
saving
for breakfast

Forgive me
they were delicious
so sweet
and so cold

This is a poem to be enjoyed every so often. I love it for its straightforwardness, homey cadence, and ostensibly considerate message. The writer apologizes for his infraction in one swift "forgive me," but quickly moves into the sensuality of those plums. He knows the intended recipient—we readily envision its being his wife—well enough to imagine that she was anticipating having them for a refreshing snack on what was perhaps an already hot summer's morning. He begs her pardon, and in the face of his disarming apology, she can scarcely withhold it from him, even if it undermines her dismay at what he's done.

The poem captivates the listener because we inhabit the note writer's attitude as well as that of its intended recipient. We are drawn in by the writer's simplicity of expression, confidential tone, and winning self-assuredness. We are happy to be his "intimates," to share vicariously in the sensual experience of eating sweet, dripping plums—plums that weren't quite his to eat. The poet has charmingly won us over, and we'll forgive him anything, at least for the foreseeable future. It's easy to forget that his wife has been stripped of her "plums," to overlook that someone has been ever so slightly betrayed. So it is with what I call uneasy intimacy. There is the painfully delicious and deliciously painful experience of being sweet-talked, and we end up accepting a seeming psychic gain that houses within it a psychic loss.

But how far are we willing to go in being acquiescent in transgression? When do we draw the line? And conversely, how far are we willing to go in sweet-talking our way past our own bad deeds? These are the kinds of tensions that begin to accrue in uneasy intimacy. What are the outer limits? Fellow poet Kenneth Koch (2005) posed the question in the form of another poem, written in 1962, called "Variations on a Theme by William Carlos Williams," which was meant as both a parody of and commentary on the original. In it, the narrator spells out and asks forgiveness for a series of four transgressions, from chopping down the person's home, to spreading poison on her flowers, to getting rid of her entire savings, to fracturing her leg while they're dancing. Each one is purely malicious, and each justification for having done the deed sounds increasingly inane, not to mention sadistic. Koch clearly found nothing *but* a disturbing tenor in the poem, and writ so large it's more traumatic than micro-traumatic! According to Andrew Epstein (2013), Williams' poem is actually one of the most parodied poems around, in the general media and on Twitter. Which is to say that, insofar as Williams is indexing uneasy intimacy, there are apparently lots of people out there who have enough experience of what can happen in this kind of relationship—and are vexed enough about it—that they're moved to try working it through in cyberspace.

The Phenomenology of Uneasy Intimacy

One reason intimacy is so potentially problematic is that human beings are many-sided, that selfhood is by its nature a multiplicity of internal states and aspects. So we may be intimate with one another vis-à-vis *some* facets of our internal life and yet not about *others*, which may be masked, dissociated, bracketed, or otherwise withheld from the relational field (see Bromberg, 2011; Mitchell, 1993; Stern, 1997, 2010). When we are unaware of the internal parameters of intimacy we're acting under, we may give false or disingenuous cues that "everything's out on the table." If this prompts a similarly piecemeal relatedness from the other, one or both individuals are likely to end up feeling disoriented at best and betrayed at worst, should the discrepancy become apparent. The chronic, everyday variants of uneasy intimacy are look-alikes (Ghent, 1990) for normal behavior but, over the long haul, they can be just as damaging as more flagrant forms of the "fatal attraction" ilk. They lie on the same continuum as the more acute, severe versions of destructive attachment.

When the uneasy intimacy is laced with erotic overtones, it becomes that much harder for one or both persons to disengage from the emotional knot. As an example, on the way to class, a college junior bumps into her professor, a very handsome married man in his forties, for the first time after the three-month summer vacation. She's surprised when he addresses her personally, something he'd never done when she took her first class from him the year before. "Ah," he says appraisingly, "I see you've lost some of your little girl baby fat." The electricity that runs down the young woman's spine in response is partly thrill and partly chill. There is the implication that he'd noticed her body before—which she'd never have imagined—and certainly he's noticing it now. There is shame in recognizing that her "baby fat" may have displeased him before, and delight that having shed it, she is pleasing to him now. Though, of course, this could all just be in her own head; perhaps, she muses, his reaction is just a version of the fondness a father feels, newly recognizing that his little girl has grown up. But *that* thought also makes her queasy, as if they were verging on breaching the incest barrier, if only in her—or his—imagination. It is unnerving to think that she might indeed be desired by such a respected and attractive other, since acting on any such urge would have serious repercussions for both of them. Now each time she goes to class, she both hopes for and dreads another private comment from him. And she can't remember a word of any of his lectures for the rest of that semester.

Uneasy intimacy should be distinguished from blatant ethical violations of role expectations, where the disquieting attraction is not only felt, but acted upon. With its strong allure, uneasy intimacy may sometimes be a *prelude* to transgression, but more often, it stops short of this. Nor does eroticism have to be involved: employees may be under the excessive sway of a particularly compelling superior, children under the undue psychic press of their parents, analytic candidates under the sway of a certain supervisor, without it necessarily evolving into an explicit transgression of psychosocial limits. Role boundaries are more like regions than sharp edges, and within such a region, there is much room for the push and pull of confidence-sharing, attitude-influencing, over-identification with another's internal objects, and so on. Up to a certain point then, there can be emotional bending without clear breakage of an I–thou social compact. Many role relationships permit considerable latitude in the personal dimension, and becoming more personal than a given role relationship explicitly calls for can be extremely productive. It sometimes becomes evident only in retrospect that one has gone farther into the private sphere of self or other than might be optimal. (For situations in which uneasy intimacy *did* flower into flagrant sexual boundary violations in the therapeutic context, see Celenza, 2007, 2014; Celenza & Gabbard, 2003; Gabbard, 1996; Gabbard & Lester, 1995.)

Actually, the fact that uneasy intimacy tends to fall below the ethical radar helps make its effect more potentially insidious, while not being flagrant or egregious. And one way or the other, it can lead to a kind of emotional exploitation in which one or both participants can neither leave nor thrive within the relationship. This effect—the curtailment of thriving as opposed to outright emotional or psychological abuse—significantly differentiates uneasy intimacy from a boundary-violating relationship. This blockage in one's own and the other's psychological development will be apparent in my work with James, whom I introduce now and whom I'll return to periodically throughout this chapter to illustrate various facets of this sort of micro-traumatic closeness.

James was a 35-year-old public relations director in an up-and-coming coffee-producing emporium, which was based in Portland, Oregon but was building up a large presence in Seattle, where he and his family lived. Tall, slender, and almost wiry, he was a gentleman and a gentle man, with a ready smile and an unassuming manner that belied his high-powered position and economic stature. James came to treatment with a history of intense sequential romantic relationships that somehow never worked out. Each relationship's end left him in a state of terrible anguish and loss, even though the decision to call it off was usually his own. He was excruciatingly lonely when on his own, which caused him to call or email friends compulsively as a way to fill up his free time. In our analytic work together, James and I determined that this was in part to compensate for the fact that he was noxious company for himself. He relentlessly second-guessed his actions at work, worrying about whether he'd handled each decision well enough. Then he would wonder if it was really necessary to function optimally or whether he was being too hard on himself, and so on. James would also ruminate about the most moral way to handle his underlings or anyone else who crossed his path. These struggles took on a philosophical cast, as he insisted on hashing out each action or choice for its intrinsic value as well as its repercussions on others. The result, unfortunately, was painful paralysis and a sense of inefficacy.

At times, James could be almost overly genial—probably a function of his desire for others' approval, which was itself a substitute for his parents' affirmation and ultimately his own. Particularly important was the way this played out in James' romantic life. With his non-threatening, warm affability, James easily attracted women. Soon one of these bonds would intensify, as James and the woman spent hour after hour in heart-to-heart talks about their life goals and concerns, eventually revealing their anxieties and vulnerabilities to each other. James would feel listened to and accepted by the woman, which was soothing for him. Perhaps even more importantly, he would feel needed. He would bend over backwards to resolve the woman's problems, and would lick whatever wounds life had inflicted on her, which elicited further dependence on him. However, while James was thrilled by the woman's admiration and growing involvement with him, he simply couldn't commit to her permanently, and for reasons he himself did not quite understand.

This is a central point in James' situation and in many cases of uneasy intimacy—the person pursuing it is often out of touch with his or her mixed motives and with any underlying ambivalence that might be fueling them. In his mind, James was recurrently writing his own version of Williams' "This Is Just to Say" note. James' version went: "This is just to say that you're a lovely person, but I can't stay with you and can't explain why." However, after we'd explored several repetitions of the patterning, James could see that he'd been choosing women who were notably insecure about their competency or their position in life, and that this set the stage for his pursuing an uneasily intimate dynamic. The woman was usually someone who sought more a paternal figure than a romantic equal, a role that James both loved and hated to play. Moreover, while denying this to himself, James felt intensely judgmental of the woman, which further fed the ambivalence that made him avoid an ultimate commitment to her. In time, the analytic work helped him recognize and accept that he was ambivalent, and that this ambivalence stemmed from the disapproval and disdain he unconsciously harbored toward the woman. This self-understanding made him feel terribly guilty, but it was key to his efforts to change his approach to forging a solid romantic partnership. It became clearer to him over the course of our work that being needed by the woman was ultimately an unsatisfying substitute for being respected and loved by someone he himself found respect-worthy and lovable. This perspective would allow him to let go of his uneasily intimate way of relating and was key to his ultimately being able to undo the micro-traumatic patterning in his relationships.

The experience of an infatuation—or for that matter, falling in love—can set the stage for uneasy intimacy, but under optimal conditions the relationship needn't end up there. With some self-awareness and fore-thought, both the suitor and the object of affection can try to withstand the temptation to show too much of their inner world to the other prematurely. This will be easier if they recognize that it's wisest to let closeness evolve gradually on the proving ground of mutual trust. Where there is a differentiated and yet coherent enough sense of self on each one's part, both partners are more likely to hold their own in the force field of psychic and erotic attraction.

Theoretical Considerations in Uneasily Intimate Relatedness

Fairbairn's (1952) view of schizoid factors in endopsychic structuralization offers a perspective from which to view the wayward form of closeness I've been describing. To review his thinking, Fairbairn argues that the ego (or self) is comprised of splits that occur by virtue of its efforts to cope with living with a mother who "fails to convince her child by spontaneous and genuine expressions of affection that she herself loves him as a person" (p. 13). (Singled out as "worst of all" is the mother who is both "possessive and indifferent.") The child's solution is to regress to a simpler form of relationship and concentrate on the mother's breast as a part-object. The regression entails a depersonalization of the object and a "de-emotionalization" (p. 14) of the object-relationship, so that affect is repressed and thinking becomes overvalued. In this way, the real external other can become a part-object "thing" to be dealt with rather than a full-bodied other to be related to. This "dealing with" rather than "relating to" the other is a facet of uneasy intimacy.

In Fairbairn's further theorizing, the ego responds to trauma by internalizing the bad object, which splits into exciting and rejecting internal objects; the "central ego" splits off from itself and then represses two subsidiary aspects, the "libidinal ego" and "internal saboteur." An individual with this sort of painful early relationship with his or her mother and the excessively strong internalized objects and split-off aspects of self described by Fairbairn might, I would argue, more readily project the exciting object onto a real external object in the outside world. This individual would then seek to woo and win—while still keeping at arm's length—the projected-onto external other in order to compensate for the constant internal attack against the self waged by the internal saboteur and inner rejecting object.

Further, the allured one (as opposed to the alluring one) with the intensely negative internal saboteur might be someone whose libidinal need has been aroused through prior life experience to attach to someone who implicitly invites being treated as a better-than-good object. This would be someone who, like James, is inherently intuitive, empathic, and rather intense. Such a person, functioning as an exciting object, may to all appearances seem to be a healthy external object— that is, the allured person "feels" that the other is a balanced influence and can't discern the problematic qualities of their closeness. These conditions in both the allured one and the alluring one might call forth an overly close relatedness that, in the end, proves sterile and relatively counterproductive—in other words, uneasy intimacy.

From another quarter, Michael Eigen (1999, p. 1) uses a feeding metaphor to get at the miscarriage of closeness associated with uneasy intimacy. He echoes Fairbairn's view of the "tastiness" of some of what the exciting object offers:

> Emotional toxins and nourishment often are so mixed as to be indistinguishable. Even if they can be distinguished, it may be impossible for an individual to get one without the other. In order to get emotional nourishment, one may have to take in emotional toxins . . . A life can so sour, and a person so accommodate to high levels of toxins, that he or she may develop aversive reactions to less polluted opportunities for nourishment. Life may not feel real without large doses of emotional toxins. Some people cannot take nourishment that is not embedded in psychic poisons.

This description fits James' own early development, in that his overreliance on his mother for emotional nourishment was a similarly mixed blessing. The youngest of three children in a lower-middle-class family, James decided early on that he did not wish to compete in the same arenas as his elder sister and brother. Instead, he became the playful rebel, marshalling his considerable intellectual and verbal skills to challenge his parents' values and expectations of him. At the same time, James drew considerable support and pleasure from long, late-night talks with his mother, who offered time, attention, and seemingly warm understanding. He would try to convince her that he should be allowed greater freedoms in the household, more flexible standards, and so on, and she would listen carefully. However, in the end she would always side with the father's categorical, authoritarian prohibition. James never, to the best of his recollection, won one of these arguments. Yet, up until the middle of his analysis, he was under the illusion that they were intimate, satisfying contacts. This was simply his family's version of intimacy—and, as such, the best he could imagine. In keeping with Eigen's description of toxic nourishment, James had developed a taste—or craving—for female approval and comforting from this childhood closeness with his mother, such as it was.

James transferred much of the earlier mother–son scenario to his courting behavior. He would sway the woman with his warmth and piercing attention, thereby winning her over to his side (and away from the Oedipal father's). And if, by chance, she sensed his underlying disdain or otherwise recognized that they were not a good match and therefore pulled back, he would pursue her all the more ardently, offering understanding and sensitivity to overcome her qualms. This unfulfilling, precarious engagement would feel to him like intimacy, because it resembled the aborted recognition he had experienced so often with his mother. In the end, the woman, being weak herself, could never give him the ultimate affirmation he'd craved from his own mother and, of course, his father. She was trapped, but so was he—stuck being the father–lover, never the full-bodied equal mate and partner.

Khan (1979) elaborated on distortions in the healthy capacity for intimacy based on disturbances in early attachment between mother and child. In his view, some individuals with this sort of history (he singled out the sexual "pervert" as his exemplar) engage in the "technique of intimacy" that replays their earliest psychic disturbance. Says Khan: "Through this technique another object is appealed to, involved, seduced and coerced to share in the enactment of developmental arrest and cumulative trauma resulting in identity diffusion which constitutes this infantile neurosis" (p. 20). A "make-believe situation" is set up that involves the "willing seduced co-operation of an external object" (p. 22). The person creates an "emotional climate" in which he or she can engage the other as an "accomplice," where the two people merge through intense sexual or bodily intimacy according to the perpetrator's psychic needs and game plan. However, the perpetrator "cannot surrender to the experience and retains a split-off, dissociated manipulative ego-control of the situation" (p. 22), and therefore he or she is never satisfied by it. Having it fail in this way causes him or her to want to repeat it over and over. An interpersonal game such as this dramatizes but offers no real object relatedness and hence no psychic nourishment. The individual may use half-hearted, insincere confession and self-disclosure as a doomed strategy to substantiate the intimacy (and presumably to engage the other more closely). Khan emphasizes that the pervert in particular "tries to use the technique of intimacy as a therapeutic device and all he accomplishes is more expertise in the technique itself" (p. 24). In all the foregoing description and explanation, Khan is taking up an extreme form of pathology. However, I would argue that the overall shape of his thinking applies also to those who are more within the normal range, those who do *not* seek out relatedness for sadistic or hypersexual purposes. In fact, elsewhere Khan (1966) applies much the same reasoning—minus the sexualization—to those who are schizoid. I would extend his reasoning yet further. People like James invite the other into a falsely intimate-seeming alliance without malevolence and with nowhere near the desire to humiliate or degrade the other that the true pervert has, nor the need to maintain an unbridgeable distance that the schizoid has. But they are still using a semblance of intimacy in ways that undermine the other's needs and don't end up meeting their own either.

For another quotidian example of someone's employing a technique of intimacy, this time in a brief and limited way, consider a phone call placed by a middle-aged man, Walter, to his college fraternity brother. Living several states away from each other, the two habitually got in touch by phone three or four times a year. On this particular occasion, Walter noticed early on in their conversation that his friend seemed somewhat detached, as if he were not much up for talking to Walter. This raised the uncomfortable question as to whether their relationship was no longer as much of a priority for the second man. Walter could have let the phone call come to a natural (if earlier) close, giving things time to see how the friendship would evolve. Instead, though, he stepped up his efforts to engage his friend by raising his worries over some marital flare-ups and then various financial concerns. He seemed to be making the case that he really needed a good sounding board. The frat brother, a caring person, had the niggling feeling that something was "off" in his friend's manner, but he nonetheless got drawn into asking for more details. In the process of exploring some avenues for resolving Walter's problems, the friend even admitted having a few financial problems of his own, probably hoping to assuage any embarrassment Walter might feel at being in difficult straits. The conversation ended up lasting far longer than the second man had initially felt like talking for.

Nonetheless, later that same day, an additional suggestion occurred to him, and the frat brother called his friend back. Caught off-guard, Walter now sounded absolutely fine and not at all distressed. He was upbeat and breezy, and more or less waved off his friends' added input. With that, the frat brother came to the realization that he had been "had." Walter must have been exaggerating his anxieties in order to hold his friend's attention, and he (the frat brother) had swallowed the bait. The goal for Walter in engaging his friend's sympathy was to make himself feel important and worthy of attention. What was valued was the "prestige" (in Sullivan's terms) that the intimate attention conferred upon him, not the friend himself. This was a micro-traumatic realization for the frat brother, who felt foolish for having believed his input was valued on its own merits.

But uneasy intimacy takes many guises, and often its impact is considerably more significant than an unpleasant exchange like the one just described. As one illustration in the arena of clinical work, O'Shaughnessy (1992) describes a situation where a certain unsettled quality in the intimacy between herself and the patient threatened to compromise the treatment. Miss A, a high functioning woman, sought analysis because she was concerned about not having found a partner with whom she could have a child, as her previous romantic relationships had all ended up failing for reasons she couldn't explain. After some time of seemingly constructive and mutually "well-attuned" analytic interactions, some of which even included intimate-seeming explorations of the analytic relationship itself, O'Shaughnessy realized that their relatedness was actually superficial. Although the patient seemed to have strong feelings, there was "no real punch" in whatever aggression the patient expressed. There was, in fact, a "lack of unconscious depth" in much of what the patient said. Moreover, the analyst came to see that she as yet had little grasp of who she was to the patient in the transference, how this related to the patient's "unconscious phantasies," and how all of it linked to the patient's history or even her current extra-therapeutic life. In other words, the patient had up to now been presenting a thin, socially acceptable version of herself, which didn't permit the analyst to understand her well enough to make any sort of intervention that could truly have therapeutic traction.

O'Shaughnessy (p. 603) explains this sort of situation as the patient's having set up an "enclave," the writer's term for a kind of constricted relatedness characterized here by an appearance of intimacy and candor, where that closeness is actually primarily designed as a "refuge" from unbearable anxiety and disturbance:

Reflecting on this analytic situation, I saw that I had mistaken, just as Miss A herself does, over-closeness for closeness, and mistaken, too, a restrictive and restricting part object relationship for full contact between whole persons. My dissatisfaction with the 'you–me' interpretations that I had been making was now clearer. These interpretations were not part of a full interpretation, which in principle could eventually be completed, and involve internal objects, the interplay between unconscious phantasy and reality, and the reliving of the past. These interpretations were intrinsically denuded of such connexions [*sic*].

O'Shaughnessy goes on to warn us that "some degree of acting out by the analyst inevitably occurs" (p. 603) as the patient's relations with her internal objects emerge in the transference. The author speaks of her own prior temptation to forge "there and then" transferential interpretations of the patient's overcloseness with her as a *continuation* of the enclave, in that it allowed her (that is, the analyst herself) to avoid the anxious recognition that she did not truly understand who she was in the transference to the patient.

O'Shaughnessy notes that once the analyst catches on to the enactment, he or she will intuitively alter his or her stance in a way that promotes the working through of the problematic defensive posture. Later the author cautions: "As important as not enacting an enclave with a patient is not pushing and forcing a patient out of his refuge" (p. 604). She takes a tactful approach with her patient:

When there were relevant dynamic indications in her material, I spoke about her over-gentleness and over-closeness, her exclusion of other life, hers and mine, present and past, her control and impoverishment of me, and anxieties about herself and myself which seemed to lie behind her need for so limited and limiting a contact, which, as we now saw, stopped the analyst from disturbing Miss A and Miss A from disturbing the analyst.

(p. 604)

The key technical implications, as I understand O'Shaughnessy, are first, that the analyst cannot entirely avoid this type of enactment when the patient "needs" an enclave; second, that the analyst's willingness to recognize the constrictedness of the enclave is a critical way-station in his or her ability to understand the patient's subjectivity; and third, that there is no one right way for the dyad to work its way out of such a bind, though

ultimately doing so is essential to the success of the analysis. Neither interpreting within the transference nor extra-transferentially will necessarily
release the patient from the need to establish an illusion of resonance with
the other. In Miss A's case, a dream came that exemplified the uneasy
intimacy of their enclave, and the analytic pair's exploration of it seems to
have facilitated the opening up of the analytic bind:

> Important unconscious phantasies emerged. She had a dream of
> homosexual seclusion, in which two figures, like a pair of erotized
> instruments, played and touched each other, so that there was no dis-
> cord between them. Miss A's over-close, secluded relationship with
> me was thus revealed as a homosexual refuge, an erotized intimacy
> between similar, highly attuned instruments. Miss A was alarmed
> at the homosexuality, but very relieved by the interpretation of the
> mutual touching and playing in her dream, as the placation she felt
> was necessary between her and me for fear that, otherwise, we might
> become violent to each other.
>
> (p. 604)

Does the plum-eating writer of the note in Williams' poem intend to create
an "enclave," in O'Shaughnessy's terms? And if he does, is this a dodge
to avoid recognizing his own aggression? If we're to believe the speaker's
voice in the poem, his motives are uncomplicated. So is his pull for intimacy. He automatically, without forethought, draws the other in—he can't
help but use the poetic capacity that is intuitively his. But, like any highly
developed competency, it can take on a life of its own, one with complicated
and consciously unintended consequences that are not necessarily positive.

Articulating Intimacy in the Clinical Engagement with James

And what of the other enclave-builder, James? Certainly, he had various
"techniques" for establishing his own version of an enclave, and these
were in evidence in his therapy. The following clinical exchange occurred
about three years into this four-times-a-week analysis. James wrestles
with himself and with me, as he tries to judge whether being overly attentive and generous in the early stages of dating a new woman is at all problematic. In the meantime, he's playing out another incarnation of uneasily
intimate relating in which he tries to evoke maternal nurturance in me by
presenting himself as exceedingly and appealingly weak:

James: So I'm in the throes of thinking about my search for "a better
           mother" thing. I realize it'll never be satisfying. I know that I'm
           doing this again with H. I understand the problem intellectually
           but obviously not at the emotional level.
Analyst: Somehow I feel that in your saying this, there's a plea for me to
           supply the answer, for me to mother you.
James: [jovially] Yeah, if I could do it myself, I wouldn't be here!
Analyst: Ah, and *that* feels like an angry, *insistent* plea for mothering.
James: I'm angry at myself for playing out the same dance . . . I've cor-
           responded with three or four new women lately . . . I didn't tell S.
           that I didn't want to have a relationship with her. I'm struggling
           with it—don't want to have that difficult conversation. Since I
           don't know what a healthy relationship is, it's difficult for me to
           make these kinds of judgments.

In the session, James alternately courts my goodwill, confesses his weakness, and attempts to persuade me that certain suspect actions on his part
are actually healthy. The self-deprecation and help-seeking are rather worrisome after all his work in our analysis and the two treatments preceding
it. I fight not to succumb to either my frustration or my concern about him.
I know that I'm in O'Shaughnessy's enclave for better and worse:

Analyst: I'm not sure what you mean, when you say that you don't know
           what a healthy relationship is.
James: I know I'm drawn to unhealthy relationships, ones that are
           unhealthy because they make me replicate unhealthy behaviors
           I've had. So if I'm drawn to somebody, then they'll inevitably
           evoke unhealthy behavior in me!

This circular, sophist reasoning shows how bound up and frustrated with
himself James feels. It also illustrates how he seems to present himself
as inadequate partly in order to evoke the actively caretaking, maternal
aspects in me. Once again, I experience the pull of those early mother–son
talks, so hard to resist getting sucked into:

James: I have a good reason not to trust my sense of chemistry. I feel
           this because I can't tell what's healthy and what isn't. Unless
           the goal is to accept that I have these kinds of unhealthy rela-
           tionships and to stop worrying about it—but I don't seriously
           think that *is* the goal we're working toward here.

At this juncture, I suggest that James has painted himself into a corner and then magically leapt out of it. If there is no "best" answer, then this seemingly gives him permission to give up and do whatever feels best in the moment. I don't have to add that we both know this ultimately won't wash:

James: A mutuality of seeking out, I mean, a woman wanting me as much as I want her, is a good indicator of a healthy relationship. So if it's one-sided, with me always being the one to do the calling, it's not healthy.

Analyst: Umhmm.

James: Yesterday morning and today I finally went back to a tai chi class. It was good for me, but . . . I'm always looking for the breast. I notice it when I'm alone, that I notice women and my attention is particularly pulled to their breasts . . . I'm fixated on them.[1]

Analyst: What's going on in the "fixation"?

James: I'm noticing their breasts, which I associate with wanting to get close, be comforted, the feeling of being taken care of. A deep part of me really wanted to follow H. around. I so wanted to be taken care of; I wanted to be told what to do. Because I don't know what I want to do a lot of the time, I don't really care. I have no firm sense of my own direction. So I want someone to keep me oriented, comfort me, guide me.

Analyst: So it feels to you as if the woman knows what to do and can guide you, but you yourself *don't* know?

James: Right . . . or more that *nobody* knows what to do, but I want acceptance for that being the case. "Nobody knows, but it's okay, you'll figure it out, give it time."

Now James' associations take a new direction:

James: You know, the tendency for me is to *not* be fully engaged in things. When my father had his open heart surgery, the whole family just sat there in the waiting room, as if each of us were completely separate from the other . . . and you know, my dad had the same issue . . . He wouldn't articulate those things. He'd give someone the shirt off his back, anyone needy in his office, especially some of the retired women that he'd kept in touch with, but you'd never hear that he'd done it, or why . . . I could never tell what his feelings were until some anger fell out.

> But his reserve was typical of men of his generation . . . and for men in general, not to be transparent about one's emotions. Where it's gotten dicey is that not expressing your feelings doesn't mean you're not in touch with them—you may be, or may not be. The ideal is to be in touch with and be able to express one's feelings, but not to need to.

James had invested women with the power to heal him, and it appeared that his own warm, caregiving approach to a woman was in part (and paradoxically) a means to access those feminine healing powers. On top of his long practice at trying to be intimate with his mother, we hear in this session that James may have picked up caretaking from the father's secret "random acts of kindness." James absorbed this solicitous way of being close, and though it often came out in a constructive, genuine way, it could instead function as a vehicle for extracting emotional supplies from romantic partners. Perhaps the unconscious fantasy was that one day he might match his father and woo away the mother–lover who handed out the laurels of her attention and involvement with him in those late-night private conversations.

The above material illustrates several other elements frequently at play in uneasy intimacy. It calls attention to the attunement, the genuine sensitivity, and the desire to gratify the other often found in the "courting" individual. James was unfailingly considerate of me, seemed to respect my opinions, and—unsolicited, of course—gave me good recommendations for restaurants, worthwhile plays to see, and so forth. These were sincerely offered, but I had to watch closely lest I fall into step with his ingratiation, which would have led to a confining closeness between us that would reenact rather than allow us to analyze his central issues.

The tendency to present oneself as emotionally weak and therefore meriting help is another striking element in the analytic exchange between James and me. It echoes the example I gave earlier in which Walter used a "technique of intimacy" with his frat brother, à la Khan. Seeming needy creates a pressure in the other to offer the "weak" one nurturance and support, which oddly enough tends to feel like giving affection and again creates a semblance of closeness, but a closeness that is thin and unreliable. I felt this frequently in my work with James, where playing out the "strong, nurturant one" to his "weak, needy self" seemed somehow necessary to our bond, while at the same time it felt like it was getting us nowhere.

Another feature of this problematic form of intimacy is that the person being courted is sometimes kept on tenterhooks, not knowing when the suitor's hidden, dissociated subjectivity will emerge from its cave, causing a precipitous downtick in one's desirability to him or her. All of a sudden, an email will go unreturned, a planned date will be forgotten, a criticism will shoot out from left field, or something equally wounding will happen, introducing a new discordant thread into the fabric of their mutual involvement. Though the one being courted senses that there's more than meets the eye to the other's overly positive regard, it still feels terrible to have this confirmed in action. And the suitor him- or herself may come to feel trapped and frustrated in the self-subordinating role of cozying up to the other. In short, one or both parties in the uneasily intimate bond runs the risk of ending up feeling damaged, dropped, or betrayed.

This played out in the combative undertones of the patient–analyst exchanges I've reported. James in general seemed to keep me in the know vis-à-vis the details of his daily life and stream of thoughts. However, like O'Shaughnessy with Miss A, I was actually often in the dark as to their deeper emotional significance. James would get caught up in obsessive ruminating, absorbed in his internal self-arguments. If I challenged any one perspective, he responded with a knee-jerk contradiction; if we came to some shared understanding, it soon vanished into thin air. The obsessionalism was his way of keeping open the possibility of becoming worthy, should he land on the right answer, and it probably also kept a considerable degree of fury at himself and others at bay. Meanwhile, in terms of our relationship, it was as if we were engaged in a paradoxical dance, with James enacting the seductive, domineering masochist, and I the courted, submissive sadist (and I'm using these oxymorons advisedly). He felt hopeless and depressed due to the ongoing internal self-attack and "meekly" but powerfully demanded that I guide him, only to balk at the guiding when it occurred—and it was in this opposition that he found a semblance of autonomy, a modicum of self-respect. Returning again to the paradoxical enclave, my attempt to offer guidance around the obsessional blockade was a countertransferential element that played into that defensive dynamic; however, not guiding him ran the risk of a fatal blockage in analytic progress, as the absence of such direction left him spinning his wheels. (See Benjamin, 2004, on the doer/done-to dichotomy.) Together, we were trying to engage in the natural rhythms of intimacy between the "averagely needful patient" and the "averagely helpful analyst," but it turned into a tangled knot of thwarted intentions.

Notwithstanding the enclave and knots, however, there was a steady accretion over the course of the analysis in James' ability to recognize and work effectively with his own deeper needs and urges, particularly the ones that evoked his self-criticism. I attribute this to our persistent effort to understand his uneasily intimate way of relating to his significant others, including the analyst, but I credit just as much his remarkable determination to reach the authentic within himself and others. As James became more frank with himself in exploring less constructive uses to which he put his capacity for emotional attunement, his relationships with himself and others took on a more substantial quality, encompassing more of the bitter along with the sweet, the disappointments along with the satisfactions.

Overcloseness Early in Life and its Later Impact

Nancy Chodorow (1978) describes a situation in which a mother might pull for certain types of emotional overinvolvement with her child, especially to the degree that she experiences her husband as emotionally detached and is attempting to compensate for this. Chodorow emphasizes the daughter rather than the son as the one most likely to be targeted for this excessive closeness, but in my experience, the bonding between a sensitive son and an overly needful or overbearing mother is just as likely to occur. Nor is it exclusively the mother who is involved. When the parent inaugurates this type of confidential relationship with the child, the latter is gratified by the special singling-out, and he or she realistically benefits to some degree from the emotional lessons that may be precociously learned through their tie. However, the child is at the same time also constricted and perhaps even co-opted by the growing emotional resonance with the parent. That resonance can lead to a sense of inordinate responsibility for the parent's psychic well-being. The advantages and disadvantages of an intensified mutual involvement can appear so evenly matched that even the most perceptive child can become ensnared in it and remain so into adulthood, as can the most well-meaning, otherwise astute parent. What we could call "arrests" at an overly enmeshed phase of adult separation/individuation (Blos, 1967; Crastnopol, 1980; Mahler et al., 1975) eventually take their toll on both parties, and this can be true whether the adult involved is the parent or some other close relative who might have unmet wishes and a strong but underused capacity for emotional relatedness. As in the case with romantic adult partners, neither the elder person nor the younger one is a villain in this scenario—though of course the elder one implicitly bears central responsibility for its consequences.

Heightened sensual and affectionate currents, like the sexual ones I spoke of earlier, also play a strong role in an uneasily intimate bond. Both the thirst for and the capacity to provide emotional intimacy become inscribed in each person's psyche-soma through biophysiological pathways, rhythms, and pleasures. Consider a 10-year-old girl who is sent for the first time to visit her grandmother, with whom she's spent little time before, in a distant part of the country. For two weeks, the grandmother showers her with concentrated attention, praise, and stroking: "Darling, you're so adorable, and as clever as can be! I just *love* having you here with me—next time we'll have to make it a longer visit," and so on. There are constant affectionate words and caresses, and as they snuggle together in bed in the mornings, her grandmother asks about her likes and dislikes, her hopes and wishes. The girl feels her grandmother really listens, unlike so many other adults in her life. She reels with the extravagant involvement, all the while dimly wondering in the back of her mind what it will be like when it's time to say goodbye. When the vacation does come to a close, the little girl agonizes at having to leave someone she believes she's now gotten so close with. Yet at the same time, she doesn't know why they hadn't spent time together before, how her grandmother could all of a sudden be so very open and welcoming, and whether her involvement will continue in some form or not. The girl feels close to but vaguely unsure about her grandmother; their visit was sweet, but also bittersweet.

And once they're no longer together, her grandmother does indeed disappear again from her life. Few phone calls, no emails, not even a present when the girl's birthday rolls around. The girl misses her grandmother with an almost physical ache. It leaves the girl wondering if she'd done wrong or been foolish to get so attached. She's left with a yearning that isn't quelled for some time—the fruits of uneasy intimacy, and then an unkind cutting back. Thinking back on it in later years, she realizes that what the grandmother had offered was only a forced, condensed *show* of involvement, one that was perhaps driven by a desperate wish to carve a place for herself in her granddaughter's heart.

Overinvolvement with a child comes in different flavors and leads to different styles of uneasy relating. Victoria Secunda is an author, journalist, and lecturer who has written a probing book called *When You and Your Mother Can't Be Friends: Resolving the Most Complicated Relationship of Your Life* (1990). Secunda conducted interviews with 100 mothers and daughters whom she found through friends and a local newspaper. Her findings are based on these interviews, but for theoretical context, she draws from the work of the psychiatrists known for their research on temperament, Alexander Thomas and Stella Chess (Thomas & Chess, 1980), and from a wide range of other mental health professionals, including a few psychoanalysts.

Before I say more about Secunda's work, it's worth noting that micro-traumatic relating has long been a staple of psychologically minded books for the general reader, dating back to Eric Berne's thoughtful 1964 best-seller, *Games People Play*. Indeed, micro-trauma has been pretty well represented in certain seemingly "pop" psychology books that are positioned in the market as self-help guides, but that are based on actual empirical anecdotal research and on good scholarly understandings of the issues under discussion. In fact, these books have sometimes done a better job than the mainstream psychoanalytic literature in depicting micro-traumatic moments and making them accessible and understandable for a reading public that wants to make use of psychodynamic principles. Secunda's book is in this tradition and it is actually quite substantive. Secunda, like Berne, creates oversimplified, but nonetheless resonant typologies, but hers specifically concern mothers and daughters, emphasizing their individual roles as much as their interactional patterns. For the mothers, we have the role categories of the Doormat, Critic, Smotherer, Avenger, and Deserter. Daughters are classified as the Angel, Superachiever, Cipher, Troublemaker, and Defector. Relevant to our exploration of uneasy intimacy is the "smothering" type of overly intimate mother:

> It isn't just that Smotherers identify with their daughters—all mothers do that, to a degree. Rather, it is that their maternity is a mandate to coerce their daughters into the mother's image of what a "happy childhood" is all about, and to that end will sacrifice themselves with unsullied moral certainty and tireless stamina . . . The Smotherer wants to boost the odds that her daughter will be carefree and popular, the happiest little girl in the world. That desire, shared by many parents, seems to be set in motion by normal maternal concern. But, like a zoom lens, the Smotherer lunges forward in her loving zeal, enlarging her role and narrowing her focus to the exclusion of a healthy perspective. She wants only the best for her daughter, and she alone can provide it. Whatever you want, I will give it to you. *Do as I say*, because I will never fail you, and no one loves you more. Give yourself up to me, and I'll make everything wonderful.
>
> But it is the Smotherer who decides what the daughter wants. She defines her child's happiness in terms of her own needs and perceptions, rather than the child's: "I'm cold," she says, "put on a sweater."
>
> (Secunda, 1990, p. 114)

At this point, I'm reminded of a colleague who told me about having been on a shopping errand with his mother when he was a 13-year-old boy. As he recalls it, he remarked to her that often when he ran track at school, he would get a side stitch. But now he'd figured out how to deal with it, so it had become less bothersome. His mother jumped in helpfully, "Of course, honey, just distract yourself from the pain and it'll subside before you know it." The son was stopped short—maybe that *was* the answer, but his own solution had been almost the opposite—to enter into the pain, recognize it as part of himself, get to know it so it would be less threatening. This had seemed like a wonderful and useful approach to him. Tentatively he responded with his alternative—*his* alternative—but it seemed to hold little weight with his mother, who'd already moved on to another topic. Frustrated, the boy thought it over and generously construed the situation as his mother not being able to bear the idea of his experiencing any pain whatsoever, and he let it go at that. There is a lot going on in this memory—13-year-old boys don't often talk to their mothers about their bodily sensations, and mothers don't always ignore their children's self-care solutions, or for that matter, rush in to advise ignoring bodily pain. Now that the boy has grown up to be an analyst, he sees just how complicated this supposedly "connected" mother–son moment really was.

Secunda identifies two personality types as the cultivars of a smothering mother, a "spoiled" little girl and a "fearful" one. About the first kind, Secunda quotes John Crewdson as saying that a child made to feel overly entitled is "denied the opportunity to discover a realistic sense of himself [or herself]. He [or she] receives so much attention, affection, and praise that the narcissistic cord is not only never cut, it is never even stretched" (p. 116). In relation to the "fearful" child, she quotes James Garbarino as saying: "Smothering can create a child who is unfit to live a normal life because he or she is so anxiety ridden" (p. 117). In fact, necessary "self" functions can fail to develop due to the mother's having "over-provided" these functions herself as a self-object.

What I would add to Secunda's explanation is that this type of smothering interaction often becomes two-way. The child of an over-providing parent may come to rely and eventually insist on his or her continued excessive involvement. Even if the parent comes to recognize this as unhealthy and tries to ease out of the bind, the child may buck the change. Often, neither parent nor child can readily let the other resist the pattern, as each person's identity has become predicated on that untoward closeness.

Developmental Aspects of Intimacy: Case Illustrations

Turning from Secunda's typology, I offer some clinical illustrations of uneasily intimate relating between parent and child that, in all their complexity, don't fall into one particular, generalizable category. Jade was a 25-year-old woman who was in analysis with me three times per week some years ago. She was someone who had been extremely close to both parents all her life, even after she'd left their hometown to pursue her advanced education. Jade's marriage at the age of 23 did little to diminish her intense tie with her mother, a renowned professor of statistics. However, once this young woman began dental school, a field quite different from the mother's, Jade began to sense a rift growing between them. In the past, her mother had always seemed eager to hear about her feelings, hopes, and plans, but now she appeared indifferent to hearing about her daughter's experience of the training process and made no effort to get a feel for what life as a dentist might entail. A demanding class schedule made Jade less available during the rare moments her mother had free, but the latter seemed reluctant to find alternate times to talk—a "cutting back" on the mother's part that was painful and frustrating for Jade. There was no way to penetrate the mother's underlying feelings or motives, as she insisted that their infrequent contact was purely a logistical problem. At the same time, when they *were* in contact, her mother in some ways acted as loving and positive toward her as ever. All this put Jade into a tailspin, with periods of anxious dependency alternating with indignant fury, both leading her to feel depleted and worthless. And yet, notwithstanding her current distress over the situation, Jade continued to insist that her mother was unconditionally approving and, bottom line, that she was nearly as perfect as was humanly possible. In short, Jade's feeling of intimacy with her mother had become fraught with conflict. Jade's passage through this "second separation/individuation phase" of young adulthood (Blos, 1967; Crastnopol, 1980) had been compromised by the earlier intensity of the mother–daughter bond, and now she was thrown for a loop in having that "love affair" trail off so precipitously—if that's actually what was happening. Adding fuel to the fire of Jade's upset, a similar scenario soon played out in another micro-traumatic separation, this time between Jade and her best friend, who on becoming engaged to be married, started acting flaky and unreliable when Jade tried to make plans to get together with her.

Intimacy issues naturally arose in the analytic relationship as well. Jade seemed somewhat detached and self-enclosed in our sessions, leading me to wonder whether a fear of having yet another enticing but unreliable bond was at play in the transference/countertransference currents. Perhaps she was afraid of the impact of becoming attached to me. After hearing me read the above account in the service of my obtaining her permission to write about it, Jade confirmed my suspicions:

Jade: Yep, well I *told* you I didn't want another mother! It's like an addict, I don't want to stop one thing and become addicted to something else. My first inclination would be to attach to someone new, but it just doesn't feel safe.

Analyst: Yeah, if it's *only* a repeat of the relationship you'd had with your mom, that sure wouldn't be good.

Jade: I just don't trust myself to know what's good and what's bad attachment. What if it went awry and my attachment to you went horribly like my mom? I know you like to cook—if you make one thing horribly, how can you trust yourself to make it again? How do you trust you have the right *tools* to make it right the next time?

As Jade articulated, one of the worst consequences of miscarried intimacy is that it damages the person's sense of trust in his or her own compass for plotting future relatedness. It sows the seeds of self-doubt that sprout and become deeply rooted, even affecting the person's capacity for the analytic connection they so badly need.

As the session went on, I asked what felt risky to her about our closeness. It turned out that it was the asymmetry in our positions that troubled her—she told me everything about her internal and external worlds, and I told her very little, if anything, about mine. This replicated the imbalance with her mother, by which she felt quite belittled:

Analyst: Then there's a power differential here, in who gets to know what, huh?

Jade: Umhmm! . . . Yes, and my mom has to be the good one, the "helpful" one, and I know she's like that not only with me, but with members of the statistics department, and other people too. But it's still upsetting . . . I feel that if my mom really wanted to be close with me, she'd have started sharing more about herself with me once I became an adult. It goes back to the power relation . . . I'm not equal to her! I spill my guts to her and I'm still the little girl.

Analyst: Yes, so it sets up the illusion that she has everything together and you don't.

Jade: Yeah, and that I'm not worth sharing with . . . It's that I don't matter enough to her, or that I'm too lowly. I tell her everything, she dispenses her wisdom, and that's it, like that's supposed to be the paradigm and I don't like that. And that's the paradigm with you too—ok, here it's not quite as rigid as with her [Jade gives a little laugh here] but it's a similar dynamic.

I replied ruefully that I could certainly see how this therapeutic setup might feel that way to her. My acknowledgment of the actual asymmetrical nature of our analytic relationship opened up into a further discussion of how other unequal-seeming relationships had "burnt" her—that is, made her feel devalued and humiliated—in the past.

An especially satisfying aspect of this exchange was that it was "performative," in that it *enacted a solution* to the problem of felt self-diminishment at the same time as it expressed the problem. That is to say, Jade was actually occupying a position of authority as she "taught" me about her inner world, rather than my presumably doing the teaching or purporting to know more about her than she herself did. She was leading me, and I was getting the chance to be led by her, in much the same way as she'd wished could happen with her mother. Further, adopting a psychologically minded approach to her life, as she was trying to do in this exchange, had previously been difficult for her—it was definitely not something within her mother's repertoire, which meant she was striking out on her own and making use of her treatment's values to do so.

Jade went on to say that, at her stage of young adulthood, her mother's insistence on being a resource for her and her refusal to accept help from her daughter made the relationship feel really thin:

Analyst: The most painful thing seems to be your feeling that it's shallow because she doesn't value you. I'm curious about that part.

Jade: If she did value me, she'd want to cultivate the relationship with me . . . you know you're bonding with a friend when they share a problem. Then you know they value what and how you think. I obviously don't feel useful to her. What little wisdom I have at 25 years of age—it's not something she thinks would be valuable to her.

Analyst: So it's feeling respected, that both you and your way of thinking are respected, and that she'd want to access it.

Jade: Yeah! Like that one time when I recommended that book, and she actually read it and appreciated it. That was amazing. But as much as she says we're "crafting a *friendship*" now, the truth is that she loves being a *mom*, and she doesn't want to let that go. She wants to kiss my boo-boos. She doesn't want to give that up, though it's inherently necessary. Maybe when she has grandkids, then she'll be able to be different with me.

Here, Jade notes that healthy emotional intimacy implies a reasonable balance of the sharing of one person's inner life with another's. Should one withhold too much of his or her internal world, it leaves the other feeling on the one hand exposed, and on the other, undervalued or disrespected. Power is at issue here, the power of conferring recognition and sanction. If this power is unevenly divided, frustration or, worse, humiliation results. And if one passionately longs for intimacy—affectionate or sexual—with the other and is answered with a much lesser degree of longing, this too creates an unbalanced matrix of emotional involvement and emotional power—in other words, an uneasy intimacy (see Dimen, 2003, on the intertwining of power with intimacy).

That said, the generational divide between parent and child naturally alters the equation. It is appropriate that the intimacy between parent and child be constrained by the elder person's caretaking responsibility for the younger, just as the intimacy between analyst and patient is constrained by the former's responsibility for the latter. However, a certain degree of self-revelation might be increasingly appropriate and desirable for a parent as the child moves into adulthood, and refraining from this could feel like a vote of no-confidence in the younger person's capacity to respond in a mature manner to that openness. By the same token, Jade was aggrieved not because she expected to hear the details of her mother's most private emotional struggles, which might indeed cross a boundary between them. What she expected was a "reasonable and customary" degree of openness on her mother's part, commensurate with her growing maturity. But somehow this remained elusive, at least during the time Jade was in analytic treatment. Fortunately, the mother's attitude toward her and its impact on their relatedness bothered Jade less over time, as her ongoing professional development reinforced her own belief in herself, which in turn reduced her need to be validated by her mother's interest in her.

A history of over-intimacy with a parent early in life can play out in other ways as well, and sometimes it's the child rather than the parent who is seemingly in the elevated position. A 30-year-old man, Nathan, had been treated to a special closeness with his father since his boyhood. He was viewed as the only one in the family, which included an older brother and sister, with special interpersonal sensitivity and heightened emotional understanding. The father was full of praise for these qualities in Nathan. He felt free to lean on Nathan as a confidant, to call on him to mediate whatever family disputes arose, and so forth. When the brother developed a substance abuse problem, it was Nathan the family turned to for an explanation of what it all meant and how to handle it effectively. Nathan was clearly proud of his role, even though in recent years he had begun to feel somewhat put-upon by it.

In the course of exploring these issues, Nathan came to a session with a severe earache and seemed unable to function. His male therapist proceeded to take him to the nearest hospital emergency room, where he was evaluated as having a non-serious condition that would abate on its own. Once assured that the patient was in good hands, the therapist returned to the office to resume his workday. Things in the therapy continued as before, except that at the end of the month, Nathan was shocked to see that he had been charged for the session time of the day he'd become ill. After a mild protest, he let the matter drop, resuming his usual cooperative and sincere demeanor. But several weeks later, the issue resurfaced, and at this point Nathan was able to be more honest. He admitted that he'd felt a sense of violation in being charged for that session. He'd thought that the therapist cared for him, and that if that were so, he wouldn't dream of expecting payment for his time that day. Nathan added that had he known in advance that there would have been a charge, he would have scrambled to find some other way of dealing with the illness. The therapist began to experience pressure to feel guilty at his supposed greed. He was also rather irked at the patient's sense of entitlement and at his callousness to the burden it would have placed on the therapist to bring him to the hospital and, on top of that, not receive payment for their missed time. The therapist felt in a sense "used" by the patient ("used" in the sense of being taken unfair advantage of), and it bothered him that the patient had no qualms about doing so. On Nathan's end, the idea that he would have been abusing the therapist's kindness, rather than simply receiving something freely offered that was his due, was a hard pill to swallow—it would have grossly contradicted his self-image as a considerate, emotionally attuned guy.

The therapist stood his ground, trying not to sound indignant or defensive. He explained his experience of the interchange and opened up an exploration of its underlying intersubjective meanings. This paid off, and the analytic dyad was able to make valuable analytic "hay" out of the incident. Nathan soon recognized that he was leaning on a set of problematic assumptions that dated back to his childhood. In effect, he was trading on his capacity for establishing an uneasy intimacy with the other:

> I'm empathic and charming toward everybody, they like me, and they therefore sacrifice for me. As I would do for them, of course. This is the way I've always functioned, and it's what my dad valued in me and expected from me. I'm very caretaking and very complimentary, and so people want to help me in kind. The difference here is that I'd have nothing to give you back, other than being such a good, polite, gratifying patient.

Nathan had automatically accessed the tendencies he naturally had and the skills he'd learned in the relationship with his father. He unconsciously expected that having these would allow him to hold the same sway over his therapist as he did over his family. The therapist would therefore be delighted to serve him, and at no cost to Nathan himself. The exchange of warm supportiveness and attunement for practical gain that Nathan was used to making was partly automatic and partly intentional. If and when he thought about it, he liked to consider this bargain (Myerson, 1969, cited by Lionells, 1995) to be something agreeable for and advantageous to both parties. If it wasn't, with luck, the other party wouldn't notice what he was up to or wouldn't very much mind. Nathan was shocked, disoriented, and offended when his customary modus operandi didn't work in the therapy. But through the analytic work, he was able to see that his attitude was inherently disrespectful and, to some degree, abusive; it undermined the mutual trust within the relationship, since the other was enlisted in this exchange without full disclosure or the chance to buy in or opt out of it. There was no doubt that he should work further on all this within himself.

Another consequence of an early experience of excessive emotional closeness with a parent can be the feeling of needing to tolerate or even relish whatever degree of support the parent offers, in order to sustain that semblance of involvement with him or her. Especially where that support is flimsy or unattuned, the child (and later, adult) experiences a build-up of frustration and rage toward the parent, which the person is unconsciously fearful of unleashing if he or she were to acknowledge to him- or herself the parent's actual inadequacies and failings. The child is likely to grit his or her teeth and smile; however, keeping up the illusion that all's well in the relationship makes for a feeling of uneasy intimacy, either privately within the individual or between the two parties in the parent–child relationship. A 45-year-old man named Peter described his mother as an unregenerate "counter-cultural type," who had always offered him strength and support in the form of many ill-thought-out, supposedly helpful suggestions. She would volunteer nostrums such as "take a deep breath and think about the wider universe," and she'd gaze into his eyes in an urgent, soul-searching manner. His mother seemed so very hurt if he hinted that she was misfiring when she approached him that way. Given her obviously loving intentions, how could he complain? Soon after his marriage, Peter's wife was diagnosed with breast cancer. At this juncture, he was in a terrible quandary over sharing the news with his parents. His mother's airy, pseudo-spiritual handling of it would be unbearable, particularly for his wife, whom he now wanted to protect more urgently than ever. The here-and-now analytic work involved helping the patient explore his powerful fears of letting himself truly know what he knew about his mother and her impact on him throughout his life. The deeper work centered on his fear of intimate relatedness per se, as he believed that a fuller closeness with anyone including his wife would inevitably quash his individuality, swallow him up, or arouse such anger in him that he would end up badly hurting the other.

Sometimes it's not the child but the parent who is in analytic treatment. When this is the case in my own practice, I may find myself registering the power difference between parent and child and its impact on their style of closeness, and I reflect on the potential for inadvertently generating an uneasy intimacy between them as a result. Under these circumstances, I will sometimes end up taking the risk of being more directive than usual. Matt was an engaged, well-meaning man who enjoyed his three kids heartily. At one point, he came up with a screen name, signed on to his son's instant messenger service, and began chatting harmlessly with his son and the son's friends. Experiencing some awkwardness in the interchange, Matt thought it was due to the teenagers' not being used to a father being interested in them "as people." Some of the boys responded positively to his online presence, but others including his son seemed to become less talkative. This continued until Matt brought it up in his analysis and voiced his puzzlement at what was occurring. I offered some gentle analysis of the situation, hinting at a primal scene situation in reverse. But when this didn't do the trick, I flatly advised Matt to sign off. Amid some protest, he did, and certain tensions between him and his son subsided.

Recently, it now being a year or so later, we were exploring the son's defiant, hostile stance in relation to Matt's best efforts to respond to his needs and wishes. I found myself inviting Matt to avoid taking on the specific issues, which just turned into struggles for control, and to try to build more of an understanding of what fueled the son's defensive posture. I suggested he ask what the boy actually felt about what was going on in their relationship, what exactly was making him so angry. It struck me as odd that Matt had sought to get closer socially with his son, but rarely, if ever, tried to make direct contact with the young man's feelings. I knew that my suggestion ran the risk of sounding like an invitation to work his way even further into the sanctum sanctorum of his son's inner life, and I knew that his son could experience it as uneasy contact, as adolescents so often perceive the overtures of their well-intentioned elders (including their therapists). Just how the suggestion played out is not clear yet. The proof will be in the longer-term pudding—we'll have to see whether his son experiences this as a co-opting or an effort to open up a constricted space, within each and between them.

Misguided Intimacy within the Psychoanalytic Profession

We mental health professionals are a select group that has gravitated to this sort of work because of our natural propensities and longings for deep emotional contact with others. We've then gone through intensive trainings to hone those innate tendencies, so we can harness them in the service of our therapeutic aims. Ironically enough, as our capacity for sustained, meaningful relating grows, the number of outlets we have for fulfilling our needs for personal intimacy often shrinks (see Rucker, 1993). The more involved we get in our practice, in an agency, or as part of an institute, the less time we have for pursuing our emotional needs in the private sphere. For many of us, there's a blurring of professional and private spheres, with consultants becoming friends and other friends who are in the field becoming consultants, which makes it unclear who can be told what and to what depth we can go in discussing confidential matters. It is natural and beneficial that we turn to individuals within our professional context to engage in some degree of emotional sharing, mutual recognition, and the fellow-feeling of jointly appreciating how the psyche works. But there can be uneasy moments.

To complicate matters, some of the most immediate, most profound analytic work can only be done within the therapeutic relationship itself, with its web of transferential and idiosyncratically personal currents crisscrossing between analyst and patient. It's the perfect medium for cultivating healthy intimacy, but it can segue into destructive forms as well. And we cannot always distinguish the two, because much of the work is done in a transitional space between the really "real" and the psychically "real" and is dependent on both participants' tacit agreement as to that distinction. If one person inwardly disagrees with the other about what is the "real" reality of his or her closeness to the other, we have uneasy intimacy in the making. There may be no chink in the walls of the cocoon of therapeutic confidentiality through which an authorized third person could offer a salutary perspective on the proceedings.

This situation can readily lead to an unholy emotional alliance between patient and analyst in which one or both lose sight that the purpose of the developing intimacy is the patient's psychic maturation. They instead begin to pursue the emotional closeness as an end in itself, or they seek to reinstate a gratifying sense of being "the seeker" or "the one sought" (and either person can play either role). This ultimately results in one or both feeling drawn into closer closeness than they had originally bargained for.

The "uneasily intimate" moment is not restricted to our consulting rooms. In our professional meetings, our private lunches, our hallway conversations at conferences, and so forth, we analytically trained practitioners sometimes show too much of our own vulnerabilities to colleagues or elicit too many confidences from them. Later, we wonder, what was I caught up in? what was I doing? Being richly conversant in the idiom of intimacy, we can't resist reveling in it, sometimes getting carried away or even trading on it. How often does the analytic writer establish an air of cozy familiarity with the reader, thus undermining any misgivings about the presenter's position? How often does an analytic speaker offer a clinical example with questionable features, but in such an engaging way that the audience forgets to raise the obvious concern about boundary-crossing? Would that we could turn up the lights and be less afraid of what we'll find there. As Harry Stack Sullivan reminded us, we're all "more simply human than otherwise," and often our errors in intimacy modulation can be rectified and forgiven when they're understood for what they are.

Finally, inside of therapy and out, issues of emotional closeness and its uneasy variants need to be contextualized in terms of the society at large. Underlying our wishes for intimacy is a larger socio-cultural trope of Western society, in which establishing a sense of privileged knowledge and access to the other's private life has become at once a prize, a refuge, and a compensation. As the ties of community grow ever more tenuous, the natural tendency is to concentrate on a few relationships and to turn up the intensity in terms of closeness. A craving for intimacy might indeed be a byproduct of the anxieties and terrors of the current era. Facing ever intensifying threat, we naturally seek solace in the form of real or illusory closeness with others whom we invest with special or reassuring properties. From another angle, the social tendency to establish a sense of essentially hollow intimacy—based on relating false self to false self—might be an adaptation to the alienation engendered by the narcissistic challenges of living in such a competitive world. In such a society, intimacy that's uneasy may at times, paradoxically, seem safer than allowing oneself to be truly known and to truly know the other.

Note

1 This preoccupation calls to mind Fairbairn's (1952, p. 11 ff.) view of schizoid elements in psychic life, in which the child's libidinal interest becomes focused on the breast as a partial libidinal object instead of connecting to the mother as a whole person. The "libidinal attitude" that develops is characterized by taking as opposed to giving, by tendencies to incorporate and internalize, and by feelings of emptiness and deprivation as opposed to fullness. These echo some of James' own psychic tendencies and complaints, both formulated and unformulated.

Chapter 5

Psychic Airbrushing and Excessive Niceness

Part of developing greater emotional maturity involves learning to tolerate or even forgive character flaws, both our own and those of others. We work on being able to take the bad with the good, to counterbalance an appreciation of the positive with the capacity to acknowledge the negative. Some degree of downplaying or sweetening inherent problems or faults, tempering our disappointment in relation to them, understandably has a place in this process. But it can be a short leap from simply minimizing one's own or another's shortcomings to blotting them out entirely, from walking around those shortcomings to paving them over permanently. When the latter happens, the "good-enough self" one presents to the world leaves out too much of one's actual inner complexity; the darker elements, in particular, drop into obscurity.

I consider undue masking to amount to "psychic airbrushing," something we experience internally and communicate outwardly by embracing half-truths and committing "sins" of omission, commission, and distortion in what we acknowledge about ourselves and others. A partner to airbrushing is a blanket attitude of "excessive niceness," in which one responds affectively to the other as if any flaws or failings they possess are insignificant or immaterial. When people engage in either of these sorts of covering up, they and others influenced by them may sense the denied imperfections only dimly, which leaves them unable to grapple with areas of friction effectively. This obfuscation not only undermines psychological attunement to oneself and the other, it also disrupts the emotional communication between the person and his or her significant others, with consequences that are micro-traumatic. Being airbrushed or treated with excessive niceness—that is, being responded to with an exaggeratedly favorable attitude or undue enthusiasm when one inwardly knows better—may feel no more satisfactory than having one's real merits overlooked.

As I use the term, airbrushing is not the same thing as idealization, which can also lead to a minimization of the negative. Idealization is an innate process, and Kohut (1971, 1977) has bequeathed to us a detailed view of how idealization operates in development and in analysis. All of us need to have figures whom we can look up to and admire. When these individuals fail us, as Kohut illuminated, the result can be a rent in the structure of the self, with the disappointed, disillusioned aspects of the self sequestered off by themselves via a "vertical split" (1971, p. 185, pp. 241–242).

In airbrushing, the minimization of flaws is on a different level than it would be in idealization; it is more a day-to-day, regular operating procedure than a psychic cleavage. And its subtlety makes the disavowed faults that much harder to register and react to or compensate for. Also, in addition to the component of denial, a certain "beautification" process occurs in airbrushing that more fully contradicts the possibility of there being any badness to begin with. Being subtle and therefore *stealthful* in its destructiveness is a feature common to all micro-traumatic mechanisms, including airbrushing and excessive niceness.

In terms of being a defense, airbrushing would seem to be akin to Sullivan's (1956, chapter 3) "selective inattention," in that part of the trick lies in not noticing imperfections; an even greater part lies in not elaborating upon what you do notice. No implications are drawn, and the element that is not attended to is therefore all the harder to access in memory, lacking the additional mnemonic "hooks" that meaningful elaboration gives. This is what Donnel Stern (1997) has called "weak dissociation." But airbrushing goes beyond selective inattention and weak dissociation, in that the resulting picture is not simply blurry or undeveloped in places, it is positively retouched, made to look better than normal. This makes it more akin to the "hysterical dynamism" (1956, chapter 11) in Sullivan's nomenclature, except that hysterics exaggerate in both directions, positive and negative, and do so as an expression of their fundamental self-absorption. People who use airbrushing, even when they use it to cover their own imperfections, are not necessarily hysterical in their functioning, nor do they exaggerate the negative. That said, the tendency to try to cover-up aspects of self that could incur disapproval often does occur in those with a hysterical personal structure. These individuals have implicitly entered into "a hysterical bargain" (Myerson, 1969, cited in Lionells, 1986) to please and propitiate the powerful other come hell or high water, in exchange for the other's psychic blessing.

When we airbrush a particular feature we deem bad, negative, or otherwise unfavorable, we often airbrush our own affective reactions to those things as well. We may then be inclined to minimize related negative features so that the whole constellation retains its semblance of consistency.

so-and-so really *isn't* stingy, petty, or hypercompetitive, and I really *am not* bothered by hints of those things in her or him; he or she is not that kind of person, and I am not so unfortunate as to have such an intimate. Disguise spreads, breeding more disguise, and the falseness proliferates. The gap widens between who someone truly is and how that person is known to be.

Aspects of psychic life threatening enough to be blotted out and covered over are numerous. They include sexual, aggressive, and appetitive urges; criticism of or opposition to another's views; unsavory attitudes or opinions; and dark, unacceptable emotions or sentiments. We may airbrush *ourselves* in this fashion, as we do to avoid anxiety or shame, but we may also airbrush *others* when it seems emotionally prudent or exigent to do so—that is, when being frank stands to induce hurt, resentment, or reactive opposition from another. The erasure can happen unconsciously, but just as often it is conscious, perhaps as a sanctioned extension of social norms to save face for oneself or the other. Is the charade altruistic or selfish—or both? Ultimately, it is often neither; it is simply habitual.

Airbrushing grows out of the same soil as a phenomenon well-known within the field of psychological assessment called "social desirability." This is a type of bias in which individuals acting as subjects in an experiment consciously or unconsciously respond in such a way as to present themselves in a more socially acceptable light. For example, the item asks: do you fly off the handle when someone cuts in front of you in line? The options are "never/occasionally/regularly/always." The chronically explosive individual is likely to answer "occasionally" out of an unconscious pressure to downplay what could be perceived as a flaw, to retain a measure of implicit social approval and avoid censure. Moreover, the test-taker is prone to respond in a socially desirable way *whether or not* he or she believes that someone will actually be privy to the answers and judge him or her negatively for them. It is the inner representation of the other, their "reflected appraisal," in Sullivan's terms, that one defends oneself from most of all.

This kind of response bias has bedeviled social psychological researchers right along. For example, it makes it especially difficult to get truly representative results—that is to say, honest answers—on any kind of questionnaire research on sexuality. Indeed, though his sampling methodology was ultimately flawed, one of the strengths of Kinsey's original research (see Christenson, 1971; Gathorne-Hardy, 2000) was that he designed a multifaceted structured interview that would crisscross a given aspect of sexual behavior from different angles and thus ultimately elicit more straightforward answers. All who were exposed to the structured interview, including representatives of funding agencies making site visits to Kinsey's research center, came away impressed by the authenticity of the responses thereby obtained.

More generally, test developers of different stripes have developed ways of sniffing out and counterbalancing their results to account for this bias in responding. Notably, this has led to the so-called "validity scales" on the MMPI (Minnesota Multiphasic Personality Inventory), a much revised self-report measure. In its original 1943 incarnation, it contained 504 true–false items. There were 10 clinical scales, which were "criterion-valid"—that is, one scored high, say, on the paranoid scale by giving the same answers as those given by patients with established diagnoses of paranoid conditions on those same questions. From the first, however, it was necessary to supplement the clinical scales with validity scales designed to detect tendencies to give socially desirable answers, thereby masking psychopathological indicators. Famously, these were the L scale (L for "Lie"), which meant the test-taker was trying to present him- or herself as favorably as possible, and the K scale ("Defensiveness"), which could mean that the person was socially well-off and functioned at a high level *or* that he or she tended to minimize the extent of his or her psychopathology. But the phenomenon in question—responding according to social desirability—does not give up its secrets so readily on a pencil-and-paper measure. In subsequent revisions of the test, new scales have been added, including the S scale ("Superlative Self Presentation"), the Mp scale ("Positive Malingering"), and the Sd scale ("Social Desirability"). All of these scales tap different strategies that might be used in airbrushing, whether the object of the airbrushing is one's self or someone else; however, to explore them further requires great familiarity with this much traveled and psychometrically now quite intricate test. Let us just say that when an individual airbrushes in the context of a significant relationship, he or she implicitly presents a narrowed vision of the self or other that disrupts genuine contact. The airbrusher also implicitly indicates that flaws are intolerable in either self or other and that he or she lacks the ability to absorb and work with those limitations where they occur.

As noted earlier, sometimes airbrushing takes the form of a generalized manner of excessive niceness toward the other. Being nice is of course seen as a virtue in Western society, in familial and social interaction as well as most business and professional settings. Norms of civility do much to facilitate the hard work of relating to one another across conflicting agendas and needs. Our mutual ethical responsibility to one another (high-lighted, for example, in the thinking of Emmanuel Levinas, 1998) requires that we make efforts to offer some protection to the other's sense of pride and well-being. This involves some dampening of one's negative reactions to things in the other person we find distasteful, hurtful, vapid, stupid, or wrong. But when this niceness is kneejerk, nonspecific, and pervasive, when one airbrushes the other's bad aspects as well as one's own capacity for irritation and non-acceptance, one may be engaging in cruelty in the form of supposed kindness.

Necessary efforts to mask unpleasant truths—whether to protect one's narcissism or for reasons of survival—are memorably explored in Hans Christian Anderson's fable, "The Emperor's New Clothes," wherein the monarch believes he is lavishly dressed in a fabulous new costume as he parades before his subjects. All the while, he is in fact stark naked. His subjects, by and large, "airbrush" the situation; they *need* to be excessively nice in order to avoid provoking their liege's ire were he to realize or admit to himself that he is actually unclothed, that he has been duped by unscrupulous tailors who have played on his vanity. In recounting the tale, one invariably moves quickly to the moral: it takes having a child's innocence to see what there is to be seen—a markedly naked emperor. But let's stay for the moment with the "admiring" horde and the emperor himself: what is going on with all these people, emperor and subjects, as they busy themselves admiring what isn't there? What sort of uneasiness mounts within them? Do they dread the day when the hoax becomes apparent? This is the kind of uneasiness that begins to accumulate in the wake of airbrushing. One knows one stands on shaky ground somehow, even as the airbrusher continues on. The risk is that one day the protective mantle of the other's gaze may drop off. Such exposure of one's imperfect state is potentially quite humiliating for the airbrushed individual—and others taken in by the subterfuge. The truth-telling child escapes censure in Anderson's story, but often the one exposing the deception lives to rue the day, as nobody is happy to have the pretty picture called into question.

The term airbrushing comes, of course, from photography. In this medium, we appreciate the photographer's general effort to make us look good; indeed, we rather expect it. That's a "good picture," we say, or a "bad picture," leaving it hanging just a bit whether it is the picture or the view of ourselves that is good or bad. But airbrushing proper—that is, actual retouching—takes us further still. We may appreciate what can be done to enhance ourselves on our behalf, but we would be mortified if people found out. Why is that, exactly? We expect a photographic likeness to be factual, a visual historical record, in a way that we do not expect a painting or drawing to be. A certain artistic license is granted the portrait painter to beautify the subject, perhaps because we're used to the artist of yore glorifying his or her subjects in the name of aesthetic principles (not to mention, to flatter the patron!). But in a photograph, the same leeway does not obtain. Something has been falsified, we feel, if the photographer goes beyond merely being skillful with the lighting and the camera angles and makes further changes. Something like denial is entering in. And denial has consequences for everybody it touches and retouches.

For a fuller understanding of the consequences of *psychic* airbrushing, we need look no further than the comments of Spencer Cain (2012), celebrity editor at *Stylecaster News*, blogging on the subject of *photographic* airbrushing on its website. Cain observes that the "prettying up" of celebrity photos can go too far. He notes that many young girls will be exposed to these idealized images of the women they idolize, and they'll think these perfect-seeming appearances are entirely real. This then sets an unreachable standard for these girls, setting the stage in later years for eating disorders and damaging their sense of self-worth. But Cain is clearly ambivalent about all this, as he explains that retouching a photo within the celebrity industry is nonetheless an absolute must. He admits that he can't be judgmental of others, since he himself would go to great lengths to improve his photo if he thought it would become widely visible. It's especially absurd, Cain concludes, when the picture is airbrushed to such an extent that it looks unnatural and artificial. And he proceeds to parade a sequence of such false-looking images for the reader's amusement.

Within the world of celebrity and the media, photographic airbrushing is obviously an ever-present temptation, if not an imperative. Among those who trade on their good looks, appropriate degrees of airbrushing may indeed influence their employability and, in turn, their economic livelihood. For the non-celebrity person in the street who airbrushes the image of his or her own *persona*, it is one's *psychic* survival that is seemingly at stake. But in both cases, the airbrushing creates an illusion that can be maintained only with greater and greater determination not to deal with the obvious—that we are as we are, for better or worse.

Jean's Need to Look Good

I worked for several years in twice-weekly therapy with a young woman, Jean, who was notable for being consistently gracious and considerate. One day in particular, she began her therapy session in an upbeat mood, while avoiding mention of having abruptly cancelled an extra appointment time I'd set up at her behest. She also knew (but didn't bring up) that she was behind in her payment of the bill by several months. I had had to prompt her about this before, and she had promised to make good on the payment right away but had failed to do so. I was tempted at that moment to overlook these lapses, as addressing them felt petty in the face of Jean's niceness, which did feel genuine to me. However, catching my wish to avoid unpleasantness, I went ahead and interrupted Jean to ask whether those two matters were perhaps still on her mind. Jean froze for a moment, and then took on the look of someone who'd been caught and truly seen. No, she hadn't forgotten her lapses, she explained, but neither did she feel like bringing them up and acknowledging them. Doing so meant she'd be branding herself as irresponsible, which she didn't want to do. It seemed better to let these things slip from view. I responded that her infractions were certainly not in themselves especially troublesome or significant, but her seeming erasure of them *was*. It made me feel discounted at best and taken advantage of or manipulated at worst.

Jean immediately understood what I meant and quickly revealed that this sort of thing happened at work as well. She would overcompensate for missed deadlines by acting unusually helpful and accommodating toward those affected by her slippage. Her superiors would often automatically flex those deadlines without calling her to account for missing them. Within her circle of intimate friends, Jean strove to present the image of being well-adjusted and on top of the demands of her life. She didn't want others to sense the limitations with which she privately struggled. But her closest friends, intuiting that there was more to the story than met the eye, often complained that they didn't truly know her. She couldn't be as two-dimensionally (we might say, excessively) nice, as "together" and easy-going as she seemed. Then too, when under strain, Jean would slip up on a social arrangement—arriving late or double booking herself and then cancelling abruptly. Or she'd allow a sharp critique or complaint to escape her customarily cheery lips. This left her friends sometimes befuddled about her behavior and burdened with covering for her—yet more airbrushing—with members of their larger circle.

As we talked further, it emerged that Jean was terribly fearful that her self-perceived inadequacies—being under-disciplined, disorganized, too passive—would become too clear to her friends, and that these weaknesses would in turn reveal her as somehow fundamentally defective. The latter possibility, so at odds with how she came across, evoked deep shame in her. We traced this constellation of attitudes and feelings toward herself back to her childhood experience of having a mother who had herself grown up quite poor in a family that functioned badly. The mother's family was so destitute that oftentimes in her childhood, she had only two outfits presentable enough to wear outside the home, and each morning before school she would debate which one to wear that day.

Jean and her brother could both sense the mother's residual humiliation and anxiety about her background, about her own family's impoverishment, and about how socially backward and "untogether" the family was. The two children learned an important lesson early on: at all costs, they should avoid showing any hint of there being a lack of any kind or any hint that their own family might be in any way dysfunctional or inferior. These were the messages conveyed, even though Jean's mother had in fact provided amply for her own children, both materially and emotionally, and had shown great competence in her juggling of familial and professional responsibilities.

Carrying her mother's wound, the adult Jean still had to disguise her limitations—material, social, or psychological. She airbrushed her faults and frailties in a way that put them "off the table" for comment, critique, or attempts at repair. Here was an instance of the intergenerational transmission of trauma (see, for example, Faimberg, 1988; Fraiberg et al., 1975), in which long-forgotten or previously unregistered hurtful situations in a parent's life end up being restaged in the relationships with his or her children, thereby passing the injury down to the next generation.

In Jean, as in others, this problematic defensive strategy evolved in such a way that it touched some of the deepest areas of her life. She unconsciously felt inadequate because of having glossed over rather than tackled her deficiencies. Jean also airbrushed feelings about her husband, even as she reported comments by her friends that suggested he could be quite supercilious and even mean. She downplayed this aspect of him in part because she got vicarious enjoyment from the self-assertion and power his manner conveyed, if not also from the arrogance and nastiness itself. It was a compensation for her own meekness, self-abnegation, and dependence on others' approval. She needed to sustain the illusion that he was extra special, since it was having him as a partner that conferred value on her in her own eyes.

Airbrushing as Extreme Sport

In a satiric novel of Hollywood mores and manners, *This One Is Mine*, Maria Semple (2008) portrays a gallery of vain and self-deluded characters.

Among these is a personal trainer, Sally, whose mission in life appears to be to snare a wealthy husband so as to erase her substantial personal debt. The reader is at first repelled and disgusted by Sally's Machiavellian pursuit of her ends: she latches on to a sports statistics savant, Jeremy, and doggedly campaigns to get him to propose marriage to her by portraying herself as madly devoted to and very happy with him. This is despite the fact that his detachment and seeming cluelessness actually frustrate her no end. Haplessly caught in her snare, Jeremy does succumb and marry her against his better judgment. Sally is ecstatic, but her glee is short-lived—soon after the knot is tied, she comes across a description of a type of person who is brilliant but also "repetitive," "literal minded," "socially inept," "obsessive"—in short, autistic.

Sally is shocked and horrified to realize that her new husband's quirky characteristics mean that he, too, is autistic, and that she'd managed to miss or gloss over all the signs to this effect. For an extroverted, hysteric-type individual like Sally, this dooms her to a marriage made in hell. (To be clear, Jeremy is portrayed sympathetically as both solid and viable; it's clear that the incapacity is Sally's, and the barrier to their relationship is in her own flawed character and not attributable to his being autistic per se.) To top it all, Sally had gotten herself pregnant in order to clinch Jeremy's willingness to marry her, and she now learns that his autism is highly heritable. Ergo, the child she's carrying could also be autistic, she is taken aback to realize, a situation that would be way beyond her limited capacity to handle. She has managed to undermine her fondest wishes and goals by averting her eyes to what could have been quite obvious.

By this point in the narrative, however, the reader has come to feel some compassion for the scheming Sally, as we've learned that her father had died when she was young, leaving the family in terrible debt. Sally herself was discovered to be a juvenile diabetic, a condition requiring considerable care that her ineffectual mother couldn't provide. For decades, Sally had masked her chronic illness from everyone but her brother, who'd been her only caregiver. Lacking other capacities for bolstering herself psychologically or otherwise, Sally more or less *had* to develop a capacity to "airbrush" herself (her diabetes, her abject insolvency, her dependency on others). But she is now "hoist with her own petard," because she has hidden from herself the truth about her marital partner (airbrushed him to herself, as it were), thereby potentially ensuring her own unhappiness.

In just this fashion, the novelist seems to be saying, the person who disguises, disavows, and negates intolerable self-aspects simply lets these run rampant under the surface; she or he never learns how to manage them

effectively. (Sally's uncontrolled, fluctuating glucose level further sym-
bolizes this.) The shame is never confronted and so never resolved. Sally's
frantic airbrushing operation also distracts her from getting to the truth
of her financial situation and its potential solution, which she learns only
late in the saga—namely, that if she declared bankruptcy, all her debts
would be forgiven by society with only minor disadvantage to herself. It
is, of course, splendidly ironic that salvation appears in the form of being
"bankrupt." But the canny Semple gives this character her life lessons in
the end, forcing her to acknowledge her failings despite herself. This being
a comedic novel, Sally is left not only wiser but happier, to the ultimate
satisfaction of Semple's readers.

Motives for Airbrushing Oneself and One Another

From an interpersonalist psychoanalytic viewpoint, airbrushing is rooted
in the way the parent conveys to the child the components of a "good
me," the version of the self that will garner approval and avoid censure,
thereby reducing untoward anxiety. Insofar as the parents praise the child
for something, the child will seek to include that in his or her sense of
self—whether or not he or she actually has the trait. Many are the children
who have learned that if they act like everything is okay, then maybe everything will be okay. Conversely, they also learn that displays of anxiety,
guilt, shame, or the other trappings of the "bad-me" may make already
tense situations considerably worse. So the child works his or her way into
the airbrushed niche the parents create—and, in the process, ceases to be
governed by his or her own affective reactions.

But children learn how to regard the self not only through direct shaping by the parents' praise and admonitions, but also by watching how the
parent relates to his or her *own* strengths and weaknesses. If a parent airbrushes *herself*, the child loses the capacity to trust her perception as to
what is good or bad in the other. Personal experience becomes suspect,
which generates or deepens the rupture between genuine and inauthentic
self-experience. On the other hand, if a parent airbrushes her *child*, then
the child may come to "inattend to" or suppress an awareness of his or her
own flaws. Paradoxically, this denial can make having a flaw seem cata-
strophic rather than merely unfortunate. The amplification of the shame-
fulness of being flawed of course fosters further denial and erasure. When
a child masks personal weaknesses or difficulties from the parent, a number of problems may arise. Left largely in the dark, the parent is unable to
reflect constructively on the child's weakness itself and on his or her own

role in contributing to it. The parent may intuit a problem area but is powerless to help the child cope with or repair it. When the child airbrushes the *parent*, it can generate pressure in the parent to continue seeming superhuman. This demand in turn can disrupt the parent's connection with the full scope of his or her inner life, warts and all.

Airbrushing operations are common among those whose overall orientation to the world is excessively nice, goody-goody, or Pollyanna-like. In such people, the denial of the negative and suppression of aggression may occur because the antipathy is so strong that one fears its acknowledgment would lead to someone's annihilation; in other words, airbrushing oneself or others avoids the risk of one's anger destroying someone. Or the individual may sense that he or she lacks the psychic tools that would be needed to help soften or repair the damage incurred by expressing a negative truth. Here, too, airbrushing may seem like one's only recourse.

Often a person airbrushes a negative attitude because there is an unconscious (or subconscious) recognition that speaking the truth will arouse defensiveness in the other, who might respond with an equally harsh truth in return. The response might come as straightforward information or charged with the spirit of revenge. The airbrusher is fending off the possibility of a more challenging exchange than he or she can handle. In effect, he or she counts on the precept that "no one would shoot an unarmed person, right?" The result is a deepening of dishonesty that undermines contact between the two.

The father of a young adult woman asked her whether she was planning to arrange for repaying him the cost of some concert tickets he'd purchased for her and her friends. Noting an edge in his voice, the young woman protested that of *course* she'd arrange the repayment: "Were you doubting that? Are you angry?" The father demurred: "Oh, no, no. If it sounded like I was doubting you, I apologize, I didn't mean it that way at all." The daughter seemingly accepted his reply, and the moment passed. In an analytic session later that week, however, the father realized that indeed he *had* been feeling put-upon by the daughter, and that his demurral airbrushed his true (if partial) view of the daughter as something of a freeloader. He hadn't wanted his actual view of her along those lines unmasked. He feared seeming ungenerous and worried that an honest discussion of how much financial support he should now provide might risk disappointing her or even diminishing her affection for him. His doubt and vulnerability about this reflected his own insufficient love and valuing of *himself* as a man and her father. The daughter, on her end, seemed ill at ease during the exchange, but she appeared to accept the father's airbrushed protestation as the honest truth—or she simply let it pass.

However, it is this sort of response from a loved authority figure that could make a person confused and feel undercut. The young woman in this case at first seemed to perceive something in the father's tone that suggested some degree of disapproval of her. This could have aroused self-doubt in her. *Was* she perhaps prone to being overdependent on him? Taking greedy advantage? Irresponsible financially? Was she kidding herself in viewing herself as "pretty together"? Could there be some deplorable propensity hidden within her that the father perceived? If so, would it come back to haunt her in some other context? With her father denying it and reassuring her falsely of his undisrupted approval, she could have become "mystified" about herself, without being able to grasp the source of her unease. Too many of these kinds of airbrushed communications can leave one in a pretend role with pretend self-esteem, while developing a mistrust of the other's genuineness.

Alan's Need for Things to Be Fine

A 50-year-old engineer, Alan, came for treatment maintaining that his life was basically "just fine." So why did he seek treatment? Well, he was afraid his marriage might be breaking up, which he was determined to avoid. Whatever was wrong in the marriage must surely be easily remedied, and apart from that, everything really *was* "just fine." This attitude persisted through the first eight months of his three-times-per-week analysis. There was something to it, as Alan was extraordinarily successful, having received steady accolades for his contributions to the engineering field. This recognition, and the wealth that accumulated in its wake, gave considerable support to his high self-esteem. Alan was married to his second wife, with whom he had a 10-year-old son. He came from a large family of Scandinavian descent that had been pioneers in the Pacific Northwest. Alan described his father as a "great guy," who had taken Alan into his engineering firm shortly after Alan finished college. Alan had risen through the ranks quickly and, in time, was running things. He suggested an early retirement for his father, who accepted the idea "happily" according to family lore. Yet the father seemed to lose interest in spending personal time with Alan and Alan's family shortly after leaving the partnership, which suggested he was *less* than happy with his departure. (The father's posture of supposed gladness sounded like his own "airbrushing," and the cessation of socializing like the form of micro-trauma I described in Chapter 2 as "unkind cutting back.")

In addition, Ralph, Alan's longtime business partner and best friend, was now showing signs of wanting to leave the firm as well. If this were to occur, Ralph would likely take some of their important shared clients with him. Alan was completely perplexed by this. All their projects had gone so well and been so successful. What could be amiss in his relations with *both* of these men, his father and his partner? And could the same unnamed problem also be going on between him and his wife? Alan puzzled over all this, but denied responsibility for his situation hour after hour, as he subconsciously propped up the sagging smile that went from buoyant to rueful and back again. If this wasn't just bad luck, if indeed there *were* something amiss, no doubt it was minor. I could set him straight soon enough and teach him what he'd need to know to forestall its happening again.

In time, I began to hear the story of a micro-traumatic childhood lived among airbrushed, not to say thoroughly white-washed, "good objects." Alan's parents, divorced since he was young, had always "done right" by their four children. As they traded off parenting duties, they not only provided for the children's basic needs, but also gave them "novel" experiences that supposedly allowed them to experiment and venture out on their own. These were euphemisms for leaving them to their own devices in a home with few comforts or conveniences, in a neighborhood far away from other children. In essence, it was benign or not-so-benign neglect. The mother and stepfather with whom Alan and his siblings lived were nonetheless reported as caring and creative people; and the more emotionally detached father, whom they saw only on the occasional weekend, was nonetheless viewed positively as someone who was steadfast in his involvement with them.

Alan painted a favorable picture too of his relations with his father and stepmother in the present day, despite the fact that they seemed to have "a bit of a drinking problem," masked as "sleepiness" in the late afternoon. Alan was unable to grasp why his son seemed ambivalent about visiting the grandparents, who gave the boy very little attention when he was with them. "Isn't it just great going there, playing on their wonderful property, riding their horses?" Alan would ask, implicitly demanding his son's agreement. It was a repeat of the way his parental figures used to characterize their "novel, experimental" lifestyle, trying to instill an airbrushed sense of its being positive rather than depriving and frustrating for their children. In essence, Alan's parents had appropriated his own negative subjective experience and tried to recast it as positive, and in an intergenerational transmission of micro-trauma, he was now unconsciously doing the same to his son.

Originally a landscape designer, Alan's mother had gotten retrained to work in a mental health-related profession around the time she and Alan's father divorced. The mother was supposedly always positive and encouraging in her manner, but so far as I could determine, she did little or nothing during his childhood to actually help him succeed in school, establish friends, or make a life for himself. In Alan's adult years, she'd continued to show interest in him, asking about his feelings about his current marriage, about parenting his son, and so on. But again, little was done beyond this to help him grapple with the complex issues he now faced. His mother would sometimes lecture him about her own view of his problems, offering advice that tended to be overly upbeat, clichéd, and not very applicable to the specifics of his situation. Given Alan's extreme personal competence and self-sufficiency, not to mention the family norm of smoothing things over, it was easy for him to brush off his frustrations with his mother as being paltry and not worth dwelling on or addressing. In this fashion, Alan denied and prettified his parents' damaging, hurtful, and disappointing treatment of him, past and present. I only learned about it in passing and stripped of any emotional weight.

To give a more specific example, Alan's father would recount an instance from years ago when the little Alan refused the offer of a certain flavor of ice pop. The father would relate the story in company, commenting, "What kid refuses ices on a hot summer's day? He wanted a different flavor! Only Alan would do that—Alan, you've always been so particular, always known exactly what you want!" The patient shared this with me to illustrate his reputation for having a tenacious character, even in early childhood. But I myself heard a hurtful edge in the account—and microtraumatic relating often has this bittersweet, confusingly multi-layered, ambivalent quality to it. It seemed to me that the story carried an implicit (if veiled) criticism of Alan for having his own particular preference. Alan was expressing a wish to retain his individual desire and direction rather than being accepting and compliant like "most kids." His father's anecdote was a discordant mix of admiration and put-down. This is the kind of situation that fosters the child's learning that discriminating between "good me" and "bad-me," and relying on those feelings to guide action, is a losing proposition; this is because happily accepting the disappointing ice pop flavor doesn't feel good, but risking censure by holding out for the one you want doesn't feel good either. The father's account also undoubtedly airbrushed the context of the situation, in which the young boy was probably hurt and disheartened by his parents' general "benign indifference"— illustrated in this instance by Alan's not having been invited to select the ice pop flavor he most preferred. Events like this occurred again and again, in which he was expected to conform to his parents' expectation that he be delighted with the excellent upbringing they were providing, when its excellence was actually quite open to debate. Alan had to learn from a young age when it might be possible to advocate for his own needs, and how to mask his disappointments and sensitivities when it wasn't. Defensively downplaying his wishes would have contributed further to the father's misattunement to his son's needs. It must have been unsettling for Alan that when he did reveal his wishes in relation to something like an ice pop, he might have been superficially accepted or even praised for having them, but that underneath this lay the attitude that his "pickiness" was inconvenient and annoying. It's worth emphasizing that Alan's father's anecdote was offered as if it were a simple, straightforward observation of his son's character—ostensibly he wasn't being critical of his son. In this family, no one spoke ill of anyone else. Areas of dislike were to be minimized, glossed over, and borne with a tight smile. And someone's inner world was not to be plumbed.

Alan's own negative feelings, hidden from himself, eventually led to his retaliating subtly and not so subtly against those who had disappointed him—his father, his partner Ralph, and his wife. And his analyst pretty quickly joined the ranks of those he sweet-talked and then strongarmed—never with any real malice, but out of a determined need. By way of illustration, the following session occurred midway through our work together. The patient awaited my arrival sitting on the front steps of my office building, intently reading a new self-help book. As we entered my office together and sat down, Alan got down to business:

Alan: Nice day, huh? Say, have you read this? This is transforming my life. It's about how we use our "ego" to be pleasing to others, about how we try to manipulate the world to make it be the way we want it to be, how we get distanced from our "real" self, and don't even know what our real self *is*! Does this seem true to you? Talk to me, tell me what you think about all this.

Analyst: Hmmm. Well, I'm not sure exactly what to say . . . I'm glad you've found something that captures some meaningful ideas and feelings you're having. But, paradoxically, I feel that in bringing it up with me right now, you are perhaps also using it to show me that I myself am not enough for you, that maybe your analysis isn't giving you enough of a grasp of what's going wrong in your life.

Alan: Oh, come *on*! I hope you know by now that this work is very important to me. But, at the same time—yes, I need more of a conceptual framework—maybe that's wrong of me, I'm sure this book is just "Psychology 101," but I think I need it as a reference—it'll be great reading how they apply it to helping people. Sometimes what we do in here seems so very slow, and I want to get it now, soon. I often come out of here gaining so much! It's definitely worth it! But you want me to grasp it lying down—*really* "lying down!" [This was a reference to using the couch.] So we work on it little by little, and sometimes I just feel I need it to come together more quickly.

Analyst: It's hard to bear the inner bad feelings of all this conflict still going on with Ralph, of things not being "right," of things not being made to go better, and right away.

Alan: Yeah, it's time to get it fixed, corrected. I like to handle things head on . . . I've always been that way, I'm willing to be honest with myself and see things as they are, and then I make things go right.

Analyst: You are used to doing things on your own, being self-suffi-cient . . . your parents taught you that you should be grateful for what you get, and you've really tried to learn that lesson. I'm thinking of your father's comment implying you should want the flavor of ices he was offering you, as if he were taking such good care of you that it was ungrateful of you to reject it. So you try hard to like what's given to you, to not complain about things head on, and then to do whatever you need to on your own to make things go right.

Alan: Well yeah, you've got to roll with the punches. Anyway, why *not* do it that way?

Analyst: Staying with our relationship for the moment, I think this may make you act especially approving of me, more so than you truly feel. You try to show that you're grateful toward me and you try not to press me too hard if I don't give you what you feel you need at a given moment. You funnel that discontent with me into finding a book or some other source to give you what I deprive you of. And this helps some. And you are really pretty sure you know what will help you! But you figure you have to keep me happy if you're ever to get more of what you want from me . . . though, since I don't seem willing to cooper-ate at points like today, you might find ways to nudge me to give things to you in the form you want.

Alan: Well, yeah, that's true. I don't know what else to do . . . And again, what's wrong with that? And what difference does this make?

Analyst: Well, the anger and frustration you feel isn't directly expressed or explored. So we never come to grips with the deeper underlying tension between what I give and what you want. You just put up with it, with a show of being good-natured. And then you try to revamp this process into something you're sure will be helpful to you. This all acts as an invisible wedge between us, and underneath it, you're very angry, and your frustration with me builds. Soon, that frustration becomes disdain, which of course I sense. All of this pushes us further and further away from each other.

Alan: How can you be so sure?

Analyst: Well, it seems to me that this plays out elsewhere too, of course, like in your not telling Ralph the ways in which you view him as ineffective. You just end up overriding him without his knowing how or why. You don't want to cause "bad feeling," so you put a nice spin on things and only speak about the good stuff. But Ralph senses something's wrong, without knowing what, and it unnerves him, so of course he starts making plans to leave.

Alan: God, yes, I know I do this . . . I get critical of someone, but I don't want to show it. It would only lead to hard feelings. I want people to like me! So I try to push for what I think I should have, and make things go the way I want them to, and get other people to handle things the way I want them to. If that fails, I just figure I should make it look like it's okay, I'll deal with it myself. Though I do feel pissed about it inside.

Ok, so lately this isn't working, and maybe it didn't really work before either. Look, I need certain understandings from you about what I'm doing wrong, so I can learn to do better with people than I do now, so I won't screw things up as I have in the past. But I can tell you're getting at something beyond that . . . you seem to have something else in mind, you seem to think it's not something that can be taught or learned. I'd like to understand what this experience is that you're trying to give me, and trust in it, but I just don't know how, and I don't know where it'll get me.

Here we get a sense of the pressure Alan brings to bear interpersonally. I was quite moved by his obvious longing to get better and his fervent wish for my help with this, both of which felt genuine. However, it also seemed to me that he was engaging with me in a kind of controlling way that shed light on what was backfiring in his central relationships.

From the outset of this exchange, therefore, I made a strategic choice: I could have chosen to explore what was of such value for him in the book. After all, as Kohut pointed out, some patients have a positive knack for finding things that speak to them at crucial junctures in the treatment (see Kohut, 1977, p. 21, note 3); I wouldn't want to have thrown away such an opportunity without good reason. But at this point in the treatment, it seemed more important to examine how the self-help book was a vehicle for holding our relationship at bay, while seeming to offer a route toward smoothing out our difficulties (that is, his focus on the self-help book was an airbrushing operation). And at the same time, Alan's lauding of the book's ideas seemed like a sugar-coated, indirect swipe at me for not yet having solved his problems, framed in a way that could obscure its being a swipe. I hoped that exploring this mixture of his longing for constructive connection with me and his angry disappointment about the analysis would help us probe the mixed messages he conveyed to his loved ones as well.

In the course of our exchange about all this, I suggested to Alan that rushing to make things "work right" at the engineering firm, in the analysis, and also in his personal life, amounted to an enacted form of airbrushing, whose meaning I explained. He wanted a bible of sorts, because if he had one then he'd have the formulas that would label and explain everything, which would then lead to a rapid fix. I told Alan that I felt a poignant desperation in his efforts to manage his dealings with me and to "cut to the chase." I explained that his urgent efforts to influence me weren't entirely unpersuasive, but that they made it hard for me to pursue the understandings that I felt had the highest likelihood of truly helping him.

The analytic interactions just described triggered some progress. In fact, at one point afterwards, Alan blurted out, in apparent frustration with himself: "My God, I artificially inseminate things with positiveness, and in doing that I miss what's really important. I burn all those I love in the process." It was a hard-won recognition, but only a first step in what was to be an extended struggle to grasp and alter his defensive patterning, which continued to vacillate for some time. To be fair, part of what made it difficult for Alan to renounce airbrushing himself and others was that, in certain respects and with many individuals within his sphere of influence, airbrushing had worked pretty well—he had the external signs of success to prove it. Where it hadn't worked, it was unclear to him that being more honest would guarantee greater happiness for himself or his loved ones. It is extremely difficult to renounce partially successful defenses to choose an alternative "we know not of," as Hamlet mused. And given his familial history with disappointing but cheerful others, Alan was strongly predisposed to use airbrushing as a defense against intimate dependency that could only backfire. Better to access others' helpfulness through their formulations, advice, and precepts than to let them in more deeply as influential figures in his internal world. There was a lot to overcome in the analytic work.

Alan would say in upcoming sessions that he was closer to resolving certain dilemmas at work and home that would leave him freer to "dig in" psychically and probe the sources of his conflicts. But shortly thereafter, he instead retreated, saying he thought he would need to cut back on our session frequency, as the schedule was becoming even more "inconvenient." Alan came in next time skipping over that warning, and demanded advice about the appropriateness of an entertainment he'd planned for his son. He brushed aside my inquiry about the psychic meanings of this question and renewed his appeal for direct counsel on the matter. When I relented, most unwisely, he summarily brushed off my offering as if it were off-base and moved on to another topic. I had gotten what I deserved. It felt like a retaliatory undoing of the earlier move toward more intimate engagement in the analytic process. Once again, Alan manifested but then airbrushed his disdain for the potentially nurturing but frustrating other.

However, on the bright side, when I opened up the enactment for our shared exploration, this time Alan saw it too. The starkness of what had just happened between us—with him attempting to control rather than absorb my influence—was eminently clear to us both. From here onward, Alan was better able to reflect on his micro-traumatic modes of relating, and the analytic work gained more traction.

A Fairbairnian View on Alan's Airbrushing

During the phase of the treatment I've discussed, I believe Alan handled me as we saw him handling his mother and, more problematically, his father and business partner. (Similar issues had arisen with his wife as well, though I haven't gone into the details here.) I was the "mostly good other," whose supposed beneficence he felt he better not challenge directly. In Fairbairn's terms, the parts of me that could be seen as an exciting object, no less than the parts of me that could be seen as a rejecting object, needed to be split off and repressed. These are the devices of a central ego that cannot access either its love or hate. So he flattered and cajoled me a bit, and tried to elicit cooperation from me in the specific form he desired—conscious, rational, stepwise counsel. Alan airbrushed out his own fury and vulnerability and simultaneously airbrushed what he viewed as my failings and inadequacy in relation to our work. He also masked from himself his own desperate fear that he might not be able to grow, no matter what technique was used to help him. He tried to enact the good little boy who enjoys the delicious food his mother gives him, but he was actually also enraged at how unnourishing it truly was, and he tried to change the menu at every turn. At the same time, there was a constructive aspect to Alan's way of airbrushing me. He was using these measures in a sense as an attempt to "cure" me and make me a fully good object. He put forth the appearance of being innocent of critique or anger so that I could remain the unsullied, well-meaning object who, feeling loved and admired, might therefore eventually cough up something useful to him. In the same breath, while masking this with bonhomie, Alan would not so subtly tell me I was insufficient for him. In his urging the book on me, I had to wonder whether he was unconsciously trying to evoke feelings of shame and inadequacy in me, since this was at other times his way of motivating his underlings to meet his expectations of them.

These strategies on Alan's part had the function of making me into an object that his central ego could deal with apart from the suppressed and dissociated aspects of himself. I struggled to "stay alive" in relation to Alan's airbrushed denial of angry dissatisfaction with the treatment and his unconscious critique and efforts to control me. I had to tolerate repeatedly having to confront—with increasing intensity—his pattern of hurting me, his loved ones, and ultimately himself. I found myself adopting a forceful tone, which at times seemed the only way to get Alan's attention and cut through the cloyingly nice manner and complacent self-justification. If this aggressive stance on my part didn't have a micro-traumatic effect on *him*, it did on *me*!

As we became more engaged, and Alan could access more of his loving and hating feelings, the treatment relationship became somewhat tempestuous. As a Fairbairnian exciting object, I tantalized but then disappointed Alan (sometimes arousing countertransferential shame), at which point he experienced me as a rejecting object. Linda Sherby (2007, p. 192) offers an apposite account of the analyst's role as exciting object from her own practice:

Perhaps the patient leaves a particularly productive session feeling good about himself and experiencing me as the wise, all-knowing analyst. But I am not with him constantly; perhaps his good feelings evaporate, for I cannot make everything in his life all right. I am like his exciting object, I offer wonderful gifts but do not live up to my promise. As a result the patient feels frustrated, deprived, just as he did as a child. He responds to this deprivation by becoming rejecting himself, that is, canceling sessions. When he has repeatedly dismissed me and treated me with contempt, he becomes fearful that I will be angry with him. He now sees me as the rejecting object; he again must attempt to win me so that he can feel safe and given to. I am once again in the role of the exciting object with all the supplies, while he is the needy child—and the cycle is repeated over and over.

Sherby shows how an analysis can thus feel like a roller coaster ride between elements of overly positive and overly negative transference. A continuing theme in Alan's analysis as well was how we could even out that roller coaster ride. I tried to acknowledge Alan's fearful reservations about the usefulness of input from me that was interpretive and symbolic rather than directly educational and pragmatic. I implicitly asked him to try to suspend his customary judgment, judgment that had actually served him extremely well at times in his engineering career. I encouraged this, acknowledging the risk that I might feel to him like his mother, offering what he fears would be useless or even dangerous input. If he could reserve judgment, he could see whether he might find unexpected feelings and attitudes within himself that might guide him, rather than his trying to prize "the right precepts" out of me. Perhaps he could eventually let go of the tendency to airbrush me and himself, and perhaps this would mean he could discover what genuinely lies within me to give and within him to receive.

Perhaps once he became more conscious of his own inconvenient (and sometimes not so pretty) needs and expectations, Alan would be able to accept the other's and his own imperfect goodness and have honest shared communication about it. This could lead to more satisfactory relationships despite their not being perfect. In just this way, Alan's significant others might come to know and relate to him as a less upbeat and irrepressively positive figure but a more real one. An exploration of distortions and discrepancies within himself and vis-à-vis others might eventually be the key to Alan's transcending the veiled micro-destructiveness in his inner world and intimate relations.

On the Cruelty of Kindness

A person's minimization of undesirable attitudes and feelings can be consciously manipulative or simply out of his or her awareness. Sometimes, both conscious and unconscious elements are at play, particularly in intimate relationships. In a number of couples I've lately worked with (and akin to James' situation, discussed in Chapter 4), the man, ambivalent about remaining in the relationship, offered a veneer of niceness and being well-intentioned, while at the same time subtly conveying lack of interest in or even scorn for his female partner. He either downplayed or actually hid from himself—and thus also from her—the fact that certain qualities in her badly bothered him. This masking often arose out of the fear that the partner was too fragile to tolerate hearing his criticisms, which indeed was sometimes true. Muddying his complaints about her and letting her (unbeknownst to herself) continue to irritate him repeatedly, the man metaphorically gave the woman enough rope to hang herself with. Denying the sources of his disappointment also functioned to keep the man seemingly in control of the relationship's future. This sort of airbrushing established a false sense of innocence on his part, an air of implied good will that fended off the possibility of retribution from the woman, should she realize that he was in fact critical of her. The man would thereby keep the woman "on the hook" through the airbrushing. But the woman often colluded with this defense, if she portrayed herself as too readily wounded by authentic feedback.

In another variant of airbrushing, the man in such a couple may also subconsciously take on the relational issues as primarily his own fault, but he cops only to a lesser charge—say, that he "always has trouble committing." He pleads guilty to the facile, culturally sanctioned charge against himself as a "red herring," a distraction from the actual issue. He smoothes over and masks the woman's perceived failings, diverting attention to something in himself that he views as an irremediable condition. The woman is thereby rendered powerless to effect change between them. In this airbrushing situation, as in many, the damage for the other lies in his or her failing to learn what doesn't work. She fails to learn how to tolerate and survive criticisms and how to negotiate a compromise between the needs and wishes of the self and the other. Here, I've described the man as the airbrusher, but of course the shoe can just as easily be on the other (i.e., the woman's) foot.

An extreme or pervasive underplaying of the negative—through targeted airbrushing, or airbrushing that occurs as a generalized excessive niceness—can lead to significant misreadings within oneself and between two individuals in a relationship. These misreadings may in the moment allow the one airbrushing and/or the one airbrushed to feel less anxious or shame-ridden about the denied "badness." But this occurs at the expense of building up the capacity to tolerate and eventually learn from the less favorable elements within ourselves and in our relations with others.

Chapter 6

Chronic Entrenchment and Its Collateral Damage

Certain individuals are mired intractably in their own problematic psychic structure and subjective reality. This condition of "chronic entrenchment" is sometimes ego-syntonic—it feels familiar and in some way suited to oneself. But even when being stuck in this way feels unpleasant or for that matter, hellish, such people may be loath to change, and doing so may feel well-nigh impossible. Much of the person's energy goes into proving that trying to grow would not only be folly, but psychologically disastrous. The entrenched person's stance recalls the old saw that certain patients enter psychotherapy to perfect their neurosis rather than to overcome it. What keeps the person trapped is a combination of rigid characterological tendencies and resistive psychodynamic elements that militate against constructive influence. Put another way, the chronically entrenched person is shackled by his or her own subjectivity. The psychic intransigence of such individuals may lead to their own enduring misery and the thwarting of their fondest dreams. We see this vividly, for example, in someone such as Willy Loman from the 1949 drama *Death of a Salesman* (Miller, 1998), a character whose fixed illusions regarding happiness, popularity, and success are his ultimate downfall.

When a chronically entrenched person is in treatment, the therapeutic pathway is strewn with discarded interpretative approaches. The thwarted psychoanalyst joins a string of significant others in the patient's life who have been frustrated by this person's inability to change. Whether the entrenchment is manifest in a particular psychic structure, pattern of relatedness, or worldview—or all of the above—it becomes the person's signature way of being in the world. Others in the person's sphere can only do their best to withstand its draining, disheartening impact.

Many years ago, I worked with a vivacious, street-smart clothing manufacturer. Our therapy ended when I moved out of New York City, but she still sends me a box of marzipan each year on my birthday, without fail, with a card that says, "Eat this and you will be happy!" Over the eight years we spent together in twice-weekly sessions some 25 years ago, I learned much about her quirky upbringing, the family's worldly European background but reduced circumstances, and, most troublingly, her symbiotic enmeshment with a childlike mother. Despite being quite personable, successful, and canny in her business dealings, this woman was tense and lonely; she tended to be highly reactive to her friends' slights, and quick to anger at her colleagues' mistakes. I came to appreciate this woman deeply and wanted to support her own expressed wishes for economic security, good friendships, and a special loved one with whom to start a family. But a year or two into our work together, she pretty much conveyed to me that she had gone as far as she expected to go in her emotional development and in life itself, and now it was just a matter of playing out her fate—though she'd be glad if I would accompany her for the journey. I tried every angle I could imagine, both interpretive and directive, to overturn that life sentence—to no avail. How heartsick this made me! Now in our yearly phone call to thank her for the birthday gift, I catch up on her current life circumstances and hear that she is indeed exactly as I left her. It is as bitter as it is sweet to hear that she's scrappily carrying on but neither happier nor more fulfilled than before. It's patients like her who inspire me to think about psychic fixity and its ripples.

Entrenched people who come into treatment saying they want and intend to grow often make only half-hearted efforts to implement change. When they make efforts to try to do things differently, they abandon them before they could possibly yield fruit. In general, these individuals cannot manage to remember and employ whatever understandings emerge from potentially healing encounters.

The psychoanalytic literature has generally addressed this sort of individual in the context of discussing work with a difficult patient or dyad (e.g., Bromberg, 1992), examining the role of "impasses" (Kantrowitz, 1993), or in terms of an analysis becoming "stuck" (Chaplan, 2013). The trend in recent decades has been toward viewing these situations as a co-constructed dynamic between analyst and patient, rather than as something inherent in the patient's self. The two-person matrix is of course always a factor in a treatment's stalling. However in some cases, a sense of stalemate is chronic and pervasive in the patient's life, and the patient has long been recognized by others, and sometimes by him, or herself, as being psychologically immobilized. This brings to mind an acquaintance named Grant, a truly nice person with a serious, even grave demeanor. Greatly troubled with depression, Grant none-theless likes to render his situation with grim good humor: "I had this depression when I was small. I had it when I grew up. I've had it all my life when I had nothing else. And nobody is going to take this depres-sion away from me!" In the case of someone like Grant, most of the person's dealings with others—including but not limited to the analytic situation—have the same quality of stasis after a point. It is that sort of patient I'm addressing here.

The chronically entrenched person may be obsessional or phobic, mis-erably depressive and masochistic, superior and grandiose, profoundly detached, avowedly hyper-rational, or in some other state. Compared to patients who are highly resistive in certain specific contexts, these entrenched individuals are thoroughly trapped in their psychic situation. They may recognize that their fixity creates problems for themselves and others, but they just don't feel ready or motivated to rock their own boat. Alternatively, they may be blind to or actively deny the situation. Many externalize their issues, insisting that their "problems in living" are attrib-utable to inequities, inadequacy, or stupidity in the world around them. They themselves are just as they need to be or should be.

Should entrenched people become aware of the difficulties their condi-tion engenders for themselves and others, they may expound on the nature of their fixed inner state and the outer circumstances that inevitably sup-port it. It is as if they feel they will shed them magically if they manage to articulate the difficulties in great detail, and they rehearse and bemoan them at length. But the rehearsals do not lead to action. It is not unlike Hamlet's (Shakespeare, 1938, p. 688) "To be or not to be" soliloquy, where he rues the effect of his own obsessive rumination:

> And thus the native hue of resolution
> Is sicklied o'er with the pale cast of thought;
> And enterprises of great pith and moment,
> With this regard, their currents turn awry,
> And lose the name of action . . .
> (Act III, Scene 1, 84–88)

The famous "problem" of Hamlet as a play is precisely that he does not move to "action," at least not for the longest time, even though his path would seem clear.

Though entrenched individuals differ in the nature of their condition and in the extent to which they are aware of and bothered by it, one area they have in common is that their stuckness often creates *collateral psychological damage* in others. Since we are all "relational by design," as Stephen Mitchell (1988) memorably put it, we inevitably turn one another into witting or unwitting partners in our own internal psychic drama. *Any* degree of psychic fixity, conflictedness, or dissociation will generally implicate and involve intimate others in its psychic knot (Wachtel, 1980, 2014). So if I'm entrenched and you're psychologically close to me, you're likely to be held hostage to my entrenchment as well, and in so doing you may well sustain collateral damage. You—or any significant other—may be drawn into a pattern of enacting some unhappy role in the unconscious scenario. To avoid doing so requires one to steadily fend off that role's pull, which takes its own toll in psychic energy.

By the same token, the collaterally damaged significant other sometimes has interlocking pathology that contributes to keeping him or her fixed in place in a complementary role. Lachkar (1992) offers a compelling example of this in her study of couples whose disturbed interactional dynamics are shaped by the borderline tendencies of one partner and the narcissistic tendencies of the other. Two people prone to psychological entrenchment may more deeply paralyze one another over the years. What was once a rigidity of certain personality traits in one of the partners might become a hyper-rigidity in both. Similarly, both Sullivan and Kohut have described couples who seemed tied together by mutual hate rather than love, as each member belittles the other in order to prevent that person from having the stature to do the same back (Kerr, 2014).

The phenomenon of extreme psychic fixity I'm describing might sound like what we encounter in those with character disorders. In my view, this is not necessarily so. Some individuals who are entrenched are not necessarily character disordered, and some with character disorders are not so deeply stuck in them. An important part of entrenchment is a subjective sense of being mired down or encumbered on the part of the person or those around him or her. There is also a particular *focus* on that state, a concentration on the need to grapple with the stuckness, to announce it, if not to work around or overcome it. Those with personality disorders may, but may *not*, experience this kind of preoccupation or engender it in their loved ones.

It's hard to generalize as to why some people fail to retain the psychological fluidity they would need in order to be able to profit from growth-promoting experience, influences that under other circumstances would help the person overcome his or her psychic arrests, conflicts, and other inner strictures. Many of those entrenched are terrified of self-alteration of any kind. (Another friend of mine in this situation puts it succinctly: "All change is bad.") In addition, there are often one or more specific anti-therapeutic elements in the person's background. These might be influences that promoted the entrenched characteristics to begin with, discredited other states of being, or undermined the value of developing reflective thinking or psychological mindedness. Obviously, entrenched people must experience considerable secondary gain in remaining as they are—or they did once upon a time. A state of chronic stasis can cause others to pay more attention and even to remain more attached to the frozen individual than they otherwise would. This can generate a reciprocal dependency that becomes its own problematic reward.

In addition to being shaped by psychodynamic factors, cases of deep entrenchment are often underwritten by certain hard-wired features, likely to have been psycho-physiologically inscribed early on, or to have become so over time. Among such features are a reduced capacity for meta-cognition, self-reflectiveness, or psychological-mindedness per se. The tendency toward concrete thinking certainly lends itself to psychic fixity (Tuch, 2011). Limitations in one's other intellectual capacities, and anxieties about those limitations, may also come into play, restricting psychic responsiveness to generative influences. Other factors that may sometimes contribute to the stultification include having a mood disorder, being on the autistic spectrum, being alexithymic (unable to access emotional life; see Taylor & Bagby, 2013), having sociopathic features, and the like. These pre-existing (constitutional) conditions deprive the person of the tools needed and the vantage point from which they might jumpstart psychic progress.

In a rough and ready way, I distinguish between two broad types of entrenchment based on the quality of self-regard associated with them: those who are "self-diminishing" have a dysphoric emotional tone, while those who are "self-contented" are neutral or upbeat in feeling. Self-diminishing individuals are overly conscious of their flaws and limitations, while self-contented ones are insufficiently attuned to them. It may feel more urgent to help the self-diminishing person, but the self-contented one has just as much need for aid in removing the blinders that disrupt growth. The category of self-contented entrenchment may include the so-called "inflated narcissist," the self-satisfied individual, or the unreflective, complacent one. It also includes those who are overly developed in one particular cognitive style (say, being excessively systematic and technical, or overly emotional) and who turn a blind eye to the difficulties associated with this style.

To be sure, the distinction between self-diminishment and self-contentedness reflects the dimension of self-regard, but it does not capture all the layers and complexity of psychic currents underpinning it. For example, the self-diminishing person's actions are in some respects self-aggrandizing, as the humiliation points to a fantasized "ideal self" that one could reach if only one strove harder. And the self-contented person is often unconsciously fending off potential self-abasement.

Mabel Waring's Chronic Self-diminishment

As an example of self-diminishment, we can look to Virginia Woolf's (1927) nightmarish short story, "The New Dress." We enter into the story as the 40-year-old matron Mabel Waring joins a chic gathering in the drawing room of an acquaintance, Mrs. Dalloway. Exquisitely self-conscious, Mabel catches a glimpse of herself in a looking glass wearing the yellow dress she had painstakingly commissioned for the occasion. Mabel recoils from her image in abject horror, thinking to herself:

> No! It was not right. And at once the misery which she always tried to hide, the profound dissatisfaction—the sense she had had, ever since she was a child, of being inferior to other people—set upon her, relentlessly, remorselessly, with an intensity which she could not beat off . . . for oh these men, oh these women, all were thinking— "What's Mabel wearing? What a fright she looks! What a hideous new dress!"—their eyelids flickering as they came up and then their lids shutting rather tight.
>
> (Woolf, 1927, p. 1364)

Mabel is wretched indeed. She had resurrected an old-fashioned style for the gown in the effort to seem original and adventurous. Now having arrived at the event and seeing herself through the imagined gaze (Steiner, 2006) of the other more sophisticated guests, she recognizes her miscalculation. The dress, she realizes, is foolish and unbecoming. She plunges into a sea of self-contempt and despair, having once again proven to herself her own social inferiority. (The reader, if he or she is anything like me, can't help but cringe in sympathy.) At the same time, Mabel deplores her inability to transcend the need for the group's approval and acceptance. It is a double jeopardy. Philip Bromberg (2011, citing Helen Lynd, 1958) observes that we may be ashamed about a minor inadequacy within the self, and then, adding insult to injury, we feel ashamed about the state of being ashamed itself. This magnifies the upset exponentially. A little thing goes wrong, and then everything goes wrong. This Sisyphus-like condition is *chronic* for Mabel, who has *always* been trapped in her own self-mortification, endlessly struggling with it and endlessly failing to transcend it. (For a closer look at the interplay between chronic depressive and masochistic issues, see also Brandchaft et al., 2010; Friedman, 1991.)

Mabel's choice of the yellow dress and the psychic longing associated with it sets up what I would call the entrenchment's *reconfirming event.* Such events are common in the lives of entrenched individuals of Mabel's kind. That is, while consciously longing and striving to find relief from their psychic pain, these people are also always aiming unconsciously to prove the necessity of staying as they are. Mabel's wearing of the dress is a re-enactment of the hurt self and hurtful object scene that the self-diminishing person is fated to seek out compulsively, thereby deepening his or her psychic impasse.

In a related viewpoint, Weiss and Sampson (Sampson, 1992; Weiss & Sampson, 1986) offer a broader context for my describing Mabel's foray as a reconfirming event. These analytic clinician-researchers believe that many troubled individuals suffer from having "pathogenic beliefs," that "[link] an inner motive or goal—for example, a normal developmental striving—to a grim, intensely undesirable consequence" (Sampson, 1992, p. 515). The conviction that something awful will occur if the person directly pursues that goal or motive causes him or her to repeatedly function in a maladaptive way that is crippling and destructive. However, the individual will tend to seek self-cure by unconsciously trying to test out his or her pathogenic belief. This is accomplished by projecting it onto the external world (including the analytic relationship) in the hope of disconfirming it. Mabel's yellow "retro" gown in Woolf's short story is just such a test, one that "tries" her belief that it is impossible for her to be acceptable, adequate, or admirable. But of course her belief is—almost predictably—*not* disconfirmed by the assembled guests as she would have hoped, but quite the opposite—it is reconfirmed with a vengeance. For individuals who are entrenched, unlike the average person or the exemplars invoked by Weiss and Sampson, the wish to disconfirm their belief is counterbalanced by what may be an equally strong or stronger urge to reconfirm it, for the various unconscious gratifications doing so provides. So, often, the very way that they test their belief tends to reinforce it instead. Furthermore, the entrenched person is far more likely to register and weigh heavily whatever confirms rather than disconfirms the troubling perspective.

Woolf's depiction of Mabel's situation also demonstrates a type of dynamic I described in an earlier chapter as destructive connoisseurship, here turned against oneself. In this micro-traumatic mechanism, one excitedly comes under the influence of a more sophisticated other, who tacitly or actively offers to induct the person into the nuances of a given style, field, art form, or endeavor. One becomes engrossed in achieving a high level of refinement within that métier. However, too often this devolves, as it does for Mabel, into an invidious comparison of one's level of sophistication with an ever higher standard. One thereby diminishes oneself in one's own eyes. Now, Woolf's main focus in this particular character study is not so much Mabel's striving for refinement or her attempting to gain admittance to a higher social stratum; it is instead her foreordained, over-determined self-abasement and her compulsive urge to articulate its contours, to wallow in it:

> She knew (she kept on looking into the glass, dipping into that dreadfully showing-up blue pool) that she was condemned, despised, left like this in a backwater, because of her being like this, a feeble, vacillating creature; and it seems to her that the yellow dress was a penance which she had deserved, and if she had been dressed like Rose Shaw, in lovely, clinging green with a ruffle of swansdown, she would have deserved that; and she thought that there was no escape for her—none whatever.
>
> (pp. 1368–1369)

Mabel has failed at her attempt to disconfirm her inferiority. What follows, as is often the case for the entrenched individual, is a profound demoralization that ends up tainting her view of humankind as a whole:

> We are all like flies trying to crawl over the edge of the saucer, Mabel thought, and repeated the phrase as if she were crossing herself, as if she were trying to find some spell to annul this pain, to make the agony endurable. Tags of Shakespeare, lines from books she had read ages ago, suddenly came to her when she was in agony, and she repeated them over and over again. "Flies trying to crawl," she repeated. If she could say that over often enough and make herself see the flies, she would become numb, chill, frozen, dumb.
>
> (p. 1365)

In her defensive reverie, Mabel briefly visualizes the other attendees as "meager, insignificant, toiling" flies, too. But she quickly revises this image, realizing that it is only she herself who is the "dowdy, decrepit, horribly dingy" insect. Though Woolf shows the other guests treating her with reasonable good will and tolerance, Mabel curses them in her interior monologue as insincere, hypocritical, and cruel for not rescuing her from her self-disdain. Her bitterness contaminates her perception of others.

The guests themselves appear largely oblivious, if not impervious, to Mabel's disgruntlement and distress—her being "ruffled," as one man calls it. They neither receive nor absorb the projections. But we can imagine that her closer circle might not be so lucky. For self-diminishing individuals like her, what of their spouse, their children, and other relatives? Are they also devalued in the entrenched one's eyes, made inadequate by their association with him or her? And if so, are they scarred by the scorn? Does the unrelentingly critical self-consciousness infect them too? Do they, through a process of emotional contagion, become equally morose?

Living side by side with someone drenched in his or her own misery is often in itself enough to sap a person's life energies. It then adds insult to injury, to be the object of the pathogenic demands of the entrenched person's unquenchable neediness. In addition, being entrenched often leaves a *void* where some other more healthy affect or attitude should be. The significant other then ends up suffering from the absence of the emotional supplies that under ordinary circumstances would be forthcoming from the person in the entrenched one's role. So, for example, a hypochondriac might be entirely unable to offer support to a spouse who develops an actual medical illness.

Returning to Woolf's portrayal, what we could describe as a state of masochistic identity-diffusion (see Erikson, 1956) has curtailed Mabel's capacity to nurture and love others. Mabel thinks of herself as *always* having been "a fretful, weak, unsatisfactory mother, a wobbly wife, lolling about in a kind of twilight existence . . . " (p. 1370). By her own admission, Mabel's absence of will, conviction, and constructive authority undermined her effectiveness as mother and wife.

A psychoanalytic observation of parenting deficits offered by Shengold (1991) jibes with the novelist's characterization of Mabel. Shengold believes that parenting suffers when the adults in question are "feeble," "vacillating," or lacking in "conviction," as Mabel describes herself, due to an inability to trust their own authority and to a pervasive desire to please and indulge the child. In three psychoanalytic cases involving adult offspring, Shengold highlights how the parents' general inability to be "forceful and firm" in setting limits or establishing meaningful values and consistent standards left their children with significant narcissistic pathology. In their formative years, these people suffered from lowered degrees of self-discipline. As adults, they found it difficult to moderate their own levels of anxiety, rage, and paranoid ideation. In addition, they were chronically self-righteous, an attitude that stemmed from guilt-laced feelings of having been beleaguered in various ways; they seemed angrily indignant over the massive disappointment of their unrealistically grandiose wishes. All three of Shengold's patients appeared to make some improvement, but they terminated analysis prematurely and with a dissatisfaction shared by patient and analyst alike. From the author's description, the parents of these patients seem to have been significantly entrenched in a self-diminishing, non-authoritative state of lowered self-worth. The children's character pathology in adulthood represented the collateral damage of their parents' entrapment in an anxious, emotionally immature, vulnerable state. And as adults, the offspring seemed psychically entrenched themselves and therefore unable to profit much from their analyses.

The Shaming Gaze

A key feature of Mabel's arrested internal condition has to do with pathological dependence on others' real and imagined appraisals of her, as Sullivan (1953) would have put it. Since Mabel experiences others as judging her negatively, bringing about her humiliation, she comes to hate them and wish them ill—a kind of adult "malevolent transformation." Yet what triggers this transformation is not another person's explicit criticism, it is Mabel looking at herself (she kept on looking into the glass, dipping into that dreadfully showing-up blue pool).

For John Steiner (2006), seeing and being seen are key elements in faulty narcissistic regulation, whether this manifests itself in excessive pride, excessive humiliation, or a swing between the two. In Steiner's analysis as in Woolf's account, seeing and being seen are literally about how one's bodily appearance and demeanor are evaluated, and symbolically about how one's whole being is esteemed. Steiner believes that the narcissistic individual is often someone who has entered into a "psychic retreat" that functions as a haven from scrutiny and disapprobation. (The nature of a psychic retreat varies depending on one's personality organization, but in general, it offers shelter from a particular dreaded anxiety, and while in place, it precludes the individual's further growth.) Once that psychic retreat becomes untenable, the person comes out of psychic hiding. Now he or she must face the humiliation of seeing and being seen, which exposes oneself as a separate individual replete with weaknesses and vulnerabilities:

Vision plays a central role in *seeing*, as the object comes to be observed from a distance, and also in *being seen*, where the expectation of a hostile gaze which threatens humiliation can become so prominent. Anxieties arise from *looking* and from *being looked at* and both may lead to an intensification of narcissistic defences. The situation is complicated by the way gaze can be used to re-establish the narcissistic relationship, in particular by using the eyes to enter objects to take refuge there, and to once again control and acquire the properties of the object. I describe material that suggests that it is when the eyes have been used in this way that the humiliation is particularly feared, as if the patient expects the object to respond in a vengeful way. I believe that it is this quality which gives humiliation such a priority and which may become the determining factor that drives the patient to take urgent defensive measures and which cuts short a situation where development might have been possible.

(p. 940)

Steiner's thinking closely captures Mabel's condition. We encounter her as she ventures out of a state of cozy (if unsatisfying) psychic retreat—concretely her own domestic life, and symbolically her conviction of inevitable inferiority. Mabel desperately hopes to have her sophistication, as evidenced by her dress, affirmed by the august assemblage. But as we have seen, she only ends up confirming her pathogenic belief that she is unworthy, that she is really nothing, almost as if that were her internal fate. A feature that Steiner emphasizes is the way the self-shaming person's own gaze becomes an attempt to enter into, find a haven in, and control the supposedly "judging" other. In Mabel's case, this taking possession of the other through the eyes is mediated by her anticipation of how she, and she-in-the-yellow-dress, will be regarded. The exquisitely self-conscious person over-identifies and tacitly merges with the other in this way, and doing so, the person potentially sharpens his or her critical attitude and intensifies his or her own self-scrutiny.

In general, people who are entrenched in self-diminishment are both preoccupied with how they *might* be seen and have given up considering and working through how they are *actually* seen. The whole prospect of being seen in a different light becomes problematic, almost uncanny, even if the view might somehow be positive. They can't "see" themselves doing anything different from what they are doing, and they can't begin to imagine other people seeing them in a different light either. This is what makes Mabel's misadventure so poignant—she has at least tried to present another version of herself to be looked at.

How might Mabel and others like her undo the shame engendered by the other's gaze and move beyond their tendency to project disdain and contempt and then re-introject it from the other? The first step is to make connections between the current tendency to humiliate oneself and experiences with earlier significant others. It's helpful to home in on understanding the tone of formative interchanges in which the child was taught, questioned, or critiqued. We can explore the degree to which these experiences were laced with a devaluing of the child's whole self, rather than merely a correction of the child's functioning or behavior. It is also important to consider whether the person is absorbing self-shame through identifying with parents who are or were themselves self-abasing. Often parental efforts result in instilling a fantasy of there being a *hierarchy* of worth. The analyst can bring an existential perspective to bear in contradicting that hierarchy. Weakness, flaw, lack—these human qualities must be stripped of their exaggeratedly horrific associations. Ferreting out all the sources of shame linked with these qualities—which we *all* possess—can be an extensive process for someone entrenched in self-denigration.

The Soured Dedication

A professional acquaintance, Simon, tells the following anecdote about himself and his chronically self-abnegating mother. This woman had failed to achieve the professional heights to which she aspired and had never come to terms with that. Simon recounts how, several decades earlier, he had devoted his master's thesis to studying parent–child relationships in adulthood. On completion, he chose to dedicate the thesis to his mother. His intention, at least consciously, had been to affirm the positive influence she had on his professional life and in this way to share the credit of his accomplishment with her. The feeling behind his wish is perhaps captured in D. W. Winnicott's unpublished autobiographical poem "The Tree," in which Winnicott says of his relationship with his weeping mother, "I learned to make her smile/to stem her tears/to undo her guilt/to cure her inward death/To enliven her was my living"[1] (cited by Phillips, 1988).

Simon's effort along these lines, however, went badly astray. In the dedication, he acknowledged his mother's influence, praising her many strengths while noting that being human, she might also have had "foibles and failings." That last phrase proved fateful, dooming his hope of pleasing the mother. She had read the dedication in an early draft and had appeared gladdened and gratified by it. But it leaked out over the ensuing months that in fact the mother had been greatly offended and hurt by her son's mention of her having flaws. With the benefit of hindsight, he could now see how this might have bothered her. However, he had been alluding— as he felt she would have realized—to one of his study's central points: that *any* parent has both strengths and weaknesses. Simon's comment had been meant as a generalized statement, not a personal indictment of his mother. He was not yet in touch with the unconscious ambivalence that undergirded his unflattering comment.

Simon would have been only too happy to alter the dedication had he recognized his mother's offended response in time. But by the time she had allowed her hurt and anger to emerge, the thesis had been published and couldn't be amended. The son was sick with guilt and remorse at the seemingly irreparable damage this did to his mother, which naturally spoiled his gratification at completing the thesis. He was left struggling for some time afterward with the view of himself as a heartless, hypercritical, ungrateful son. It felt as if his professional strivings were dangerous and inherently destructive. The mother's chronic sensitivity to criticism and her silence about it at the start were outgrowths of a self-defeating entrenched state. In not conveying her hurt feelings directly and in time, this entrapped woman also entrapped her son. There was no way to make amends, to repair the damage. This type of irremediable bind can readily arise when one or both people in a relationship are psychically entrenched.

That said, in reflecting back on the incident, Simon realized that he had probably chosen to mention his mother's flaws in the dedication because he had unconsciously needed or wanted to vent underlying hurt or frustration toward her, whether or not it would aggravate the mother's low self-esteem. The unconscious assault on his mother's self-worth could have been an irrational expression of frustration that his mother had never managed to work through her self-disappointment, despite the many years of psychoanalytic therapy she'd undergone, ostensibly to overcome it. Whatever it was, there was certainly an element of reciprocity in the micro-traumatic interplay between mother and son, each injuring the other in turn.

Entrenched in Proving One's Worth

A 56-year-old woman, Catherine, was in her earlier years belittled and intimidated by her brilliant, harshly exacting father. This experience resulted in a fixed view of herself as inherently inadequate, as someone who would always stand in the wings of life and never be onstage. Yet, contrary to this profound self-negation and to her credit, Catherine was able to institute a crusade to reverse the negative self-judgment within one sphere at least, that of family relations. She strove to become—and to be recognized as—a worthy daughter, wife, and eventually mother. Pursuing achievement in the extra-familial world was not even a possibility, as she was unable to imagine putting herself in the position of being evaluated by anyone outside the family sphere. It was treacherous enough to be judged "in house!"

An introspective and emotionally attuned person by nature, Catherine had originally gone into psychoanalysis years before with the express purpose of not spoiling the relationship with her daughter by criticizing her as severely as she herself had been criticized by her father and as she now criticized herself. (There was also a much older step-son, who was already away at college by the time she married his father; she was less concerned about her tie with him, as she didn't feel quite so responsible for his development, given the circumstances of the blended family constellation.) Catherine knew she needed to soften the denigrating tendency if she didn't see her way to ridding herself of it. She tended to indulge her daughter during childhood and on into adulthood. This seemed to arise in part out of relief at now having a role she could succeed in and that she clung to—we might call it the "good mother" entrenchment—and perhaps also as part of the defense against her own hostility at having been denigrated herself. Courting her daughter's approval by being ever-gratifying, Catherine projected the "judge" representation onto the daughter as if the daughter were her father. She locked herself into appeasing this judging daughter and getting the latter's blessing. The daughter had every right, in her mother's eyes, to have her needs and expectations met, and to judge Catherine negatively if they weren't, given the daughter's illustrious and therefore overburdened state. The daughter thus had the power to confer blessing on the mother, and Catherine did not want to relinquish this channel for enhanced self-worth. It was as if the grown child were now a monster she herself had created, a monster whom she both adored *and*, at the unconscious level, hated.

At the start of our work together about 18 years ago, Catherine's inner relationship with herself was much like Mabel's—unrelievedly self-doubting and self-abasing. In fact, it sometimes seemed to me over the years that she actually *accepted* her debased status as a paradoxically comforting badge of identity, a badge she fought to keep—thus entrenching herself while at the very same time trying to disprove it. She was further entrenched by her strategy for self-repair, which involved two iron-clad demands on herself that were often mutually contradictory. Neither of these demands could be much relaxed for the first eight years of our analytic work. Catherine felt she must be a good, approved-of mother to her daughter. At the same time, she must drive the daughter to be as successful as possible, to finally win the approval of the internalized, demanding father of her own childhood. Neither aim could be compromised, even though the second goal, goading her daughter to achieve, threatened to undermine the first, the daughter's affectionate attachment to her. Catherine was strongly fixated on these imperatives, rather than being in conflict about either of them. Nor did she seem to care that the two were often in conflict with each other. She wanted to hone her influence over her daughter to ensure the latter's unconditional love, and at the same time, live through the daughter's stellar achievements. Each offered an important potential source of self-esteem and a vision of "good selfhood" for her. Though not entirely so, she was to some degree like those patients I spoke of earlier who want to perfect their neurosis rather than resolve it.

Catherine's psychoanalytic work was naturally geared toward helping examine and soften these rigid expectations of herself and of her daughter. However, she was so fearful of trying new activities or making new friends that she could not renounce the need to pursue these aims, deleterious though they were. Few other pathways for expressing herself seemed possible. Catherine enjoined me to keep trying to help her but paradoxically also to accept her supposed psychic restrictions. For the psychoanalyst treating the entrenched patient, this can present a key and tricky challenge—we must be accepting enough for such patients to trust in our regard for them and for them to feel they have the space to explore their inner world, yet we must refuse to be *unduly* accepting if we are to be useful. Finding the balance between the two is a large part of the art and challenge of working with such patients.

No doubt feeling the weight of their enmeshment, Catherine's daughter decided to move to Canada when the time came to pursue post-graduate training. She did well in school there, married, and gave birth to a little boy. At this point, the daughter insisted that Catherine either make extended visits, or uproot herself permanently to emigrate to Canada and live nearby, so that she could provide the daughter's family with emotional support as well as steady childcare. Based on her mother's report, the daughter sounded to me unduly self-doubting, fragile and overly bound to her mother. It seemed to me that through this needy plea and the clear expectation of having it met, the daughter was evidencing the collateral damage she had sustained over the course of her childhood through their symbiotic bond.

Catherine was not ready to relinquish getting her daughter's blessing as a channel for enhancing her sense of self-worth. However, here some conflict did enter the picture—she *did not wish* to have to move or devote herself exclusively to caring for the grandchild. Yet at the same time, she could not or would not release herself from the shackles of having to enact the "bountiful mother" role, one of the few things that made her feel worthy. She was stuck courting her daughter's approval while resenting having to do so. She bemoaned the bind, which to her seemed inextricable and unavoidable. She understood and was emotionally in touch with the way in which her current situation repeated the early tie with her own father, but—and this is key—her having an *intellectual* grasp of this didn't translate into loosening up her inclination to play it out currently—a hallmark of entrenchment.

Meanwhile, further collateral damage seemed to be occurring in that the daughter struggled with doubts about her own capacity to manage both career and childrearing without the mother's involvement. This was a difficult joint trap, with the mother's compulsion to be a "good mother" generating unrealistic dependency in the daughter. In my analytic role, I had to be content with tugging one way in one session, then another in the next, in the hope of loosening the knot that would eventually permit Catherine to release herself from depending on her daughter's judgment. I hoped this in turn might release the daughter from dependency on her mother.

A complicating factor was that I was often experienced transferentially as the judging father/daughter internal object, who demanded that Catherine break free of her constrictions, be a "good patient," and grow. She experienced me as potentially contemptuous of her if she didn't do "the healthy thing," and she would lecture me about her need for my ongoing empathic acceptance of her. In her view, things that *felt* impossible for her simply *were* impossible for her, and I should know this. This self-righteous, dogmatic attitude is often characteristic of the entrenched person and can itself be disempowering and therefore micro-traumatizing for those connected with him or her. Also characteristic was that at times I myself became another potentially entrenching influence, as Catherine dug in her heels to resist being "forced" by me to choose between the two self-defining dicta.

So Catherine and I underwent repeated enactments in which I urged her to reconsider her stance and she experienced me as judging her disappointedly. She then would have to fight off my supposedly judgmental attitude by opposing me and the analysis. I had not only to analyze this, but also to protest it with both warmth and vehemence for her to regain me as a usable and constructive force in her life. Through a combination of living out the strains in our relationship—what Bromberg (2011) felicitously calls "living through the mess"—and our gaining insight into the early submissive bond with her father, we tried to unravel Catherine's need to live her life through her daughter.

Notwithstanding all the difficulties of our fraught relationship—which, by the way, was also quite affectionate—a year into working on her conflict over a move to Canada, Catherine's defensive posture began to soften a bit. Why? It's hard to say for sure. One component was that she had begun to have a positive impact, through their long-distance video connection via the internet, snail-mail gifts, and the like, on her daughter and grandson. We could say that she had discovered a "good new object" in herself through the uncontaminated gaze of her grandson, to hearken back to Steiner's ideas. Her realization of this began to outweigh her own entrenched sense of inferiority. Perhaps she was indeed more creative and loving than she'd given herself credit for. She was emboldened to experiment with seeing whether, if she struck the right tone, she could explain her own needs and limitations to her daughter without resulting in the latter's becoming disaffected. Perhaps she could withstand the daughter's ire. Ever so gradually, the knot between mother and daughter seemed to loosen up, with Catherine becoming incrementally less entrenched in her conflicted dependency on gaining the daughter's love and approval. She also started to show more self-respect, in that she became able to assert her needs and wishes—with tact and constructive impact—in her relations with others outside the family sphere. In time, she began investing herself more in personal relationships outside the family. Once she would have discounted those very gains—and discounting signs of growth (which in turn reinforces one's sense of inner impasse) is an important feature in those who are masochistically entrenched. Now she could acknowledge and give herself at least a small degree of credit for the gains.

One final note about Catherine's sometime attitude of self-righteousness and dogmatism: the entrenched person needs to convince the appropriate stakeholders of the necessity for his or her stance. The campaign to win over the analyst or other concerned parties in turn generates anxiety, confusion, and frustration in the ones supposedly there to help, who as I mentioned are themselves made to feel disempowered and deskilled. As Catherine began to emerge from the inner impasse, her transferential opposition to me as an encroaching authority also began to give way, and her trust in our working relationship was strengthened.

Self-contented Entrenchment

As I noted earlier, individuals can be in a state of psychic entrenchment without consciously finding that condition painful in and of itself. For instance, people in certain obsessional states or those who are hyper-rational and emotionally detached can be quite comfortable with their own fixed states of mind and feeling. Other individuals in the self-contented camp are frankly narcissistic, grandiose, and self-absorbed. Whereas the self-diminishing entrenched person cowers under the gaze of the other, the self-elevating person may seek to preempt the other's gaze by projecting a glorified "mask" of who they are; at the same time, he or she reduces the other's role, as Bromberg (1983) has beautifully delineated it, to one of simply being a "mirror" of the self or perhaps of the self's mask.

Furthermore, a person's chosen social or professional role will some-times carry an implicit expectation or demand that one remain immersed in a certain state of mind. Over time, this becomes inscribed in one's psy-che as an incontrovertible "must." As a result, it may directly affect one's relationships with others—for better, when that other is the beneficiary of one's services, or for worse, when the other is the professional's spouse, child, or parent. Or, as in a situation I'll describe later, someone's deeply etched way of being may be at odds with the psychic state favored by his or her particular professional or social role. If indeed the person is entrenched self-contentedly in being just as he or she is, the result is a problematic chafing against those within the broader setting.

But first let's consider what happens when the personal self and the pro-fessional milieu are fairly synchronous and only getting more so. I think here of the intensive-care physician—or any sort of urgent medical ser-vice-provider—who comes to feel he or she must adjust instantaneously and seamlessly to any change in hospital schedule or demand on his or her expertise. Anything less than perfect performance in these areas becomes a cause for chagrin, while meeting the challenge becomes a source of self-approval that cannot be given up. Family members are expected to bow to the entrenched provider's exigent need to play out this aspect of his or her self-identity. Those loved ones often experience a certain diminu-tion in their own sense of worth or importance by dint of what they are made to tolerate, as they skirt the risk of seeming selfish for complaining. Shared family celebrations are cut short, the children's sports or arts per-formances are not attended, and other needs for emotional involvement are forced to the bottom of the list by the weight of the entrenched pro-vider's "unavoidable" demands. The expectation felt by the individual to meet inhumane standards for professional performance can lead to serious burn-out over time. This compromises the person in question's energy level for family involvement, with the family feeling emotionally deprived as a consequence.

Another example of professional role-related entrenchment can be found in certain overly self-sacrificing members of the clergy. In their early career phases, these clergy may have happily embraced a life of service and its likely accompanying low income. At some point, however, underlying envy and resentment may crop up at having to live with certain needs continually under-addressed. This can eventually taint the spiritual leader's relationships with congregation members or disciples as well as with his or her own family. But medicine and the clergy are hardly the only professions that can generate a deeper psychic entrenchment—the psychological makeup of software engineers, political campaign operatives, and many other professionals in highly demanding fields may also be swayed by their vocation's all-encompassing psychic impact.

Regardless of whether the entrenchment reflects career or personal dynamics, the collateral impact on the other is usually what generates a referral for therapeutic work. In situations where the entrenched condition is sufficiently self-gratifying, the person rarely comes for analytic treatment specifically to undo the entrenchment. Instead some other issue propels the quest, or it is a significant other who urges the person to seek analytic input as a way to work through its problematic effects.

Focusing again on the personal dynamics of the self-contented narcissist, McWilliams and Lependorf (1990) address the interpersonal impact this stance may have in their study of the "narcissistic pathology of everyday life." Given that narcissistic individuals go to great lengths to promote a view of themselves as superior, prime defensive operations are a continual denial of remorse and an inability to convey gratitude. Instead of offering a heartfelt apology, narcissists who have harmed another person use one of a series of dodges to evade such an admission: they seek to magically undo the injury; they engage in self-justification regarding their good intentions; they further explain their actions rather than owning responsibility for the consequences; they engage in rote self-recrimination; or they deflect the blame. Instead of thanking another for a service or kindness done, the narcissist confers approval for the other's "good behavior," reversing roles as if to humor the other; he or she similarly protests an accolade or compliment, or expresses excessive gratitude that implies its actual absence—anything to avoid being simply grateful. Here's how McWilliams and Lependorf (1990, p. 448) describe the resulting collateral damage:

We have put particular emphasis on the psychological encumbrance borne by the objects of essentially narcissistic transactions, whose usual response to the prolonged substitution of other behaviors for expression of sorrow and thanks includes confusion, self-criticism, loneliness, and diffuse irritation—an overall sense of having been, as one of our patients put it, "mind-fucked." The state of confusion induced by narcissistic defenses may say something about why it took so many years for psychoanalysts to develop a rich and specific literature about narcissism, comparable to that on the more "classical" psychopathologies.

The misguided sentiment that the purpose of engagement with the other is to elevate and perfect the self is, in my view, what predisposes many such narcissistic individuals to become seriously entrenched. And their ability to "mind-fuck" their interlocutor, as was so delicately put by one of the authors' patients, is part of what keeps them there. As this attitude of one's own superiority gets expressed and impressed upon others over and over, it becomes something the narcissist is increasingly dependent upon. To tolerate having one's grandiosity "called out"—that is, named as false and destructive—becomes more and more threatening.

A Self-contented Social Climber

The character Winn Van Meter in Maggie Shipstead's novel *Seating Arrangements* (2012) is an excellent example of someone comfortably self-satisfied with his own entrenched psychic state. The only fly in the ointment of Winn's contentment is the difficulty he's having bringing his wishes and expectations of life to fuller fruition. In the meantime, his self-absorption wears on his daughters and long-suffering wife. They have already been harmed by Winn's character defects, and in time they are further burnt by Winn's bankrupt values and superficiality, to which he is blind.

Winn is not only narcissistic in the ways McWilliams and Lependorf describe, but he is also unaware of himself, concrete and literal in his thinking, self-congratulatory, and prone to repeat the same errors in understanding and judgment. Shipstead steadily builds her portrait of Winn's obsessive preoccupation with reaching the top rung of the social ladder as he strives to "win" by his own "meter." A successful but aging Harvard man, Winn prides himself on what he thinks of as his fine New England pedigree, though in the course of the novel he comes to find out that this lineage is not what he thinks it is, a realization that should have made him rethink his grandiosity. Yet the discovery seems not to quite register with him—another indicator of his entrenchment.

In the novel, Winn has come to his island vacation home to join his wife and two daughters in anticipation of the wedding of the elder daughter, Daphne. Two issues are rekindled for Winn in the course of the nuptial activities that will culminate that weekend: one is his frustrated desire to sleep with his daughter's bridesmaid; the other is his wish to "right a wrong"—his having been (in his own estimation) unfairly excluded from membership in a desirable country club on the island. His boorish efforts to force the issue, along with other kinds of public acting-out, humiliate his wife, Biddie. Once he learns that his rejection from the club is final, Winn's sense of narcissistic injury fuels a seriously offensive speech he makes at the daughter's wedding, in which he seemingly curses marriage. This of course horrifies and alienates the bride.

The reader also gets a sense of the lifelong damage Winn has steadily done to his younger daughter, Livia, by virtue of his monomaniacal preoccupation with social status. Winn has no meaningful commitments in life to anything other than himself, so it is inexplicable to him that Livia would be avidly studying biology at Harvard, planning to pursue a doctorate later as a marine biologist. She has become enamored of and pregnant by Ted, the glamorous, well-positioned son of a woman Winn had earlier jilted. When Ted in turn jilts Livia, leaving her devastated, Winn is incapable of sympathy for her and is only annoyed by her inability to get over the relationship sooner. At one point in the novel, he sees her from a distance looking paralyzed with despondency, as if she'd just finished crying. Though this arouses some tender feelings in him, he sidesteps going to soothe her, which would place too much of an emotional demand on him.

Livia's longing for paternal approval is probably an important part of what led her to pursue the relationship with Ted—someone not unlike her father—to begin with. And having lost that relationship, she despairs of ever being able to make this match that will validate her in society's eyes, even while she herself shows signs of transcending such a need. Winn views his daughter as being inexperienced, emotionally overreactive, and prone to being angry at anyone and everyone. Her anger at him arouses his defensive anger back in response. Livia unconsciously exacts a tepid revenge against both Ted and her father by announcing at their shared college club, which Winn holds dear, that she's pregnant by Ted. Throughout the novel, Lydia struggles to free herself from her father's incomprehension and negative judgment of her, and also from her residual attachment to Ted. It would have been tragic for Livia if she had indeed ended up with Ted as a look-alike substitute for her father; she would have recreated the stultifying world her father created for her mother. So the reader is relieved that she ultimately frees herself from Ted.

Having gone through all the trials and follies that could lead to psychological epiphany and reform, Winn matures little if at all over the course of the weekend's fateful events. In the end, he is still entrenched—sadder, and if anything, only marginally wiser. His power to inflict collateral damage on his wife and daughters, however, has been diminished, as they've caught on to him and developed better skills for containing his self-absorbed excesses. Shipstead has beautifully captured how being mired in pursuing narcissistic self-affirmation takes a profound toll on those one supposedly loves.

A Self-contented Personable Guy

Ben, a warm and extroverted 47-year-old man, had failed to advance beyond the mid-level position he held at an online real estate listing company. He entered psychoanalytic care wondering whether the higher-ups doubted that he was strong enough in the skills his position demanded, given that it was a role that blended data analysis and product management capabilities. But, entrenched in his own temperamental tendencies and a belief in their value, Ben felt that his sociability and also his considerateness toward others should be sufficient to ensure his worth to them, even in the world of e-commerce. He defensively insisted that his interpersonal connectedness should compensate for any gaps in his knowledge base, analytic skills, or approach to business. His genuine warmth was undeniable, and I found that it clouded my being able to tell whether there might be some degree of lapse in his technical know-how. We examined these matters from many angles for several years, going around and around the issues. It seemed to me that there was a self-defeating quality to Ben's compulsive campaign to get his interpersonal skills recognized in this particular work environment. He believed himself to be indispensable to his manager, who clearly seemed to like and enjoy him. It made him feel he was well-regarded, notwithstanding his obvious failings and lapses, like his having turned in imprecise, vague financial reports for some months in a row. Ben minimized the importance of his report-writing performance to the job as a whole and was firmly convinced of the value of his own way of being for the role he was in—and after all, being primarily "people-oriented" was the only way he felt he *could* be.

So it came as a huge shock when, midway through our work, Ben was abruptly fired from the company. The purported reason was that the company's focus had shifted, that Ben's project was no longer a priority. However, it was clear from innuendos in the exit interview that Ben was actually viewed as an underperforming member of the group. He was astonished, dismayed, and yet still in denial that he himself could have invited this treatment. He plunged into a deep depression that lasted for many months.

It became apparent to me that Ben's entrenched conviction vis-à-vis the value of his interpersonal skills was in part an effort to deny probable weaknesses in his technical expertise. His characterological tendencies generated a worldview that he could not step outside of long enough to appreciate its distorting effect. Ben came from a family that prized business and its lucrative upside. This inherited value set impeded his ability to pursue a vocation in some meaningful but less lucrative area such as the social services, where his strengths might well have been more fully appreciated. There was a stark incongruity between Ben's temperamental endowment and the professional work life to which he insisted on clinging.

In the course of our work together, Ben was receptive to exploring the "usual suspects" in terms of psychodynamics, including explanations involving Oedipal issues, separation-individuation conflicts, and whatever else seemed to hold promise for helping him think differently about himself or his situation. But over time, it became clear that this was not helping Ben bracket his urges to rely on his extroverted "people focus" rather than a depth of organizational knowledge. I had to work steadily over many years to help him accept the idea that his attunement to others might not be valued highly in all sectors of human endeavor. (Though I certainly appreciated and shared his concern that where such proficiencies *were* honored like in the nonprofit world, they might not bring home the most bacon.) His strongest capacities couldn't necessarily be parlayed into a high-paying position in business, especially if they were being relied on as a substitute for developing strong product management skills.

Fogel's (1995) work on the functioning of psychological mindedness as a self-deluding defense is relevant to Ben's situation. Fogel found that in patients such as Ben who were seemingly sophisticated in their mental reflectiveness, "psychological and other formulaic understandings were prematurely applied to offset overwhelmedness and other unarticulable experiences; the patient's talents for ambiguity, irony, self-soothing, or responsiveness to others were, in effect, exploited at the expense of full psychological growth" (p. 793). So too Ben's fixed self-identity masked massive anxiety about being a different sort of person than his own parents valued, consequently requiring a different pathway toward personal efficacy than they would have envisioned.

Ben's self-contented entrenchment ended up having negative consequences for his wife and children, whose lives he was deeply and intimately involved in. He had difficulty taking on a position of authority in relation to his three children, two of whom had moved into a troubled adolescent testing period during the time of the analysis. (This echoes the Shengold findings I alluded to earlier.) Ben tended to think that offering understanding and emotional closeness would deter his teenagers from dicey choices and bad company. He was unduly permissive, setting rules for them that had wide margins of error. As a consequence, his children only strayed further from constructive pathways. Fortunately, Ben was able to call on the school principal and the family minister to take the authoritative stance that he himself couldn't, so the collateral damage to their developmental course could be to some degree curtailed.

Ben's loss of his job and the steady reduction in his career prospects took direct tolls both on his morale and his income. As a result, Ben's entrenched denial eventually undermined his family's economic and social well-being. His being in limbo itself was confusing and worrisome to his loved ones and may have contributed to his children's own indirection. He became increasingly distraught after being fired, but for a long time, he could tolerate the idea of no other vocational pathway. I concentrated on analyzing and relieving the shame that barred his climbing out of the entrenched state, and eventually this began to seep in. As our work wound to a close, partly due to his financial straits, Ben began to come to terms with his own limits. He slowly resigned himself to earning much less than his wife and worked to find other ways to contribute in the world, including through volunteer activities. Over time, his depression eased up, and from our sporadic contacts since then, my impression is that he found a modus vivendi and measure of self-acceptance that had more grounding in his actual aptitudes, which indeed were many and not inconsiderable.

Entrenchment and Imprisonment

Entrenchment overlaps to some degree with the concept of psychological imprisonment as it has been previously examined in the analytic literature (Brandchaft et al., 2010; Hymer, 2004; Miller, 1981; Ogden & Ogden, 2012; Schafer, 1983). Schafer (1983) in particular offers an elaborated exploration of this concept in his discussion of a "narrative" or "storyline" of imprisonment. Schafer treats imprisonment as a subjective perspective on oneself that is oftentimes conscious. While the two notions, imprisonment and entrenchment, are related, they not identical. One way to put the difference between the two concepts is that imprisonment feels like something that is *done* to one, whereas entrenchment feels like what one *is* (D. Goldman, personal communication, March 2013). But some entrenched individuals do indeed have the storyline of imprisonment that Schafer describes. Individuals who feel imprisoned, according to Schafer (1983), convey the sense that they are locked in by intrapsychic, interpersonal, or social circumstance that permits no release. He goes on to explain:

> Being imprisoned does lay down a powerful storyline in that its potential for multiple function and complex meaning is enormous. For example, imprisonment may serve not only to punish the guilty self; it may serve as well to indict the world and to torture the allegedly innocent through implied or stated masochistic incrimination and recrimination. The analyst as jailer is a familiar figure in the psychical reality of transference. And it is not unusual for the analyst to note the analysand's efforts to imprison him or her in the role of jailer—the prisoner can be imprisoning.
>
> (pp. 257–258)

Schafer notes that the imprisoned patient may readily feel confined or trapped by his loved ones, his life circumstances, or within the analysis by the analyst. These others are viewed as "guards" who must be "propitiated," as one "atones" for one's "crime." In the treatment, the person may avoid being spontaneously emotionally expressive or conveying an independent thought, for fear of incurring the analyst/guard's harsh punishment. These individuals may resist embracing the idea that they have improved, because this could imply that they were "bad" to begin with and "don't deserve to be better," as Schafer tells us. Their imagined prison ends up being locked up that much more rigidly. The analyst may come to feel guilty anxiety about imposing the customary demands and restraints on the patient, both through the structure of the analysis (fees, schedule, etc.) and the interpretative mode itself, with its "judicious abstinence" and other constraints. Schafer warns that the clinician must do his or her best to avoid enacting the countertransference by relaxing those expectations, which only reinforces the patient's avoidance of looking at the underlying psychic meanings they carry for the patient. As time goes on, the analyst patiently helps expose the fallacies inherent to the storyline of imprisonment and all its variations. In so doing, the individual comes to see inbuilt self-delusions in the narrative for what they are and discovers avenues of actual empowerment heretofore masked.

Clearly, some patients will become entrenched in Schafer's imprisoned position, and if that entrenchment is strongly structured around the imprisonment scenario and its associated anxiety-ridden beliefs, then having those beliefs dispelled will relieve the entrenchment. Nonetheless, I think that the role of building rapport and trust within the therapeutic relationship—the analyst as a new, freeing object—is underemphasized in Schafer's formulation.

Moreover, imprisoned themes and metaphors are not simply a subjective storyline one tells oneself. Sometimes they capture certain developmental and psychosocial verities of one's existence. Hymer (2004) details how a sort of psychological imprisonment can be an actual feature of one's early childhood. She draws on Alice Miller's (1981) well-known study of how parents may indeed "bind" their children, not only by unreasonable overt rules and expectations but, in more severe cases, through emotional manipulation and indoctrination of the child to feed the parent's own narcissistic needs. Hymer elaborates on Miller's account to suggest that a kind of emotional blackmail goes on in these situations, where the child must keep close to the parent and play out scripted roles that curtail the child's own separation and individuation. In Hymer's view, such imprisonment constitutes "attachment gone awry," a description that captures something of Catherine's relationship with her geographically distant daughter. The writer goes on to talk concretely about how the childhood home, both the family and the house itself, can be unduly confining. The body and its limitations, especially when traumatic medical conditions are present, can also generate a sense of imprisonment. Stifling social norms, as evidenced in the famous Ibsen play *A Doll's House* (1879), can likewise cause one to become trapped in a deadening relationship. All of these states of overt psychological entrapment can lead to an internal feeling of imprisonment that can become deeply etched into oneself and therefore part of entrenchment. But whether or not they do depends on other facets of one's psyche, psychosocial surround, and somato-psychic makeup. In short, Hymer's constricting developmental patterns, like Schafer's narrative of the imprisoned self, can contribute to, but only *sometimes* develop into a state of psychic entrenchment.

An Explanation from Ogden's Fairbairnian Viewpoint

As it does with other forms of micro-trauma, Ogden's (2010) slant on Fairbairn's (1952) view of endopsychic structuralization once again offers a helpful lens through which to look at micro-traumatic aspects of self—here, the condition of chronic psychological stasis. Ogden explains that the internal structure described by Fairbairn involving split-off parts of the object and of the self gets externalized onto others. These projections greatly influence all the individual's object relationships. Now, the entrenched individual is ordinarily wrapped up in the relationship with his or her internal object world, so the emotional energies available for striking out on new paths is limited. But when someone seeks to move him or her out of the entrenched position, the inner universe of part-selves and part-objects gets more highly activated and comes to the fore. It is then that those inner aspects, now projected, most strongly and most negatively influence one's external relationships. Ogden usefully notes the adhesiveness and the particular qualities of the inner object ties: there is an *addictive* bond between the libidinal ego and the exciting object, a *resentment-saturated* tie between the internal saboteur (rejected ego) and the rejecting object, and a *contemptuous* attitude experienced by the internal saboteur toward the libidinal ego and exciting object.

We can think of humiliated states of entrenchment as being ones where the person is immersed in the painful interchange between the shamer (rejecting inner object) and shamed (internal saboteur) intrapsychic aspects. An important part of why this dynamic becomes chronically stuck is that it is compounded by the deep contempt the internal saboteur feels toward the mutual appreciation (noted by Ogden) that exists between the libidinal ego and the exciting object. Put more simply, one is mistrustful of having prideful or self-appreciative feelings. After all, one could be duping oneself, and since "pride goeth before the fall," it may feel more risky to aspire to higher levels of belief and pleasure in the self than it would to remain "humble." Likewise, it may seem safer to continue to confine oneself to feeling one's own badness just as it is right now. One is already so low in one's own estimation that any possibility of further self-diminishment that might be incurred by aspiring for a shred of pride risks self-annihilation.

I believe that this fundamentally negative, demoralized attitude fatefully extends to a discrediting of external objects who could otherwise have become new, emotionally healthy models. One's negativism extends to and sullies any other possibly "good-enough" figures in one's world. As a result, it becomes impossible to take in new views of a more gratified and gratifying other, who in turn could replenish the self (see Goldberg, 2007, and Greenberg, 1991, for discussions of the "good new object"). So such individuals stay entrenched and miserable, but not so miserable as they fear they might become if they trusted a new object.

Apropos the demoralized entrenched position, Schafer (2006) expands eloquently on the further issue of the pronounced inability to experience pleasure in the self, which is such an important feature of profound self-abasement. He explains that one can be mired in a failure to experience self-pleasure due to conflicted partial identifications with seemingly opposed external objects. In addition, there can be a tendency to "abandon the pleased self" if key significant objects lost interest in oneself when one was happy during childhood. Schafer also notes that incompatible internal standards can play a strong role in undermining the experience of self-pleasure. These incompatibilities may be expressive of differing moral self-expectations or different standards for excellence in separate realms of existence.

Then too, there is the role of the exciting object. The "intermittent reinforcement" schedule offered by a potentially approving inner evaluator can be most compelling. One could easily stay fixated there, continually deceiving oneself into believing that one is on the right track in pursuing one's usual mode of functioning. It's as if full gratification were just around the corner, one should simply try a bit harder and longer, as we saw happen with Mabel, Whim, or Ben. And the same could be said of Catherine, who seeks both the internal praise of her father's imago and the external praise of her daughter as a stand-in.

Digging Out from Entrenchment

Entrenched individuals have by definition a long history of averting, sabotaging, or simply not being able to register and profit from opportunities for change. At some level, their condition may simply be too enjoyable or gratifying to let go. (It is perversely gratifying when the entrenchment is self-diminishing and frankly gratifying when it is self-contented.) Instead of responding to calls for growth from their loved ones and other more formal therapeutic agents, they have found ways to disqualify others from affecting them favorably. They may even have campaigned others to be more supportive than challenging of their entrenched condition.

One woman seriously mired in a perfectionistic, depressive state found a long-term housekeeper who would cater to her every over-anxious whim. In the face of each new request, the housekeeper responded with the propitiatory words: "That's okay, Mrs. Johnson, we both know these things aren't strictly necessarily, but I realize how much they matter to you, so of course I'll take care of them." The employer was so gratified by this unconditionally accepting response, that she repeated the story endlessly to her teenage daughter as a model of how one should show love toward another. The message was that the good daughter would, like the housekeeper, simply tolerate the mother's neurotic self-expectations and standards with endless love and understanding. A caring child should not unsettle her mother by expecting her to reflect on and overcome her own neurotic pickiness. In this way, the mother steadily socialized her daughter out of challenging the mother's entrenched condition.

But some entrenched individuals, such as Catherine and Ben, eventually do at least *try* to open themselves up to professional help for their paralysis. How can we best approach such a patient, who is so ambivalent about emerging from the bunker? Ogden, through his Fairbairnian lens, suggests that a self-diminishing person's stuckness is a compulsive effort to re-enact the critical internalized parent's disapproval of the inadequate self. The patient can be helped to see that there are other favorable facets of self and of the internalized parent that can be invoked to counteract this stereotyped internal process. Similarly, the self-contented person's tie to the exciting inner parent can be discussed as a start at freeing oneself from the self-promoting and aggrandizing tendencies that are doomed to thwart one's deeper goals. Talking about a specific inner relationship with oneself helps concretize what is going on, so that the entrenched person can envision recasting his or her distorted attitudes in real time. It is also valuable, following Schafer's advice, to explore whatever conscious narrative of imprisonment exists in the patient's mind. Further, we can look for any explicit developmental scenarios that would have enforced a sense of being psychologically trapped (Hymer, 2004).

Then too, the analyst should make an honest assessment of the effect of any relevant hard-wired cognitive-affective limitations within the patient. Psycho-educative input can often help carve out some reflective space about those tendencies. We might, for example, suggest to the self-diminishing patient that his or her depressive affective current is itself a primary factor, tainting his or her capacity to register the goodness and feel pride in the self. Only by staving off that dysphoric pull will he or she be able to climb out of the saucer of self-abasement, to echo Woolf's metaphor about the fly stranded in a pool of milk.

In general, the analyst must hunker down and keep looking for potential openings for psychic experimentation. We need to provide emotional constancy while developing a shared understanding of what contributes to the person's specific form of stasis. We should do our best to "assimilate" and also "accommodate" (Minuchin, 1974) to the patient's adaptive and defensive postures and their psychic logic. From that experience-near position, we can more deeply grasp the meaning of the entrenchment and help the patient feel his or her way out of it. Looking together at the enormity of those factors may stimulate the person's desire not to let them thwart further growth.

In the meantime, we wait for life and extra-therapeutic forces to provide windows of therapeutic opportunity for loosening a person's fixed beliefs and patternings. Gifts sometimes fall from the skies unexpectedly. As Catherine's conflict about moving to live near her daughter came to a head, I was pleasantly surprised to hear her report that the daughter had started to let up the pressure. She had in fact told her mother in a reassuring and conciliatory way: "I'm a big girl now, it'll be okay if you don't come." Catherine was dubious about the genuineness of this sentiment at first, but it opened the door to believing that she might not need to comply with the original demand to move in order to retain her daughter's love and regard. I might also mention a different instance of an old-guard, hard-as-nails trauma surgeon, whose own life-threatening illness and grueling treatment significantly loosened up his psychic structure and way of relating to himself and others. Once the man returned to work, his bedside manner with his own patients became noticeably gentler. Entrenched states require our patience and humility, as we await life's serendipitous help to foster the possibility of climbing out.

By the same token, overcoming entrenchment may be a long and iffy campaign, especially if the fixity involves constitutional elements that yield *benefits* to the person along with their drawbacks. We need to appreciate the whole balance sheet involved in altering a person's customary way. In fact, some of our most important work with such patients may be to help them accept those aspects of self that are too deeply engrained to be mutable. Instead we can try to help make the entrenchment a more bearable one—for the person him- or herself and for all concerned, for the foreseeable future.

What can be done for those among our patients who are sustaining collateral damage from their relationship with an entrenched other? The first step, of course, is to analyze the psychic interlocking between the two individuals. The collaterally damaged person can be guided out of the introjected role and helped to push back steadily against the stereotyped, hurtful influence of the other. Whether the person in treatment is the entrenched person or the one bearing its brunt, I occasionally ask to have the other join the therapy for several sessions. My aim is to provide a safe-enough environment for the entrenched one to begin to perceive and develop concern about the unseen impact of his or her fixed state. By arousing some empathy for the other, I hope to re-stimulate his or her motivation for change. If the entrenched person is the identified patient, the hope is that temporarily including the other will allow him or her to see the potential upside of allowing an internal shift, if the patient can sense the possibility of its promoting enhanced closeness with the loved one. This may of course also be possible even without the other's direct participation in the therapy.

In some instances, an entrenched individual is not just massively reluctant, but is entirely unwilling to undergo change. Like Melville's character Bartleby the scrivener, he or she simply "prefers not to." Edgar Levenson (2012) offers an existential perspective on the way in which this "rite of refusal" (a pun on "right" of refusal) might arise. He articulates certain ontological factors that might be in play: a fear of influence; a fear of helplessness; a fear of expulsion; a fear of growing up; or the joy of blowing things up. Wishing to remain within one's own neurotic paradigm is part of the human state, and in that respect, it may go beyond our customary view of psychodynamic resistance. This necessitates a somewhat different attitude from the analyst:

> The analysts' dictum has always been "What can I do or say that would promote change?" I am suggesting a perspectivistic shift to "Why is the patient unable or unwilling to use my efforts?" We are, after all, often the court of last resort. Patients have been exposed, in their lifetimes, to many people who tried to influence them (for better or worse). They "preferred not to." Why that should be so is our enterprise.
>
> (pp. 5–6)

Following Levenson, we should jointly explore the nature of the patient's unwillingness, the whys and wherefores underneath the rejection of therapeutic help. It may take a rumbling up from the analyst's own unconscious (see especially Ladson Hinton, 2009) to fully test the fixity of the person's entrenchment by destabilizing the interpersonal context in which the fixedness exists. Here is where the analyst's proverbial "spontaneous gesture" (Winnicott, 1965), "act of freedom" (Symington, 1983), "courting of surprise" (Stern, 1990), or being part of "the mess" (Bromberg, 2011) may have their place. Yet these too may ultimately fail, if the patient insists on invoking the "right" as well as the "rite of refusal." Being saddled with such a fixed psychic identity is micro-traumatic to the self, but it is one's own burden and, in a sense, one's own responsibility. At the very least, entrenched individuals can be enjoined to examine the micro-traumatic influence their psychic impasse has on their loved ones, if they are indifferent to its negative impact on themselves. One way or the other, the therapeutic seeds we attempt to plant may lie dormant for some time, but under the right conditions, they might yet sprout and grow.

Note

1 This unpublished poem is reported by Phillips (1988), who says he received it from James Britton, D. W. Winnicott's brother-in-law, to whom Winnicott had sent it.

Chapter 7

Unbridled Indignation

In Philip Roth's 2008 parable-cum-character study *Indignation*, 19-year-old Marcus Messner, lying stricken on a distant field of war, silently reviews the life that led him to this moment.

Marcus is the only child of Jewish parents who live in gritty, working-class Newark, New Jersey. The time is the late 1940s and early 1950s, and the young man's father makes his living as a kosher butcher. Assisting in the butcher shop during high school, Marcus learns—and loves learning—from his conscientious, diligent father how to do what's necessary to get along in life. But the moment Marcus starts college, a battle breaks out between them. The father, increasingly anxious and insecure, cannot rest assured in his son's integrity, cannot trust that his aspirations are healthy. In response to Marcus' comings and goings, he insistently scolds and warns his son that he will get involved with an unsavory crowd and end up a criminal—or worse, dead. Marcus, who stays out late only to study and to avoid his father's anxious recriminations, feels profoundly misunderstood and insulted. The anguished mother can do nothing to calm the situation. The father is indignant. So is Marcus.

Bent on escaping his father's frightened, obsessive grasp, Marcus transfers from his local college, where he felt he really belonged, to a far-off one in the American heartland. There he feels disrespected and unrecognized by his new Midwestern peers, and views himself in general as being a terrible misfit. He thwarts his own prospects as he indignantly rejects the dean's offers of counsel and direction. The dean urges Marcus to try compromising with others rather than swimming insistently against the tide. Marcus interprets this advice as nothing more than oppressive control and a demand for conformity to pedestrian white Anglo-Saxon Protestant mores. Eventually, Marcus' acts of defiant self-isolation, rebellion, and refusal—tinged as they are with haughty self-importance—result in his expulsion from the college. This leads in the end to the fulfillment of his father's gut-wrenching prophecy. No longer protected by college enrollment, Marcus is now eligible to be drafted into the army. As a lowly private, he is sent forthwith to the Korean front. There he sustains the mortal wounds to which, after an extended backward look on his life, he succumbs.

What does Roth's parable have to teach us about prideful umbrage and the thwarted desire that generates it? As a reminder of its web of significance, "indignation" is the state of judgmental displeasure at something deemed unjust, disgraceful, unworthy, or mean. It is a feeling of contemptuous, scornful, disgusted, or bitter anger. It involves a mixture of being offended, hurt, angry, or frustrated at a perceived injustice or slight. Its Latin root *dignus* means "worthy," and the word *indignari* means to regard as unworthy.[1]

Throughout the novel, Marcus is seen reacting with indignation to the perceived squashing of his personal idiom. He feels unfairly reproached and severely unrecognized by his father and later by the college community. His narcissistic rage and the choices it engenders are his downfall. But even at the end, Marcus doesn't understand this to be so. Instead, he draws only the less perceptive conclusion that a person's most trivial-seeming decisions in life can end up having the biggest—and worst—impact. The character himself remains blind, but the reader knows that the true lesson lies in the book's title. Roth is showing us that "pride goeth before the fall," that the intemperance of indignant resistance can be death-dealing. Ever the astute amateur psychoanalyst, Roth illustrates how certain psychic and psychosocial situations can conjoin to ignite rampant self-righteousness. This happens notwithstanding the intelligence and percipience of the protagonist. Marcus cannot help but dig his own grave, oblivious to his complicity in bringing about his downfall.

These are what we could call the "wages of indignation." The expression of unbridled indignation in personal relations is, of course, often directly detrimental to whomever may be the object of the rageful sentiment. Self-righteous anger can stimulate reprisal and retribution rather than correction. But it can also be poisonous to the very one experiencing and expressing the indignation. As Roth's story illustrates, such micro-traumatized and micro-traumatic relating can cause further psychic bruising and eventually lead to full-scale blindness that may indeed instigate trauma with a capital T. The fear of misrecognition, of prejudice ending in persecution, pervades the fictional Messner family and the climate of the post-World War II United States. We surmise that Marcus' father, the elder Messner, suffers from the residual horrors of World War II and the Holocaust. "Butchering" of all kind—not only as the senior Messner's vocation—hangs in the air. The father also suffers from the rigors involved in creating a life and a living for himself and his family as a relative new-comer to the United States. He feels at risk of being robbed of his dignity and self-worth, with kosher butcher shops being edged out by large-scale supermarkets.

Messner the father always strives to do what he must do and do it well, but this cannot defend him adequately against the serious threats to his sense of self-worth and dignity ever-present both intrapsychically and in his social milieu. The disavowal of potential incompetence or unworthi-ness leads him to project those features into his son. This puts the son in an equivalent predicament. Thus, in an intergenerational transmission of trauma (see Faimberg, 1988; Fraiberg et al., 1975), Marcus cannot help but forcefully and angrily protest the father's projected imputation of wayward urges, to which the father responds by berating and humiliating the son in a misguided attempt to keep him in the fold.

Father and son thus become mutually abusive toward one another, and the affective soundtrack of their interplay is self-righteous outrage. The father has an intrapsychic representation of his son as an abuser. This is partly shaped by the father's own disavowed badness extruded and pro-jected into the son. But the father also feels abused by the son's actual moves toward separation, which he believes are fated to kill him. Of course, the elder Messner's own toxic micromanagement spurs Marcus' defiance, fostering his disdain and rejection in actuality. But this contemptuous distancing—akin to Sullivan's (1953) developmental concept, "malevo-lent transformation"—spreads to every facet of Marcus' life. Somehow, Marcus is always being inducted into involvement—by his father into manhood, by potential fraternity brothers, by an ardent non-Jewish coed, by his college dean—and he is always *resisting* that induction, sure that he knows better what is good for him.

Marcus ultimately does embody the wild power with which his father invests him. He embodies the father's powerlessness as well, as he him-self becomes just one more casualty in the vast social-military-industrial machinery. Finally, Marcus is no more than the psychic descendant of a persecuted people turned inductee and cannon fodder in a personally meaningless war. No wonder each of these men feels something is terribly wrong and is driven to angry protest. And what a tragedy that the most they can do is inflict their indignation on *one another*, indirectly contribut-ing to each one's miserable decline and death.

Psychoanalytic Views of Indignation

The psychoanalytic literature addresses indignation in such forms as moralism (Schmalhausen, 1921), self-righteousness (Lax, 1975), moral outrage (Kaplan, 1997), problems in the development of moral values in childhood (Morrison & Severino, 1997), resentful entitlement (Shabad, 1993), and narcissistic rage (Kohut, 1972). As early as 1921, Schmalhausen railed against the self-importance, intolerance, and self-congratulation inherent in a moralistic response. He wrote forcefully:

> Oh conceited moralist, why seest thou the hypocrisy in thy brother's eye and seest not the duplicity in thine own? Conventional morality has its deepest roots in the morbid desire for self-approval and self-aggrandizement, not in the love of virtue. So much is plain.
>
> (pp. 390–391)

This, we might say, is a vividly *indignant* portrayal of the scourge of indignation; were it not so righteous in its own wrath, it might be a fine moral for Roth's more subtle psychological study. At any rate, Schmalhausen seems to have been among the earliest in the psychoanalytic canon to denounce moralism as a narcissistic defensive attitude with widely and flagrantly destructive consequences. Further, indignation lends itself to being "performative"—that is, something one tends to express in the very act of examining it.

Later theorists have a kinder, gentler understanding of indignation and seem more compassionate toward those in its clutches. Morrison and Severino (1997), in exploring the development of moral values, note that self-righteous indignation "is experienced as restoring a sense of power and worth to the self. The retaliatory aspect of shame-induced anger seeks to turn the tables on the shamer and reclaim power for the self by shaming the other" (p. 259). The authors do note, however, that this unfortunately maintains a schism within the self rather than bringing it into harmony internally or into attunement with the other.

In a similar vein, Shabad (1993) suggests that indignation arises during childhood out of the perceived violation of rightful needs from whose gratification the child feels debarred. The needs are transformations of repressed "impossible-to-fulfill wishes," whose non-fulfillment one initially experiences as a terrible psychic injury. The "entrenched faults" in the parent's character disempower the child, who then denies the wish that meets with frustration. What is once perceived as "impossible" becomes instead "forbidden," though a fantasy might linger of its eventual gratification in a future form. The lingering, eternally frustrated need is, in Shabad's view, a concomitant of what he calls a "traumatic theme":

> [A] chronic pattern of frustrating childhood experiences suffered passively at the hands of significant others that, when repeated day after day over a number of years, may cumulatively take on the emotional meaning of a trauma. A parent's persistent nagging, moody silences, consistent breaking of small promises . . . may each come to constitute distinct traumatic themes of varying severity.

> (pp. 482–483)

This is very close to how I conceptualize micro-traumas as the stuff of strain trauma. Shabad is especially astute in his assessment of the ultimate fate of these frustrated needs, originally exiled as "forbidden," as development goes forward. The author summarizes:

> With a sense of resentment and righteous indignation . . . [the aggrieved person] may then, with a vengeance, seek to retrieve those wishes from their exile in the unconscious—by giving them a "rebirth" as entitled demands or "needs" that must be filled and indulged through action, immediately and repeatedly.

> (p. 485)

The difficulty, of course, is that the indignation may take on a poisonous life of its own. In an especially compelling account, Ruth Lax (1975) discusses indignation from a combined Freudian/Kohutian viewpoint in the context of chronic fault-finding. Like other theorists, Lax views self-righteousness as a narcissistic defense, often not experienced by the person as pathological or problematic, that may be characterological. The self-righteous individual is likely to select a significant other on the unconscious basis of "neurotic complementarity." That is, a partner is found who embodies the devalued parts of self with which the righteous one can actively disidentify. The result is an unconscious reenactment, which cyclically reinforces the dynamics of criticizer/criticized, right one/wrong one, within the interpersonal matrix. The righteous one feels entirely justified and, in fact, praiseworthy for carrying the banner onto the field of battle. Because of this, the aggression inherent in asserting one's moral rectitude comes out in full force, untempered by the guilt that under other circumstances might soften the intensity of one's self-assertion.

Naturally, as Lax details, the intrapsychic scenario also shapes the analytic relationship. At first, the analyst is experienced as fault-finding and judgmental. Projective identification causes the patient to variously experience the self and the analyst as right or wrong, attacker or victim. Once negative transference currents are quieted and the analyst's benign intentions come at least intermittently to be experienced and trusted, the stage is set for the uncovering of unconscious disavowed self-aspects deemed unworthy. After a typically stormy course of treatment, these may eventually become integrated into the patient's sense of self.

Lax observes a characteristic developmental history in those with self-righteous personalities. One parent is experienced as dominating and punitive but also loving and forthcoming; the other parent is relatively absent but accepts and therefore reinforces the domineering parent's demands and value structure. The child comes to identify strongly with the powerful, critical, but also lovingly engaged parent, whom the child views as a life-giving mainstay. Their relationship is both emotionally intense and ambivalent. The parent's values are internalized as part of the superego, and the parent as "idealized 'righteous one'" is introjected into the ego-ideal. This provides relief from the childhood narcissistic injuries and serves to replenish "lost narcissistic supplies," which is what makes a self-righteous attitude so ego-syntonically pleasurable and hard to renounce. The indignant person is in fantasied fusion with an upstanding, "upright" parental introject, and reinforcing this frequently is necessary for the maintenance of the person's ongoing sense of well-being. Putting this in a nutshell, Lax tells us that "an outburst of righteous indignation represents an acting out of an identification with a non-metabolized introject which has become a dominant aspect of the ego-ideal" (p. 288).

Lax's view of the merger with an introjected version of a beloved, righteous other goes far toward explaining the younger Messner and his tragic self-destruction. In the face of potential threats to his survival, Marcus adopts his father's obsessive workaholism. Like his father, he steers these efforts in the service of postwar American values, though Marcus applies them in quite a different direction from his father's—toward academic success, not toward developing a trade. Marcus is attempting to separate and individuate, but cannot grasp how devastatingly frightening this is for his father. He is overwhelmed by his own sense of being unjustly oppressed, and the resulting anger blocks his capacity to become attuned to his father's anxieties and to help assuage them. Marcus' pride is brittle, being based on such a narrow definition of what makes a man's life viable and valuable. His bull-headed conviction of his own goodness and his wish to do everything "just so" blinds him to the values and virtues represented by his mother and by his erstwhile girlfriend, namely the capacity to relate to others with empathy and fellow-feeling. This psychic capacity, which might have saved him, is as central to ensuring psychic safety as is autonomous self-striving. Instead Marcus repeatedly invests in his own correctness while humiliating, shaming, and devaluing others who seem softer or more dependent than he.

I agree with Lax's view of self-righteous indignation as temptingly contagious, especially from parent to child, as it offers a falsely grandiose counter to painful feelings of inadequacy and powerlessness. But I would add that indignation as a micro-traumatic characterological tendency is best understood in a broader relational, social, and even international context, as Roth himself invites us to do. The word "indignation" is the mantra Marcus chants silently to himself over and over, when having to sit through required religious sermons at college. But Marcus has gotten the word from a source with much more global significance: it is part of the defiant cry in the lyrics of the Chinese national anthem, a song sung as an expression of China's defiance of the Japanese during World War II. And there is a further and ultimate irony, not completely spelled out by Roth: it is the Chinese, now indignantly attacking American-backed South Korea, who inflict Marcus' final, fatal wounds.

My point is that sometimes an individual's moralistic judgmentalism emanates not solely from the matrix of self and other; it may develop as a defense against larger, deleterious forces beyond the individual's control. The traumatic impact of these forces merits its own compassionate attention, and doing so may help reduce the righteous defensiveness. The elder Messner's frantic fulminations are a symptom not only of a character distortion, but also of his desperate doubt as to his ability to sustain his family in the face of socioeconomic upheaval and the threat of a son's military conscription. Behind this, there is the legacy of the genocidal drive against those of the Messners' ethnic background. To fully appreciate a moralistic character, we should try to factor in the role of the larger sociopolitical context and its inexorable demands as a stressor.

Indignation's Expression in Political and Personal Arenas

One can turn to the events of the so-called "Arab Spring" to see how indignation intersects with the sociopolitical context. On December 18, 2010, a Tunisian fruit vendor, sick of police corruption, publicly immolated himself an hour after his goods had been confiscated. This act of indignation ignited protests that spread first in Tunisia and then throughout the Arab world. Three years later, there were new governments not only in Tunisia, but also in Egypt, Libya, and Yemen, and there had been major uprisings and protests elsewhere.

Shortly after that horrific example, the role of the sociopolitical context was brought home to me all over again in a more immediate way. In May 2011, Spanish protesters explicitly calling themselves *"Los Indignados"* ("The Indignant Ones") set up camp in the Puerta del Sol, an important gathering place in Madrid, to rage against the sociopolitical and economic hardships they had suffered in response to Spain's current economic situation. The protesters' makeshift tents were still in evidence in early July 2011, at a short distance from where I was coincidentally staying in preparation for presenting an earlier version of this chapter at a conference elsewhere in Madrid. The *Indignados* movement spawned further demonstrations in other parts of Spain and various other European cities, where similar privations and injustices disproportionally affect the middle and lower classes.

When the world seems more oppressive and prohibitive, the individual is more likely to respond in a unidimensional, narrowly moralistic manner. If I cannot count on you to find what there is to value in me, I may either self-deflate or self-inflate; I may strip myself of power entirely or make myself the sole authority as to my own worth and become the watchdog of its recognition. When this mood is shared by large segments of the population, a single demonstrative indignant act can bring the whole situation to a conflagration. But those are exceptional circumstances, exceptional times.

In general, when a person experiences more than the average share of injustice, disadvantage, or injury, and when that iniquity is minimized or unheeded by the person's loved ones or the society, it sets the stage for an amplified cry of objection. In one such instance, a child who was disabled both cognitively and physically was struggling in the specialized education program he'd been placed in. His parents began lobbying to arrange an "accommodation" (that is, a custom-tailored adjustment to help bypass his difficulties) for his auditory comprehension issues, which seemed to be the main obstacle. When their concerns were minimized or shrugged off by the staff, the parents reacted with indignant shock—here was one place they'd really expected their son's needs to be honored. How could this be happening? Ironically, as part of the program, the child and his family both were being encouraged to advocate for his needs in the outside world, which was—and this was to be expected—likely to be resistant to dealing with people's handicaps in general. Yet in this setting, one that purported to promote the disabled's rights, a complaint got the family nowhere. Out of indignant frustration, the family escalated their requests, but this seemed to invite only defensive irritation and disapproval from the program leaders. Moreover, it began to look like the parents' outraged stance risked their son's being ousted from the program completely—a risk indeed, as this was one of the few settings where they lived that was available to serve such a child. In time, the parents began to see the situation more clearly; it became apparent that the program had been designed primarily for those who were handicapped *physically* rather than cognitively, or both; their son's so-called "invisible" disabilities were simply beyond the scope of what the staff could or was willing to deal with. The family eventually realized that patient self-soothing would be necessary to cope with any feelings of insult or offense, if they were to reach their goal of having their son remain in and benefit from this particular setting. They understood that expressing their indignation in an unbridled way was likely to be counterproductive, no matter how valid their objections might be. Such indignation could easily undermine or discredit itself if they remained so strident.

Sometimes an expression of indignation is not especially substantive— instead, it is a "perversion" of a more healthy pride. With amplified outrage, we overidentify with the cause or value, and our insistence on our correctness becomes more a narcissistic stanchion than an argument for the sake of the thing itself. Unbridled indignation outshouts our efforts to probe the nuances of a complicated question. Even as we believe ourselves stronger and better heard, we actually undercut our capacity to comprehend the fullness of the situation, which thwarts our ability to take constructive action. This, in turn, unconsciously erodes our self-respect. Better to approach the world's impingements, infractions, and inadequacies with measured objection but without offended rage; in doing so, we foster the emotional "justness" of our inner and outer lives.

But how to reach that desideratum? Donna Hicks (2011), an expert in international conflict resolution, addresses this question in her succinctly titled book, *Dignity*. The "dignity model" she presents forms the basis for her successful efforts to negotiate rapprochements in places as fraught as Northern Ireland, Sri Lanka, and the Middle East. In Hicks' view (which follows on the thinking of Immanuel Kant), dignity represents the *a priori* birthright of each individual and, by extension, of each racial, ethnic, or national group. Each person or group should be treated "as if they matter, as if they are worthy of care and attention" (p. 4), and not simply as a vehicle for or obstacle to one's own ends. While *dignity* is viewed as a basic human right, *respect* is something to be earned through meritorious actions and worthy qualities. Hicks offers her commonsensical position in crystal clear terms:

Treating people badly because they have done something wrong only perpetuates the cycle of indignity. What is worse, we violate our own dignity in the process. Others' bad behavior doesn't give us license to treat them badly in return. Their inherent value and worth need to be honored no matter what they do. But we don't have to respect them. They have to earn respect through their behavior and actions.

(p. 5)

The writer bases her "dignity model" on John Burton's list of the universal "ontological" needs humans have for a sense of identity, recognition, security, and the feeling of belonging to someone or something. Violations of one's dignity may cause one to respond defensively in a manner that violates the other's dignity in turn. Untoward responses to a perceived offense may even undermine one's *own* dignity in the process of expressing them, thus generating a vicious "cycle of indignity." Hicks (2011, pp. 93–94) articulates a list of ten "temptations to violate dignity," many of which, in my terms, are expressions of misguided indignation. Slightly paraphrased, they are:

- taking the bait;
- saving face by masking one's bad behavior;
- shirking responsibility for one's own mistakes;
- seeking false dignity by unduly relying on others' approval;
- seeking false security out of a need for connection;
- side-stepping a healthy dispute and instead asserting a supposed "truth";
- experiencing oneself as the victim one-sidedly;
- resisting constructive feedback;
- blaming and shaming others to deflect guilt over one's own infractions;
- engaging in false intimacy through demeaning gossip.

Marcus Messner fell prey to many of these temptations over the course of his life, with sorry results. Having Hicks articulate them so clearly hopefully makes it easier for the rest of us as we try to temper our own feelings of offense and divert them toward a more constructive channel. We should be cautious about the state of feeling offended and work to temper it. We do well to listen for a buildup of convictions of righteous offense whether they occur within our selves, within the other, in the world at large, or in the consulting room, since indignation that is unbridled and pervasive tends to intimidate others micro-traumatically and often boomerangs against ourselves as well.

As Roth and Hicks each in their own way amply demonstrate, an individual who is led to feel powerless within the family matrix or in his or her larger sociocultural milieu will sometimes become defensively impassioned about the rightness of a particular perspective or cause, and he or she may impose these views on significant others and the wider world. Swayed at the visceral level, the listener may identify with the moralistic one and share the umbrage. Alternatively, especially if she or he is the target, the listener may introject the sense of badness being railed against and succumb to self-shaming. Or contrarily, she or he may momentarily embrace the attitude but eventually turn it back on the ranter. The seeming strength derived from expressing unbridled indignation is chimerical and insubstantial at best and distracts one or both from dealing effectively with the nuggets of true offense that lie within the screed. Full of "sound and fury," the indignant one can't register internal inklings that might modify his or her understanding of the apparent insult or injustice—or suggest how to remedy it.

Indignation as a Defense in Professional and Other Settings

Many ethical, legal, and moral issues get stirred up in the course of psychoanalytic practice, both in the treatment and training context. We are trying to stimulate new forms of self-expression and freedom, a process that naturally leads to the unknown—how far may one go, and to what end? This ambiguity in turn generates anxieties in both analyst and patient or supervisor and supervisee. With the opening of new pathways, sensible boundaries, limitations, and guidelines need to be in place within the clinician's or supervisor's mind. Here we're in the realm of salutary values and strictures, the realm of conscience, conscientiousness, and ideals that would be referred to as mature superego functioning within the Freudian and ego psychological frameworks. The position of authority as analyst or supervisor often involves offering oneself as a benign superego figure. But this is an area where a commitment to imparting standards can sometimes stray into micro-traumatic territory.

In order to deal with a particularly challenging maternal erotic transference–countertransference situation with a same-sex patient, a colleague of mine named Mindy, a recently graduated analyst, had re-entered periodic supervision with a well-known senior analyst. This analyst was known for her wisdom and good sense, but above all, for her attunement to the irrational currents of deep feeling that may arise in a long-term treatment.

Mindy had trusted that this particular supervisor could "go the distance" in dealing with the irrational urges and thoughts that this seductive, manipulative patient aroused in her. However, at one point in their supervisory work, while in the throes of examining a sensually charged interplay between Mindy and the patient, the supervisor burst out in a steely, moralistic tone, "What *exactly* do you have in mind for this patient?"—the implication being that the supervisor imagined Mindy might engage in a sexual boundary transgression. The supervisor's interjection was like a punch in the stomach. Mindy had in fact entered supervision—and with this particular senior analyst—in order to further bolster her intention *not* to violate a boundary. And she'd wanted to ensure that in keeping that limit she would do so in an attuned and tactful way, not letting the analytic relationship's emotional tenor become dry, stilted, or flattened out. The senior analyst's indignant intervention made Mindy feel ashamed and guilty on the one hand—was there something bad in her that she herself hadn't recognized?—and blind-sided and unheard on the other.

As Mindy describes it, she stumbled through the remainder of the supervisory hour and then privately anguished over the comment for a week, until she called the supervisor to discuss it. The supervisor's response was that she "hadn't realized" how she'd come off; she insisted that she hadn't meant to be hypercritical, accusatory, or shaming. She apologized nonetheless for having given that "impression," and the supervisory bond was to some degree patched up. But a seed of doubt was sown in Mindy's mind, and she had trouble feeling quite as secure in her stance with the patient going forward as she had earlier on; the residue of (what felt like) an indignant scolding kept her from entirely trusting her own clinical motives and decisions in this treatment, the supervisor's apology notwithstanding.

There was a coda to this incident. Several years later, with both the supervision and the analysis itself at an end, Mindy happened to hear from a credible source that the supervisor had herself likely engaged in a relationship that crossed sexual boundaries, a situation that might have been underway during the same period as their supervision. Mindy was terribly distressed at the news. She couldn't be entirely sure that the rumor was true, but it was plausible and couldn't be dismissed, given what she knew of the surrounding circumstances. Mindy herself now felt indignant—how galling that the supervisor would have impugned and punished her, as if she were guilty of the latter's own improprieties! She did her best to keep her sense of betrayal and injustice under wraps, discussing it with only a few trusted friends, as she didn't have incontrovertible proof of either the supervisor's original motives when questioning her or of her unethical behavior. Moreover, she realized that her outrage about the supervisor's possible breach was at least partially a response to her (that is, Mindy's) own narcissistic vulnerabilities, given her lingering feelings about their prior consultation. This situation illustrates how one person may impulsively (and unfairly) condemn another out of his or her own disavowed guilt or shame in relation to a similar transgressive urge. It appeared that the supervisor was projectively identifying with an unacted-upon aspect of Mindy's erotic urge, an urge that was dissociated—or not so dissociated—in the supervisor herself. She externalized this and defensively clamped down on Mindy, acting with unbridled indignation and inflicting micro-traumatic damage in the process.

In another instance, an acquaintance of mine living in southern California had developed an ailment with an unclear cause, but that was painful and seemed to be worsening. He tried all the noninvasive, first-wave therapeutic approaches he'd heard about for relieving the discomfort. This being to no avail, he went to the next level and began seeking advice from the major specialists in that part of California. One of the most touted of these, Dr. D, recommended a particular procedure that was so new and advanced that the patient's insurance company would need to be lobbied if there were any chance it would be covered. The specialist's advice sounded both knowledgeable and convincing, but the challenge of taking on the insurance company, and the length and difficulty of the recovery involved, caused the man to seek one last high-level opinion before going the route recommended by Dr. D. So it was that my acquaintance ended up meeting with Dr. E, who after careful examination told him that he didn't see any need for Dr. D's procedure unless and until the symptoms became more completely disabling. Moreover, Dr. E questioned Dr. D's impartiality and judgment, indicating that he had reason to think that Dr. D might have a financial interest in recommending that particular procedure, based on his having endorsed one of the new materials it required. Dr. E sounded earnest and sincere, but also rather scornful and indignant that Dr. D would have handled himself in this manner. The potential patient felt greatly relieved that he'd received this advice, and the doubt about the honorableness of Dr. D's advice was subsequently reinforced from other quarters. The patient decided to give his ailment more time to heal, kept using the less invasive measures to ease it, and found his symptoms became more tolerable over time.

So imagine this man's shock when, some months later, in the midst of thanking his lucky stars for having met the wise and virtuous Dr. E, he opened up the newspaper to discover that Dr. E himself had just been indicted for professional malfeasance. In fact, he was charged with having some years ago received financial perks for prescribing a particular medicine that was featured in his practice. How could Dr. E have been so sincerely disapproving of Dr. D, while knowing that he himself had similarly engaged in unethical professional behavior a decade before? The patient was nonplussed—and indignant himself—to think he could have come under the sway of a doctor who was himself unscrupulous and in whom he'd believed. It must be that similar minds in similar positions with similar temptations think alike—or as the saying goes, "It takes one to know one." However, perhaps the patient had reason to celebrate rather than become indignant about his discovery. After all, in a sense he benefited from Dr. E's chicanery, in that he was saved an unnecessary procedure by virtue of Dr. E's possibly having sublimated his guilt over the prior transgression into a usable reparation—that is, his saving someone else from another crooked practitioner's self-serving advice.

Ricocheting indignation can also be found in the world of the performing arts. Mike Daisey (Fallows, 2014; Isherwood, 2012) is a dramatist, actor, and cultural critic known especially for his one-man monologues that aim to hold the mirror up to nature about various societal ills. Not long ago, Daisey wrote and performed in a show he called *The Agony and the Ecstasy of Steve Jobs*. (The late Steve Jobs was of course the founder and CEO of the Apple Corporation.) This performance piece, termed "a work of nonfiction" in its playbill, was an exposé based on Daisey's own supposed investigative reportage of inhumane labor practices in a factory in Shenzhen, China, where Apple products are manufactured. Daisey also took aggressive aim at Jobs as a person, portraying him as inveterately self-serving and almost monomaniacal in his efforts to promote his corporate aims. Audiences came away from the performance fired up by the report of the appalling abuses of the Chinese workers, and their indignation was fueled further by a handout entitled "What happens next?" that they received as they exited the theater. This flyer was a recommendation for ways audience members could channel the outrage Daisey had ignited, steps that would pressure Apple and other similar technology companies to become more socially responsible. Now Daisey also performed a version of this material on the National Public Radio (NPR) station's program "This American Life," at which point another NPR reporter discovered significant inaccuracies in his account, most of which were designed to add intensity to the scenario. It was a sad day when the falsifications were revealed, as it undermined Daisey's credibility in relation to the elements of his narrative that were all-too-horribly true. And those who'd been swayed by Daisey's account felt understandably indignant at his actions.

Coming back to the initial performances themselves, the fanning of indignation stirs up an affective storm that temporarily focuses attention and potentially galvanizes corrective measures, and that is obviously all to the good. However, once the storm settles, or when those clearheaded enough to question its assertions do so, the original process of pursuing truth and justice may be badly discredited, and then the corrective measures suffer. The upshot of this situation in Daisey's case was a good one—he was censured publicly in a serious but non-castrating and only moderately indignant fashion. This seems to have allowed him to take the criticisms of his work to heart and to emerge a sadder but wiser social critic. And notwithstanding Daisey's poor judgment and its potential for having undermined his message, the actual ills of Chinese labor practices—and Americans' support of them—did end up being better recognized as factual in the larger sense and seriously in need of redress.

Self-righteous anger—even when its protest has validity—may be an attempt to assuage unconscious shame or to deny one's own perceived weakness, but it is almost always an inadequate defensive measure, if not a manifestly self-thwarting one. Judgmental rage can actually be *self*-alienating, if it spurs unconscious guilt or shame over one's own fury. It can, of course, also undermine the target's sense of efficacy and agency, thus stimulating a cycle of damaging reprisals, as each individual struggles to uphold a sense of self-worth.

Poets have a knack for expressing complicated things in a pithy and memorable way. In his apt, recently published poem, Ben Downing (2012) considers the impact of taking offense:

Umbrage

Taken, given:
friendships riven.

From *shadow* or *shade*,
it instantly puts paid

to hard-won clarities
and causes us to freeze

up with unearned righteousness;
it makes us less.

How much better to combat it.
We should take umbrage at it.

So true! Though, then again, rather than taking umbrage at umbrage, we should probably just adopt the personal guideline of being cautious about making judgments of another's attitude. Otherwise we may inadvertently perpetuate the cycle of someone getting a narcissistically satisfying kick out of decrying another's failing or excess.

As a coda to these reflections, I have to admit that I myself at times fell into umbrage's trap as I tried to identify forms of micro-traumatic relating and probe their impact for this book. Here and there, I found myself indignant or even outraged by what I saw and how it played out. I hope I was at least moderately successful at tempering this in sharing my observations! Certainly, indignation in the psychoanalytic writer—or the psychoanalyst proper—tends not to advance the process of discovery. One should remember that most people are doing the best they can with what they've got. As for instances where indignation really does seem called for, perhaps there is cause to say "so be it"—but hopefully, the indignant one keeps in mind Shakespeare's wisdom: "Use every man after his desert and who should 'scape whipping?" None of us is incapable of causing damage.

Note

1 These definitions are culled from Webster (McKechnie, 1983), the Merriam-Webster online dictionary, and www.latin-dictionary.net/definition/23423/indignor-indignari-indignatus.

Chapter 8

Little Murders and Other Everyday Micro-assaults

The list of ways in which individuals may further bruise one another is frighteningly extensive. Being ubiquitous, these hurtful tactics can easily slip below one's radar. The purpose of this chapter is to flesh out the catalog of micro-traumas by describing (somewhat more succinctly) other noteworthy examples. I start by exploring "little murders," or put-downs explicitly designed for psychic damage. Next comes an assortment of other mundane micro-assaults, including affective overdrive, engulfment, martyrdom, and emotional blackmail, among others. Then I will offer an instance of micro-traumatic relating that is a region-wide pattern rather than something specific to a particular two-person dynamic. I close with a clinical interchange that shows a mutually hurtful process along with the analytic pair's concerted effort to reverse its effects and learn from the experience.

Broadly speaking, these various micro-assaults all violate the "generally understood rules of interpersonal engagement" articulated by Tuch (2008) in his exploration of perverse relationships. As Tuch sees it, such rules operate on the shared basis "that one recognizes and permits the other's beliefs, wishes, etc. to influence and help co-determine how a specific interaction, string of interactions, or relationship plays out" (p. 147). Tuch elaborates:

> These unspoken rules of engagement also dictate that one interact with others in ways that show respect for the other's most basic assumptions about what can roughly be expected from others in the course of relating. No one is to violate another's basic trust by interacting with him in ways that challenge that person's orienting beliefs about how humans interact with one another, which could cast serious doubt on that person's understanding of human relations, or reality in general. Failures to respect these unspoken but understood rules often prove psychically traumatizing.
>
> (p. 147)

When these fundamental expectations are violated, the other person is left struggling either consciously or subliminally to determine what just happened, what it means, and what if anything should be done about it.

I hope it is already clear and possibly even self-evident that for such disconcerting experiences to rise to the level of being micro-traumatic, they need to exceed certain thresholds. There must be one too many of them, and they must involve a person or persons who are significant to one's sense of self. They need to be part of a pattern of relating that consistently undermines one's self-regard or sense of efficacy in the world. And the injured parties must be predisposed to be vulnerable to their effect, whether because of their youth, due to an idiosyncrasy of character, or because they have insufficient psychic protection against such an assault. When these conditions are present, often (though not always) due to factors in the person's earlier developmental history, seemingly minor psychic impingements will accumulate and eventually undermine or thwart one's "going on being" (Winnicott, 1965).

As an example, a highly competent young man named Sean, in his first job after four years at an elite college, was disappointed to find that the organization employing him had little of the vaunted effectiveness it had appeared to have when he'd first accepted the job. Worse still for Sean was that six months into his work there, he began to notice that his co-workers, whom he'd initially respected and looked up to, were overtly dismissive and scornful of the company and its stated mission. He caught them surfing the internet on personal business much of the time, giving short shrift to their assigned projects. And they seemed to look askance at Sean's own seriousness of purpose. Having started out very enthusiastic about the position as the first step on his chosen career path, Sean became increasingly demoralized and eventually depressed. He could not imagine himself gaining anything from this job experience, and the whole field started to seem bankrupt in his eyes. Being at a company that fostered such low morale and did nothing to address it was, of course, part of Sean's problem. But the *coup de grâce* for him was the ongoing disparagement of the company among the people he admired and the fact that they nonetheless continued on in their positions and, from what Sean could tell, didn't seem to try to either change the company or leave it. Sean's work-life came to feel like a meaningless, absurdist drama from which there was no escape.

At first I didn't see why it was that his co-workers' attitudes were so bothersome to Sean, who in our sessions would rail repeatedly against their slothfulness as well as their complaints. Couldn't he just ignore them and simply plan to "get the hell out of Dodge" as soon as he could? But

I gradually came to understand that the situation echoed the cynical attitude of Sean's three older brothers, who had been outspokenly dismissive whenever the question of a future vocational pathway for any of them came up. It was his siblings who influenced Sean most, since his parents, newly emigrated to the US, were hardly ever home. The parents were too busy struggling to support the family by any and all means, without the luxury to be particular about how satisfying the work was or wasn't for them psychologically. Sean's brothers' negativity laid the groundwork for his co-workers' attitudes to be frighteningly erosive and therefore microtraumatic to Sean's morale, threatening him with having to settle for a deadening, meaningless work-life. This is how an experience that would be merely *disappointing* to many could become *micro-traumatic* for a person whose history provided the underpinnings for disillusionment.

And now to the listing of additional micro-assaults, offered with the intent of sharpening our attunement to the forms cumulative emotional injury can take.

Little Murders

Little murders, straightforward or oblique onslaughts on another's sense of personal worth, are foremost among injurious modes of relating. A vast and various group of behaviors, they include off-hand insults, slights, mockery, back-biting, discounting, damning with faint praise, and back-handed compliments. I cribbed the term, as have others before me, from the title of an absurdist play of the same name by famed satirist and cartoonist Jules Feiffer (1968). Feiffer's story, a send-up of the hypocrisy of modern society, deals as much with physical as with psychic assaults. The action is riddled with random, meaningless murders and other crime occurring in the streets of the city. The satire and the horror of the play lie in the idea that this level of gratuitous violence becomes "business as usual" in modern-day society. At one point, the father of the family describes how he makes it through each moment of the day—having breakfast, taking a walk, returning to his apartment, and so on—anxiously evading being sniped at, knifed, mugged, or robbed at any one juncture. This type of defensive stance develops also with psychic hurts. When chronically trapped in destructive interpersonal patterns, we subconsciously absorb and try to quarantine the hurt, as we immediately go on the alert to fend off the next one. Each day becomes a journey through a psychic minefield, at the end of which we are depleted from the stress of the vigilance required to minimize damage.

Feiffer's play closes with the father, his son, and his son-in-law taking turns aiming a rifle out of their apartment window, gleefully shooting at passersby. The mother says she's glad the three of them are having such a good time, as she was starting to be afraid they couldn't anymore—as if shooting others were acceptable or even therapeutic entertainment! Feiffer is showing how we may resign ourselves to and even become complicit in the dangerous absurdities of modern-day life—whether they be physically or psychically injurious. We downplay and justify their toxicity so we don't have to go to the trouble to unpack and correct them. Yet there is no such thing as a "little" homicide—if someone dies, he or she is truly dead. So, too, in the psychic realm. We try to excuse ourselves for taking pot-shots at the other's well-being. We rationalize snide and snarky remarks as trivial or "all in fun," and in so doing, we give ourselves license to draw emotional blood. So much for the old adage "sticks and stones will break my bones, but names will never hurt me."

When I first went searching for a paradigmatic illustration to flesh out my portrait of these kinds of verbal assaults, I was puzzled to find that no "little murder" from my own past immediately leapt to mind. A little reflection reminded me that micro-traumas are by definition hidden in plain sight, and then it occurred to me that they might be even more deeply obscured when the one who inflicted them is now deceased. It can seem churlish, if not frankly disloyal, to dredge up hurts associated with a loved one who is dead and gone, whose memory one nonetheless cherishes and wishes to honor. But these are the very hurts that undermine us, unless we do our best to identify them and work them through.

Amid these musings, a moment did come to mind—a holiday dinner held 10 years ago as our Judeo-Christian family was celebrating the Christmas portion of our December festivities. We had sat down to partake of the dessert I'd baked, a complicated pastry called a *buche de Noel* that is shaped like a Yule log to represent the winter season and Christmas itself. My late mother, who'd always purported to be in awe of my baking, pronounced it delicious—and just like the cake she used to make for us in during our childhood.

My mother was referring to a Nabisco cookie package recipe popular in the 1950s and 1960s, in which you sandwiched together chocolate wafers with whipped cream. (My husband insists the whipped cream was in fact the ersatz product Cool Whip, making the story still worse.) The cookie stack as a whole is laid on its side and enveloped in more whipped cream (Cool Whip?). It then "rests" in the refrigerator overnight, so the cookies absorb the filling and become cake-like. My mother was comparing that—that concoction—to my *buche*. And my *buche* was from a French recipe I had carefully researched and executed, involving a complicated *genoise* (an egg-white based cake) that was filled with liqueur-laced buttercream, rolled, further iced, and bedecked with chocolate leaves flecked with edible gold. This elaborate Yule log was flanked by marzipan mushrooms dusted with cocoa to invoke the "naturalness" of earth.

On hearing my mother's comment, I was briefly tickled to think back on that childhood dessert. It was only a few moments later that the aftershock landed. Did my *buche de Noel* taste and look no better than an ersatz recipe cribbed from a cookie box? Another guest, an elderly mother of a friend of mine, and so my own mother's natural ally, noticed and later remarked on my mother's thinly veiled put-down. But I couldn't sit content with that either. Was my mother's comment *really* an intended diminishment, the product of a need to spoil on her part, or was I overreacting to a reasonable and perhaps innocent comment? I couldn't decide and couldn't put it to rest. I've never since felt quite the same pleasure and satisfaction in making a *buche de Noel* as I had before that evening.

In contemporary society, the capacity to injure—ideally with rapier wit—has been raised to an art form, through which an observing audience has a vicarious catharsis. We can think of comedians' caustic sketches and monologues, piquant *New Yorker* cartoons, *Saturday Night Live* and other satiric television series, social media offerings, and the like. That said, Clive James (2013), the Australian poet and critic, argues that Americans are *less* adept as psychological assassins than other nationalities, at least with respect to literary criticism. He spells out his position in a *New York Times* opinion piece called "Whither the hatchet job?" As someone who has been on both the giving and receiving ends of the hatchet's blade, James seems anything but ironic in arguing for the value of *sharper* critique, or what he considers to be bitchiness. He reports that in the UK, a no-holds-barred criticism is experienced as an enjoyable thrill by the public, as if it were a spectacle or sport, whereas in the US world of publishing, being disparaging toward others is very much frowned upon. James caps his piece with an imagined exhortation to a younger critic, in which he insists that one sidesteps a negative commentary at one's own peril. Being unafraid to sound harshly judgmental, in his view, makes any praise that may also be forthcoming that much more substantive, based as it is on a strict standard of excellence.

James is not alone in celebrating the bite as much as the substantive critique in a witty putdown. The supposed innocence of social teasing, which begins in grade school, obscures how it operates aggressively and competitively. Victims are left mistrusting and valuing themselves some quantum less with each jab. Moreover, given our multiple conscious and unconscious agendas, the intention behind the attack is often murky to the perpetrators themselves. Yet making a discrediting or shaming remark in public is common in contemporary life, whether on playgrounds, in executive suites, or elsewhere.

Little murders are especially potent when they're inflicted between parent and child. Being critical of a child in front of others is unfortunately all too common. A witty gloss on this can be found in *New Yorker* columnist Simon Rich's parody "Play Nice" (2008), in which the typical roles are reversed between chiding parent and supposedly "selfish" child. The writer burlesques parents' expectation that their children should play happily with the heretofore unfamiliar children of their parents' guests. His piece highlights that in this sort of interchange, what is especially hurtful is the shaming, guilt-inducing implication that one is a greedy ne'er-do-well if one doesn't rise to the occasion of sharing with others cheerfully. To go further into the specifics of the column, in Rich's imagination, a boy's mother is expected to share her "toy" with a new "playmate," the toy being her *car*—and a Mercedes no less. When the mother demurs, her son responds—in little murder fashion—that he's disappointed in her, that by now she should understand the value of sharing her things—whereupon the mother defeatedly admits she was wrong and hands over the car keys. This sort of interchange can amount to a little murder to the degree that the non-sharing "possessive" person—the child, in the real world—is being labeled inadequate for having desires that are natural and understandable at any age. The implication is that one is fundamentally faulty or even sinful if one can't be generously self-sacrificing toward a total stranger—there's something amiss at the core of one's being, and it is not just a matter of "bad" behavior in a given instance.

But turning Rich's satiric situation on its ear, hurtful, disrespectful communication can indeed go both ways. Socialization that runs upstream from child to parent is relatively neglected in our theorizing, but it can be just as harmful (or helpful) as the downstream type from parent to child that attracts more attention in our society. It's not uncommon for an adolescent or young adult to express impatience or even mock a parent for being ill at ease with new modes of technology that the younger person learned virtually *in utero* and has understood viscerally ever since. I've seen this stressful, demoralizing dynamic be especially prominent and spread to other areas in immigrant families, when the new generation grouses about its parents' and grandparents' "old country" ways. Criticizing their elders' slowness to assimilate perpetrates little murders that discourage rather than hearten the parents to take on unfamiliar challenges.

A child's judgment vis-à-vis his or her parent is all the more troubling when it is directed toward aspects of the parent's personal identity. An 8-year-old girl heard the word "slutty" on a television program about fashion and asked its meaning. Caught off guard, the mother first offered a brief explanation but then elaborated on the subject of women's role in society and its fraught presentation in the media. Her daughter interrupted, snapping: "Would you please just speak plain English? Talk to me like you're supposed to!"

The woman, who was my patient, was cut to the quick. She already felt ashamed and anxious at having to raise her daughter as a single parent. She feared that being single might interfere with her providing an adequate environment for the girl's growth. Moreover, the woman was a publicist and communications expert by trade, and so very invested in her ability to do just what her daughter demanded—communicate in "plain English." Excoriating herself for having lapsed into adult language, the mother needed assurance that even a married mother adultifies her child on occasion.

In Fairbairn's terms (1952, pp. 75 ff.), the little girl was an "exciting object" for the mother. Extremely smart with a tendency to lap up new information, this child could also be quite exacting. In part because of these qualities, she was unconsciously invested with the fantasied ability to raise the mother up from her humiliated internal state, to repair the mother's damaged self. Further underlying this painful exchange was the fact that the mother was conflicted about her own high level of intellect and education. It felt like a betrayal of her own parents, who were themselves far less well-educated than she and resentful of their grown daughter's accomplishments and upward mobility.

Framing it differently, the mother and her daughter were participants in what Faimberg (1988) has called a "telescoping of generations" as part of an intergenerational transmission of trauma (see Fraiberg et al., 1975). The woman experienced her little girl's comment as if it were a parental critique, rather than a child's. At the interpersonal level, the woman's parents had projected their sense of inadequacy onto their daughter. It was she, not they, who was inadequate, in that she spoke in a supposedly pretentious way that proved her supposed snobbery. All of this was condensed and ventriloquized now in her young daughter's scolding of her. Yet the little girl herself was probably ashamed at not understanding the mother's explanation, which could have felt like a maternal micro-traumatic attack on her. Conceivably, she may have projectively identified with and then been overwhelmed by her mother's shame and anxiety, expressed through the mother's "over-explanation." So the little girl's snappish scolding of her mother was an overdetermined counter-punch. Here there was a telescopic trading of little murders within a mother–daughter relationship that could have become toxic under other circumstances. Fortunately, as far as I could tell, the damage done here was only temporary, as the patient's bond with her daughter—unlike that with her envious, resentful parents—was fundamentally strong and loving.

A parent's off-hand judgments about a child can reverberate in toxic ways decades after the slight was administered. A 45-year-old female patient reported how her mother used to comment that she would never amount to anything. When she did get high grades, the mother would warn the patient not to get too proud of her performance, as she was likely to be brought low in the next marking period. As a result, my patient had what she called a "little dog yapping at my heels," an inner voice that threatened her with failure every time she slacked off on her massive efforts to prove her mother wrong. Having that internal yapping dog both relieved and tormented her—it could be counted on to keep her striving, but it threatened her enough that some mornings she could barely get out of bed, as she wanted to stave off dealing with the dog for a few hours longer. What was in one sense a helpful spur was actually sabotaging the life forces that could have fueled her steady advancement.

Damning judgments can be delivered under the guise of jest. After some years working on his conflicts with intimacy, a young man happened to mention to the therapist that his father, whom he loved devotedly, would occasionally respond to the young man's comedic expressions with the comment: "Watch out, kiddo—what woman will want to marry someone as clownish as you?" The father had supposedly meant it teasingly, and the man had nearly forgotten it had ever been said. When as an adult this man found himself indifferent to dating, he hadn't associated it with his father's remarks. Assertive and effective in his business role, he'd honed a droll sense of humor, not unlike his father's, that masked self-deprecation and doubt. After much therapeutic work, it became clear that what had seemed like an absence of interest in being married was actually the product of real doubt that he could be taken seriously by and retain the regard of a woman, based on the seed his father had inadvertently sewn. The ripples of little murders can be deucedly difficult to identify, as the murders themselves are downplayed by both sender and receiver; they therefore end up dissociated or otherwise unconscious.

It's impressive how little murders are sometimes endlessly traded between two individuals over the course of many years. It's as if each person's "badness" were a hot potato, too steamy to hold, so it gets lobbed into the other's hands as soon as possible—and then lobbed back. An off-hand comment whose gist is "You're bad or inadequate" leads to a quick retort whose gist is "Nope, not true, *you're* the bad one"—and on and on until the cycle erodes each one's self-worth and feels inescapably self-perpetuating.

Two sisters in their mid-thirties, Ann and Jane, lived several blocks away from each other and described themselves as always having been rather close to one another emotionally. At one point, Ann (who was in therapy with me) told me that she had availed herself of a ream of paper from Jane's closet without remembering to mention it, as Jane had extra paper aplenty in her storeroom. Jane had realized one was missing, guessed who'd taken it, and made a snide crack that her sister was being a freeloader in taking it. She added that Ann had "some nerve," given that Ann had often teased her (that is, Jane) about the latter's wastefulness with paper, citing its negative environmental impact. Ann brought up the incident in therapy feeling she'd been treated to a "little murder"—she was hurt by and ashamed at Jane's rebuke, which felt more like a thoroughgoing devaluation of herself as a person than an isolated criticism of a particular attribute. She couldn't understand why Jane would be so harsh, and how this condemnation could be triggered by something so minor—quite a petty theft! She'd have *asked* to borrow or take it if it had occurred to her to do so; it just hadn't seemed like a big deal. Jane's remark must indeed mean that, deep down, Jane didn't love or value her.

Ann and I went back over the interaction and some of its relevant history in "slow motion," something often essential for uncovering the impact of a micro-traumatic exchange. In doing so, and after further discussion with Jane herself, a deeper pattern of meaning emerged. Jane had apparently (unbeknownst to her sister) been feeling hurt by Ann's supposedly "playful" teasing about her paper usage, and this ribbing had felt like a little murder to *Jane*. Tracing these dynamics back even further, it turned out that Ann had likely been making those comments to begin with because she herself was upset that her sister had always seemed uninterested in their having a deeper, more personal connection. Teasing Jane had been a way to get a rise out of her, which made her feel they were more engaged. Ann had felt deprived of a deeper relatedness with her sister in an ongoing way throughout their adult relationship, but she was afraid to express the woundedness and frustration directly to Jane, as she didn't want to show her vulnerability or seem overdependent. So what started out as Ann feeling "murdered" by Jane's angry criticism of her pilfering turned into an appreciation of the longstanding pattern they'd had of each hurting the other through small insults. This pattern itself arose out of the sisters' fear of talking directly about the type of intimacy they each wanted with the other and what a particular degree of closeness might mean for each one's sense of self-worth. Unpacking the underlying tensions that fed the sisterly sniping led to a sounder compromise as to their level of intimacy—and to fewer trips to the (psychic) "emergency room"!

Slights, insults, and criticism sometimes amass and then fester in long-term romantic relationships, with predictably damaging consequences to each partner's well-being. An important chronicler of these is John Gottman (1994), the marital relationship specialist who heads his own institute for treating troubled couples. Gottman identifies what he calls "the four horsemen of the Apocalypse"—that is, habitual ways of interacting that insidiously undermine a relationship. In ascending order of toxicity, these are criticism, contempt, defensiveness, and stonewalling. Gottman uses Eric and Pamela's marriage to illustrate how these poisonous elements become compounded:

> What makes the four horsemen so deadly to a marriage is not so much their unpleasantness but the intensive way they interfere with a couple's communication. They create a continuing cycle of discord and negativity that's hard to break through if you don't understand what's happening. Eric and Pamela are a classic example. Their happy marriage first became blighted when they moved from complaining about specific actions to *criticizing* each other's intrinsic nature. From there it was a slow but easy slide to feeling and *expressing contempt* toward each other. Not surprisingly, this mutual psychological abuse made it all the harder for them to listen intently to each other's point of view. Instead, they responded to the vicious attacks by *defending* themselves. They each perceived themselves as an innocent victim and their spouse as an evil, abusive figure. Who wants to understand someone else's perspective when you feel under siege? Finally, Eric became so overwhelmed by the stress and tension that he ceased interacting with his wife at all. He began *stonewalling*. Once Eric and Pamela moved from poor communication to virtually no communication, they were sliding closer toward the end of the marriage.
>
> (pp. 97–98)

Gottman identifies four strategies for interrupting the destructive cycle: calming oneself to avoid emotional flooding; speaking and listening nondefensively; validating one another or the relationship; and "overlearning" the first three tactics to make them into a new habit that replaces the older problematic ones. On the basis of his own research, Gottman goes so far as to quantify his perspective, asserting that there needs to be at least a 5 to 1 ratio of positivity to negativity—or approving, accepting communications to critical, angry ones—between the two members of a couple for it to function effectively and remain intact.

Gottman's codification of this ratio and especially the nature of the negativity he spells out are useful for capturing the manifestation of little murders within an intimate pair. However, naming the horsemen and seeking to corral them behaviorally is often insufficient. Analytic work is needed to uncover the unformulated or unconscious internalizations and motivations that incite the need to commit psychic murder in order to quell the emotional violence in a sustained way.

Affective Overdrive, Engulfment, and Gushing

As Gottman points out, one can become emotionally flooded inside oneself in the heat of an exchange. In those moments, if one doesn't freeze or withdraw, one may instead flood the other, in what I call "affective overdrive." The ardent person in overdrive expresses him- or herself quite forcefully, with a long and strong flow of feeling. Another person experiencing this flow may lose touch with his or her own psychic experience, as it is overwhelmed by the intensity of the other's seeming passion, conviction, enthusiasm, or possibly warmth. (Designated mourners hired to wail loudly at a funeral engage in an intentional form of this, to the degree that they sway the other's sense of grief toward a more intense, demonstrative form.) The observing person's own experience may be undermined or even subtly discredited to the extent that it differs from the emoter's feeling.

One's own affective overdrive can be micro-traumatic to oneself as well. Jenny is a competent, independent, 35-year-old psychiatric nurse practitioner who comes into sessions absorbed in a storm of anxiety and upset, tears welling up and streaming down her face. All the while, she asks what it means that she gets so upset and whether it will ever be possible to stabilize herself. The daughter of a sociologist and a musician, Jenny frames acute psychological understandings of herself and others that sound dead-on, all the while watching me closely for my reaction. She knows that she's likely to feel and react to many emotional tones at once—this, after all, is part of her giftedness. At the same time, she is terribly frightened that her emotionality will make her seem overdramatic like her older sister, for which she is ashamed in advance. She believes she really shouldn't feel as much as she does. Worse, she worries that she will "overshare" her reactions in conversation with others and thereby co-opt their emotional experience, as her sister sometimes co-opted hers. Jenny is preternaturally expressive, but not hysteric in the sense of the common popular and sometimes clinical usage of the term as a synonym for theatrical. Nonetheless, her awareness of this "stirred up" inner tendency makes her diagnose herself damningly along these very lines. This stimulates an overly critical, negative attitude toward herself.

Excessive emotionality can blur our thinking, disrupt our ability to empathize with the other's experience, and cause us to careen blindly ahead with little attunement and no heed to the consequences. Affective forcefulness can block one from appreciating the effect, for good or ill, that one truly has on others. Too flooded to shift perspective from self-expression to receptivity, the emotionally intense person may come across as overbearing or close-minded.[1]

"Engulfment" is a term I use to characterize the taking over of another's cognitive, behavioral, emotional, or spiritual aspects. Getting too close can be equally as disruptive as its near-opposite, the distancing involved in "unkind cutting back." Masterson (1976) writes about this kind of encroachment as a key fear for many a borderline individual, but this psychic issue isn't limited to those organized at a borderline level of psychic structure. Engulfment may be accomplished or enacted through other micro-traumatic attitudes and maneuvers such as affective overdrive, relating via connoisseurship, or unbridled indignation. What is common to all these is the effect of undermining the other's separateness and sense of agency.

A patient reported that her father, recovering from the day's shift as a police detective, would take regular naps in the early evening during her childhood and would often ask her to lie down next to him so they could snuggle with each other. The little girl herself was not sleepy and quickly grew restless, but loving her father as she did, she wanted to provide the comfort she knew this gave him. She felt engulfed by his need but was loath to hurt his feelings by wriggling free of him, either literally or figuratively. She could sense that his desire for her presence came out of some inner upset, and she felt sad for him but also frustrated at having her movement curtailed at that hour, when she was still filled with energy. As an adult, the daughter remained wary of a man's possible dependent need, as she unconsciously feared a repeat of the engulfing aspect of the paternal relationship.

"Over-affectionate gushing" is a blend of affective overdrive and engulfment with a soupçon of airbrushing. It can emanate from someone who is intent on being a good object for the other. As in airbrushing, the other person is seemingly over-valued, but in this case, it is through an undiscriminating warm sentimentality aroused by the other's supposedly marvelous attributes, rather than through a cooler prettifying of them. Sometimes the person is swept away by the seeming beauty of his or her own loving, effusive, affectionate feelings. Those driven compulsively to cast a positive aura are often defending themselves against a sense of inadequacy, unworthiness, or emptiness. The over-affectionate person makes the other feel bound to him or her through an emotive intensity that isn't commensurate with the relationship's actual value for each person. Not responding to the affection carries the implication that the targeted individual is hard-hearted. To avoid the shame of seeming cold, the person may force him- or herself to cooperate with the affectionate program, thus losing touch with the "truer" self.

Martyrdom, Emotional Blackmail, and Coercion

"Martyrdom" is an attitude that, in the context of an intimate relationship, can lead some people to refrain from even the most obvious self-interested pursuits. The attitude toward someone exerting energy on their behalf to turn on the proverbial light is "Oh no, don't trouble yourself, I'll just sit in the dark." Offering to take the hit—that is, to accept the disadvantaged position—is a bid to arouse the other's guilt while also falsely promoting oneself as too "good" to put one's own needs first. Self-serving rather than altruistic, it gives a semblance of selfless rectitude that is hard to challenge.

A consideration of martyrdom naturally leads into the broader realm of "emotional blackmail." While I found 42 references to this phrase in the PEP-Web archive, none of them treated the concept to its very own article, and I will not attempt to correct that relative neglect here. Emotional blackmail in all its variety is too common an experience to seem to warrant all that much exposition. Interpersonal extortion co-opts another's psychic state, thereby generating anxiety, guilt, and shame in the other for the blackmailer's own ends.

An overt, and at the same time somewhat pathetic example involves a man, Derek, whose beloved cousin lay gravely ill in a hospital in a distant city. His brother, who lived near the elderly woman and was her designated caretaker, threatened Derek that he had better be both nice and complimentary toward him if he wanted to be kept in the loop about their cousin's cancer treatment. The brother, an immature, vitriolic man, was the sole possessor of and conduit for this information, as the hospital refused to share information with more than one family member. Derek himself lived too far away to fill this function, so he was at the mercy of his brother's willingness to convey the information. Derek felt he had been criticized, undermined, or slandered by his brother many times over, and so could only barely be civil to him, much less complimentary. Yet if he didn't accede to the brother's demand, he risked not hearing of downturns in their cousin's health before it would be too late to journey to her bedside for a final visit. Derek was enraged at his brother's effort to extract warmth from him and at the same time was saddened at how low the brother had sunk in trying to squeeze insincere approval from him. His understanding of the reasons behind his brother's ploy was insufficient to temper his outrage, as the manipulative aspect of the ultimatum outshouted his understanding. Neither giving in to the brother's demand nor refusing to do so could really work. This left Derek greatly conflicted as to how to play a role in the last stages of his cousin's life. Placing him in that paralyzing, powerless bind was itself an additional layer to his brother's revenge.

Emotional blackmail is a devious way of influencing the other, while "coercion itself is often quite direct. The experience of being strong armed to do or feel something that is contrary to one's proclivity is inherently invalidating and therefore potentially micro-traumatic to the one being pressured. It undermines the feeling of being the captain of one's own ship, eroding faith in one's own power. Studying the nature of forceful suasion in psychoanalytic treatment, Ginsburg and Cohn (2007) cite the *Random House dictionary* definition of coerce: "To compel by force, intimidation, or authority, esp. without regard for individual desire or volition. To dominate or control, esp. by exploiting fear, anxiety" (p. 55).

In fact, I had to use some coercion to get myself to read the first few pages of their masterful article on the subject, as doing so brought up painful, countertransferential "bad analyst" feelings (Epstein, 1999) that I would have preferred to fend off. But as is often the case with challenging intellectual tasks, this self-coercion paid off, as Ginsburg and Cohn's (2007) account was illuminating. The authors note that coercive mechanisms are jointly evoked by the therapeutic contract (including the technique and procedures) and by the pre-existing psychic tendencies of the two participants. In four closely discussed cases, coercive dynamics are shown to arise: within the triad of patient, analyst, and supervisor due to the training needs of the analyst; at the juncture of "converting" a psychotherapy into a psychoanalysis; in relation to the analyst's request that the patient use the couch instead of remaining face-to-face; in the patient's refusal to talk; in certain types of intervention involving interpretation and suggestion; and so forth. So many opportunities to coerce the other, even when one's fundamental intention is well-meaning!

In one instance, Mrs. X, a 30-year-old patient with a history of paternal incest, had given up a trusting bond with a female therapist in order to begin an analysis with a male clinician. Her self-devaluation and avoidance of intimacy were expressed in her remaining mute session after session. Over time, this made the analyst feel increasingly powerless, to which he responded by becoming excessively active, "barraging" Mrs. X with interpretations and queries about the silence. This approach further overwhelmed and silenced the patient, as it led to her feeling she was again the object of a male's inappropriate, possibly sexual interest. At some juncture, the analyst became able to identify his own coerciveness and understand it as a countertransferential enactment of isolated and helpless feelings, aroused by the patient's inhibited participation. In time, this self-understanding brought positive consequences:

> Mrs. X eventually became aware that her protracted silences were a form of coercion. As the analyst acknowledged that each was pressuring the other out of conflicted needs for further engagement, Mrs. X felt more valued at being recognized as having force and influence. However, she then worried that the analyst would lose interest in her unless she engaged him in a coercive or seductive interaction. The ultimate recognition of coercive elements in the analysis and their *raison d'être* proved to be an invaluable clue to Mrs. X's level of resistance, as well as to the complexion of her object world and the analyst's countertransference. During the course of a lengthy treatment, concerns about her inherent value, as opposed to her perception of being an object of exploitation, were laboriously worked through. Mrs. X was eventually able to achieve a reasonable degree of trust in the analyst as an ally in the analytic process.
>
> (Ginsburg & Cohn, 2007, p. 72)

Ginsburg and Cohn ponder what drives either analyst or patient to be coercive, and how the power structure in different therapeutic stances might lay the groundwork for this:

> We hypothesize a causal connection between coercion by an analyst and his or her need for power in response to feelings of helplessness,

frustration, and failure. Hoffman (1996) states that "the analyst's personal involvement in the analytic situation has, potentially, a particular kind of concentrated power because it is embedded in a ritual in which the analyst is set up to be a special kind of authority" (p. 120). This power is most likely to be exercised by an analyst under duress. In the opposite situation—when an egalitarian ideal for the analytic dyad is subscribed to—the analyst may surrender authority under similar duress and feel more and more a victim of coercion by the patient. There is great potential for therapeutic change in the working through of these experiences of mutual coercion.

(pp. 74–75)

As I see it, neither the hierarchical power structure of yesteryear's analytic relationship nor the current democratic style is a guarantee against coercing or being coerced by the other on either the analyst's or the patient's part. I would argue, further, that it isn't always crystal clear or objectively verifiable when exerting influence over another amounts to coercion. Sometimes the intent to wield influence is subjectively experienced as excessive forcefulness, where others might not view it as such; that is, whether or not influence rises to the level of coercion may be in the eye of the beholder. This of course complicates efforts to work through its impact. To some extent, the same is true with the other micro-traumatic mechanisms I've articulated.

Where the psyches of analyst and patient lend themselves to its occurrence, a coercive enactment may be overdetermined and inevitable. Ginsburg and Cohn spell out conditions where this may be so on the patient's side:

Coercive enactments are more prevalent in patients with certain types of conflicts and personality structures, and viewing such enactments through the lens of coercion offers a better understanding of such patients. For example, it seems likely that coercion is a major mechanism used by individuals with a predominance of sadomasochistic fantasies or behaviors. It is also probable that significant coercion occurs during the analysis of individuals with a tendency to form desperate dependency bonds, associated genetically with failures of attachment and separation-individuation.

(p. 74)

Having the enactment take place has the silver lining of revealing underlying intrapsychic elements that need attention. These elements can then be opened to analytic scrutiny and (one hopes) repair. When the problematic character structure exists on the *clinician's* side of the equation, we can only hope that the countertransference will come under the supervisory scrutiny necessary to curtail coercion on the analyst's part.

Sometimes the use of coercion is warranted notwithstanding its negative aspects, whether in psychoanalytic treatment or in everyday life. This occurs for example when the suasion's goal actually is in the long-term interest of the one being coerced. Productive nudging of oneself to take on something whose gratifying aspect comes only later is part and parcel of self-discipline and the development of ego strength. Parents may need to coerce their children to take needed medications even if they taste foul, and societies coerce their members to abide by laws and regulations that, while not immediately gratifying, do serve their own or the collective's fundamental interests. The trick is to determine whether or not the coerced individual really is benefitted by the pressure or whether it just suits the coercing one to think so. I think that the experience of being coerced, however beneficial the result, is inevitably micro-traumatic when it becomes a pattern rather than a one-time event. Habitual coercive influence ends up replacing one's ability to develop one's own sense of how to direct one's actions, whose results one can test out for oneself. An eroding sense of agency is micro-traumatic indeed.

Non-recognition

"Non-recognition" of the other is an attitude that can be exceptionally painful and undermining. It cuts to the quick because it potentially invalidates not only one's efforts, but also one's whole being. Non-recognition casts doubt on the expression of one's "effectance," the urge to put forth one's vital energy in order to make things happen in the world (see Greenberg, 1991).

A person I treated some years ago was systematically shut down and dismissed by her family for her supposed over-sensitivity. From what I could tell, this sensitivity was an understandable response to their impersonal and neglectful treatment of her. They related to her as if she were without specific qualities or needs. Her psychological-mindedness, which was astute and constructively applied, came under attack by family members at every turn throughout her life. The family's view of her changed, though only temporarily, when her grandparents' issues with aging led to serious discord between them; the granddaughter's ability to articulate the emotional issues at stake rescued the elderly marital pair from sinking into depression and a fatally divisive relationship. The other family members briefly caught on to how the woman's intervention eased the grandparents' relationship with each other. They expressed some limited appreciation, to the woman's delight. Soon, though, they went back to ignoring or forgetting her contribution to the improvement, and she was disheartened to realize that her sensitivity would likely always go back to being dismissed as more of a weakness and annoyance than a strength. Our analytic work centered on helping her mourn this non-recognition from her family and move on to greener emotional pastures, where her giftedness would be enjoyed and celebrated.

Benjamin (1990, 2004) views the breakdown in one person's recognition of the other as a route to the often-destructive state of "complementarity," or polarized relations within a dyad. More specifically, there's a split between a giver and a taker, the doer and the one done-to, or a powerful and a powerless one. The persona of each is whittled down to just a few major attributes, as either the weak-seeming or the strong-seeming one in the relational dynamic. Either of these polar roles restricts the subjectivity of oneself and the other. Other aspects of self have to remain dissociated or negated, which is at least *micro*-traumatic, if not *massively* so.

At times we ourselves fail to recognize one or another aspect of our own selfhood; whatever damage this does is compounded when this same recondite aspect remains uninvited or ignored by the analyst as well. Philip Bromberg (1994) views the analyst's non-recognition of dissociated, "unspeakable" parts of the patient's psyche as "equivalent to relational abandonment," which (in his experience) can lead to the patient feeling that the analyst doesn't *want* to know him or her. Here we are moving directly into the territory of micro-trauma. In Bromberg's view:

> [I]t is in the process of "knowing" one's patient through direct relatedness, as distinguished from frustrating, gratifying, containing, empathizing, or even understanding him, that those aspects of self which cannot "speak" will ever find a voice and exist as a felt presence owned by the patient rather than as a "not-me" state that possesses him.
>
> (p. 537)

Bromberg is highlighting how the clinician may fail to engage aspects of the patient's self that are "bad-me" or even "not-me." It is through a full appreciation of the unguarded personal relating between analyst and patient that those unacceptable parts can be apprehended, so that analytic non-recognition does not compound and worsen the patient's dissociated state. That said, actual recognition of the disturbing parts of the patient's self can have its own injurious aspect, given how anxiety-provoking it can be to tolerate one's own darker elements.

More broadly speaking, psychoanalytic theorizing durably upsets and micro-traumatizes the patient to the degree that it engages in the non-recognition or misrecognition of critical aspects of an individual's experience. One of the many ways this can occur is exemplified in Stephen Mitchell's (1988) view of the developmental tilt toward theorizing psychic life through the lens of early life, with the result that adult phenomena are reduced to mere latter-day extensions or versions of infantile modes of being. Another non-recognition involves seeing the self too narrowly—say, as the product of only two drive states—rather than acknowledging a fuller range of motivating factors, another theme of Mitchell's (1988). While these are potential potholes for classically-influenced clinicians, contemporary relational clinicians may overemphasize observable interpersonal functioning at the expense of elaborating unconscious life, another way a central dimension of self-experience may go unseen. Bromberg (1994) maintains succinctly that it is up to the analyst

> to be as attuned as possible to those moments when application of "technique" has replaced a stance centrally organized by ongoing involvement with the patient's experience. A pattern of pointless retraumatization in analysis can take as many forms as there are analytic techniques, and any systematized analytic posture holds the potential for repeating the trauma of nonrecognition, no matter how useful the theory from which the posture is derived.
>
> (p. 537)

The structure of psychoanalytic work itself, with the roles of relatively dependent patient and relatively expert analyst, can also lead to a non-recognition of other psychosocial aspects of the patient's life. I have been shocked on more than one occasion to learn from some third-party that a certain patient was functioning much differently, for better or worse, in the "real world" than I'd understood from my own experience of him or her in my office. I realize that I may inadvertently have under- or overestimated the person in a way that could have been harmful to him or her or to the treatment process itself. We have all heard patients complain about various biases in an analyst's interpretive bent or practice; we have felt their despair at being unheard or unseen in this regard. We need to watch for the potential for micro-traumatizing our patients due to our own propensities that overly highlight or create "bright spots" (McLaughlin, 1991) in relation to *some* elements, while leaving other important ones shrouded in darkness.

A different sort of professional non-recognition occurs among psychoanalysts themselves in relation to their academic work. As in other fields, when a newcomer to a particular topic takes it up, he or she may not go to the trouble of fully seeking out, acknowledging, and building upon prior theorists' contributions in the same arena. Non-recognition of earlier relevant work (now more accessible than ever in the PEP-Web archive) has the effect of seeming to invalidate or even nullify those efforts. Furthermore, packing "old wine in new bottles" is not only disheartening, to say the least, for the original writers, but it may also be disheartening for the readers who are dismayed to realize they've just wasted time retracing pathways already trodden. Of course, a colleague's prior work may be overlooked through honest mistake or chance rather than callous indifference to the matter (regrettably, perhaps in this very book!) Whatever the motive, ignoring others' work product—in our field and others—is potentially micro-traumatic to those overlooked.

Wearing Teflon, Spoiling, and Deception

A particular form of micro-trauma involves one individual figuratively "wearing Teflon," the latter of course being the coating put on metal and other materials that reduces friction and lets them slough off grease and stains. Wearing Teflon, then, is the ability to slough off one's flaws or mistakes, and it is often accompanied by the tendency to externalize and attribute them to someone or something else. Both of these aspects can have a micro-traumatic impact on the person witnessing them, especially when the blame unjustly boomerangs back on him or her, as sometimes happens. This second person registers consciously or unconsciously what is going on, but he or she is powerless to get the Teflon-coated other to own his or her own role. Something did go wrong, so the responsibility must belong somewhere. At the same time, it seems unfair to the truly innocent party to be expected to absorb the fault oneself. This generates perplexity, self-questioning, frustration and resentment, self-denigration, or all of the above in the person saddled with the disavowed culpability.

Individuals with narcissistic issues are particularly prone to the Teflon-coated moves of denying any badness or imperfection in oneself by feigning innocence over a transgression. Often they try to put the lion's share of guilt onto another while they go their own merry way. Describing the grandiose operation of "deflecting blame," McWilliams and Lependorf (1990) present a narcissistic supervisee who, being blocked from trying to inflate the number of supervised hours he'd completed, tried to make the supervisor seem like the one acting badly:

> Several years ago, one of us worked with a brilliant, attractive, talented, and quite grandiose analyst-in-training. For about a year, the atmosphere of the supervision was delightful, as both parties engaged in what amounted to a *folie à deux* of mutual idealization. The supervisor, out of her own narcissistic pathology, joined this man in believing that reported problems with previous supervisors derived from his having been insufficiently appreciated by, or even having been felt as threatening to, these therapists. Then he sought her collusion in over-reporting his hours of control analysis to the institute. (He believed that he had had so much equivalent training that his background fulfilled the "spirit" if not the letter of the training provisions, and that the particulars of the program requirements were needlessly stringent.) She refused. He abruptly devalued her, as he had his previous instructors, but since it was in his interest to maintain the relationship until he had passed a Case Presentation requirement, he stayed in supervision. When she tried to make ego-alien his narcissistic entitlement, he accused her of acting out all kinds of unpleasant dynamics, including having contributed to his expectation of special favors by her prior warmth and support, which he now labeled seductive and transferential. He was, of course, right to a considerable extent, as narcissistically defensive people, with their hypervigilant sensitivity to others, often are.
>
> He somehow structured the psychological situation as follows: "If you deny your part in the dynamic, you are self-deluded and therefore not worth listening to; if you admit it, you and I can lament your shortcomings together, construe my actions as responsive to your mistakes, and avoid looking at my own problems." It is very difficult to turn this bind into a learning situation for the trainee. We have each seen examples of narcissistically preoccupied analysts-in-training who, by structuring their experience of supervision this way, develop a set of quite prescient beliefs about each of their teachers' dynamics, with no observable growth in their comprehension of their own.
>
> (p. 444)

As McWilliams and Lependorf understood it, narcissistic supervisees like this one are threatened by having their own imperfections and dependency unmasked. They assume that the supervisor shares the self-expectation of perfection. It suits them then to try to spread around the mortification by emphasizing the supervisor's weakness, thereby appearing to level the field and reduce the significance of their own flaws. The authors comment that in interactions with a narcissistic individual—and I would say, with anyone wearing Teflon—there will often be truth in the idea that the other is also faulty, but this is a convenient side-step and is quite beside the point. In general, an individual's sloughing off of guilt or shame may be micro-traumatic for anyone else involved in the matter, as the free-floating responsibility can readily land on and be internalized by those most prone to self-doubt, thereby further diminishing and disheartening them.

Then there is "spoiling." Nearly everyone from time to time has observed or been the target of another's spoiling tactics. As Melanie Klein (1958, 1975) explained, at a primordial level, the urge to spoil another's good inner feeling or the pleasure they take in something else may be born of envy, jealousy, or spite. The spoiling may take the form of directly marring what the other relishes, or a "sour grapes" stance of evincing disdain for something unattainable that one actually covets. The person toward whom this attitude is directed can feel foolish for valuing something whose worth is newly questioned. As for the perpetrator, the effort to render another person's peace of mind bankrupt brings a temporary, superficial relief of envy, but the satisfaction is bound to be incomplete. The spoiling operation is a misguided attempt to achieve inner happiness and self-esteem by reducing the differential between one's own and another's happier inner state. But the spoiling won't come close to compensating for this in any real sense. So ultimately, the spoiler ends up feeling as empty or emptier than before, with a world seeming increasingly bereft of goodness. The spoiler is "hoist with his own petard"—micro-traumatized by his own efforts to damage things for the other.

Last on my own list—though the reader will undoubtedly be able to name more—are "active and passive deceptions." These are rarely good, but they are particularly problematic when they occur in the guise of loving concern. Being lied to can be micro-traumatic to the one deceived, in that it generates mistrust in one's fellow human being and leaves one feeling stupid for allowing oneself to be duped. Of course, the damages inflicted by sins of commission and omission depend greatly on the perceived motivation of the deceiver as well as the circumstances of their discovery. Even a "little white lie," ostensibly proffered out of the impulse to save someone else from a distasteful truth, is often distressing when it undermines faith in the other's ongoing candor, when it rings hollow, or once the fuller truth belatedly emerges.

For a period of several years during elementary school, I would play ping-pong with my father once or twice a week after dinner. These times stood out, as I saw very little of my father, a harried, overworked surgeon, during my childhood years. In fact, the two of us had no other regular shared activity that I can recall. And to add to the delight of having his time and attention, I frequently won those games. Each time that happened, I was taken aback and thrilled, as athletic prowess was foreign to me, and in our family sports activity was confined to a few turns around an ice skating rink several times each winter. Wow, I thought, if a sport didn't require much physical strength or strategizing, I might be able to hold my own. I quietly cherished the idea that there might be some nascent physical capability in me that I could one day tap and really take advantage of.

However, the day came, late in high school, when my father offhandedly mentioned—"Oh, those ping-pong games? I *let* you win those." Of course! He had only been humoring me, out of a loving impulse. Somehow my mis-impression had stayed intact all those years. On uncovering the ruse, I was a bit disappointed that I hadn't really won; but much more so, I was horrified and ashamed of myself for not having caught on earlier, for incorrectly believing that I'd won fair and square and that my pride was rightful. Somehow, for me at least, prizing one's own significant talent or skill, only to be shown that one's satisfaction is baseless, is more humiliating than never having believed it at all.

Seattle (N)ice—A Compounded Micro-assault

Micro-traumatic relating sometimes takes the shape not of one particular pattern but an interweaving of several. Often, in what we could call "compounded micro-assaults," one mechanism breeds more. And sometimes it occurs not only in a given personal relationship, but as part of a widespread social pattern.

For instance, there is a type of subtly injurious functioning that by many accounts is endemic to the Pacific Northwest, where I live. This is a tendency for people to treat those outside their immediate family or long-term social circle with a type of friendly civility that is deceiving, in that it seems to promise a greater interest in becoming closer than is really meant. Julia Sommerfeld (2005), who penned a cover story about this in the *Seattle Times'* magazine, dubbed this way of relating "Seattle (n)ice," which she identified as "our social dis-ease." She describes how on first meeting someone new and perhaps afterward as well, there will be a kind of polite considerateness, with a subsequent pulling back from further interaction—hence the "ice" within the "niceness." The author is not alone in perceiving a contrast between "Seattle niceness" and the "Seattle freeze." She provides many anecdotal instances, backing it up with the observations of Jodi O'Brien, a professor of sociology at Seattle University, who is quoted as saying, "At the university, where people are hired from all over, this is a pretty standard conversation. Seattleites are often seen as having this veneer of pleasantness but being hard to come to know." Sommerfeld ponders the sources of this pattern:

> One theory points to the cloistering effect of cloudy skies. Another has it that the Seattle Nice/Ice phenomenon is rooted in a historic inter-section of Nordic-Asian reserve. It may be the influence of weekend mountain men or the influx of socially disinclined tech workers. It could be a trapping of mid-sized citydom—small enough to manage on your own but too big to care about your neighbors.
>
> Or perhaps it's all of the above: some confluence of factors that has created a perfect storm of antisociality.

The Seattle (n)ice experience is, in my terms, a compounded micro-trauma that blends airbrushing and excessive niceness with uneasy intimacy, followed in rapid succession by unkind cutting back. Non-recognition of the other and little murders may also be experienced within such interactions as well. In the several decades since I moved from New York to Seattle, I have heard this social phenomenon described by friends and patients multiple times. Its painfulness is most pronounced for transplants, who, as Sommerfeld notes, feel rejected, isolated, and ostracized as a result. There is a strong natural inclination to take the rejection as a vote of no confidence in oneself as a *person*, with the individual assuming that one is being seen as uniquely inferior or offensive in some fashion—or at best, simply uninteresting. This engenders humiliation that in turn may cause one to shrink from trying to connect with others further. The person despairs of being able to break through the reserve and is fearful that further rejection lies in wait behind it.

For many, Seattle (n)iceness is a bugaboo because it leaves them unclear as to how they are really being perceived and received, which in turn knocks their social calibrations off kilter. When someone responds with a continual "plastic smile," as Sommerfeld calls it, when you're just being yourself—which may sometimes involve being difficult or challenging—it creates the illusion that they are recognizing and receiving you favorably, that they can tolerate your outspokenness, or what have you. But if in fact they are airbrushing aspects they don't like, or masking their indifference toward or distaste for you, then they falsely raise your hopes that your way of being is acceptable and that a relationship is being built between you. The higher our expectations rise, the harder they fall. Such a deception creates a mini-experience of rejection. It potentially stimulates feelings of personal inadequacy and the specter of loneliness.

Undoubtedly, each region of the world, not to mention each country, has its signature ways of titrating intimacy, some of which are micro-traumatic both to newcomers and denizens alike. Sommerfeld's study of the Seattle version ends on an upbeat note, with her detailing the many ways those new to Seattle learn to adjust their expectations to the surround and protect themselves from further injury. One way they do so is to band together and bond over discussing their shared experiences, a process that may begin with someone lobbing the "ice-breaking" salvo: "So, have you been finding it's hard to get to know people in Seattle?" It's both fine and fitting that comparing one's micro-trauma with others in the same boat can itself be a mechanism for beginning to detoxify the experience.

Mutual Injury and its Resolution in a Clinical Session

A good clinical example of compounded micro-trauma, here playing out in the analytic relationship, comes from the acutely sensitive Philip Bromberg (2011). His patient, Martha, is a survivor of developmental trauma that involved an early experience of depersonalization and the ongoing sense of being "driven mad" by her disturbed and chronically enraged mother. Martha needs to feel entirely in synch with her analyst, to the extent that she denies, parries, or suppresses any feeling that would disrupt the pleasant tone between them. Bromberg offers her his analytic understanding of her psychic blockages, but she habitually evades engaging with his interpretive efforts. Her implicit cutting back on him generates more and more frustration in the analyst. However, he says little about this, as he is exquisitely sensitive to her fear of attachment rupture. He is leery of identifying disjunctions between them that could feel annihilating to her. Over time, he explains: "Martha's need to control how I experienced her increased in intensity, and its oppressiveness became for me (as it had with most of her previous therapists) the primary source of tension between us" (p. 83).

On the occasion Bromberg wishes to explore with us, the analyst is probing to learn more about the patient's having failed to come to a session. Martha laughingly reports that she had gone for a run in Central Park instead, having forgotten about their regularly scheduled appointment. She is delighted that she's not being self-critical about the mistake and is surprised that Bromberg isn't also pleased and amused at the incident. She asks how come, and Bromberg snaps at her that he doesn't see the humor in it, and adds: "What do you imagine I *am* feeling?" He quickly realizes this question was a mistake in both its content and tone. He had been irritated with her unconsciously and expressed it through a stance of "seriousness" that attempted to disguise the irritation. He adds that "there was enough displeasure in my voice about what I perceived as her effort to distract us from our 'task' to trigger *her* early warning system" (p. 84). Martha shrank into herself, shifted into a frightened little girl "self-state," responding emphatically, "*I'm too ugly to answer that question!*" The analyst reports that this is a part of Martha he had never seen but only heard about. Bromberg goes on to try to speak to the scared, ugly-feeling little girl part of her, but the patient becomes furious at the inquiry, apparently feeling further shamed and threatened by it. The analyst then feels hurt at the patient's failure to appreciate his analytic sensitivity and acuity. But the patient relaxes her attack and explains that their interchange confuses her and she's not up to discussing his points. She reveals that she does hear an inner voice that suggests to her that she's healthy, but she's afraid that showing a healthy aspect will draw unwanted attention to herself. Bromberg acknowledges having been a "stuffed shirt" in his response to her earlier laughter. He confesses that he failed to grasp that she was showing him her healthy side by revealing that she'd enjoyed her time spent away from him, and also by not castigating herself for having missing the session.

In this exchange, each of the two, analyst and patient, had inadvertently slighted the other, resulting in a micro-assault on the other's sense of self-worth and equanimity. But as they get back in touch with the other's fundamentally good intentions, each one softens and lets down his or her scrappy defensiveness and conveys regret at having been hurtful. The patient is glad her analyst admits and rues that he had seemed critical of her. She responds with the gift of admitting to him that there's a secret "healthy voice" within her now. Reflecting back on their tangle, Bromberg tells us:

I had, until then, been dissociating the part of me that could pleasurably connect with that part of her, because, like Martha, I was afraid of exposing my own capacity to hurt and be hurt should I compromise the part of myself that I relied upon to protect me from exposure, the safe anchorage of being a serious, that is to say, "well-regulated," analyst.

(p. 88)

The hurtful exchange had, in Bromberg's terms, "awakened the dreamer"— the dissociated healthy, if vulnerable part—in them both.

In the hands of someone as attuned as Bromberg, such an interaction can (and in this case, did) evolve in a highly therapeutic direction. Two people can wound each other momentarily and still regain enough contact with their loving and generative feelings toward each other that one or another can initiate repair. They end up all the wiser for it, having indeed reintegrated that which had been hidden within them.

Let's now look at the interchange through the amplifying lens of micro-trauma. We can see certain injuries accruing alongside healthy self-assertion on each participant's part. We could say that Martha has a history of cutting back on Bromberg, by leaving his formulations one-sided, neither recognizing them nor grappling with them enough to correct and realign them. This leaves Bromberg feeling he has little traction with her, a most unsettling sensation for an analyst. Martha delivers the *coup de grâce*, as cutbacks go, by missing their session rather than, say, cancelling it in advance. No doubt it was, as they come to understand, an ambivalent expression of growth, separation, and independence from the treatment relationship. But being ambivalent, the cutback also has some degree of passive aggression toward the analyst and the analytic process. All of this amounts to a little murder of the analyst and his analytic function. Martha's laughing attitude toward the experience, and her belief that the analyst should find it funny too, suggests a certain sort of emotional coercion, in the same sense that she has tried to nudge him into a semblance of emotional harmony with her throughout the analysis. Perhaps Bromberg had put too much pressure on himself to accede "with a smile" to the patient's efforts to control him. He has to be "too kind" (and he therefore remains painfully isolated from her) in order to keep her anxiety at bay, and the pain and frustration at doing so in turn micro-damages him. Finally, provoked beyond his limit, he seemingly corners her, saying "What do you imagine I *am* feeling?"

I wonder whether this query, which Bromberg himself calls a mistake, poses too much of a challenge to Martha. It puts her on the spot micro-traumatically, making her feel inadequate and confused. Perhaps this is why she unravels further at this point, calling herself "too ugly" to respond. Bromberg is shocked and puzzled by the retort, but also resonates with this vulnerable part of the patient. He probes its meaning with her, offering some acute observations that he later ironically dubs "brilliant." These interventions may have felt to her like connoisseurship, being so refined or complex that they only confused her further. No wonder she becomes for the first time firmly and explicitly angry at him—and this anger is a breakthrough. Now the patient's angry criticism of him is *legible* to the analyst, and he responds with hurt and shame. It is the analyst's apparent woundedness and the patient's attunement to that woundedness, that lets the patient take a self-assertive stance at this point:

> We each "knew" the other person without questioning how we knew what we knew—and part of what was known was that we both could accept having our vulnerability exposed. It was implicit, mutual, and powerful, and in turn brought us nearer to one another without sacrificing our respective individualities.
>
> (p. 86)

Once the analyst recognizes his own sometime inadequacy and feels a degree of shame about it, and the patient can register the analyst's embracing of that shame, then the patient can feel more of an equal. The result is an increase in self-respect that is enormously therapeutic to her. Hindsight is more likely than foresight to be 20/20, but if Bromberg could have allowed himself to be less than "well-regulated," if he could have let himself know *but also sympathize with himself* for the fact that the patient's strictures were strait-jacketing him even before the skipped session, then perhaps the tension would not have built up in him. It is helpful—but a desideratum that is often elusive—when we clinicians can note and accept the experience of being micro-traumatized by our patients' psychic demands on us in real time, at each turn in the road. The analyst in this encounter does the next best thing, grasping his own distress and reflecting on it in time, so all can go well.

To generalize from this vignette, there are *inflection points* at which a chain of micro-traumatic interactions is redirected into becoming a psychically *strengthening* one for one or both parties. At such a point, one's own narcissistic need is assuaged enough, one senses enough equality between self and other, and one cares about the other's feelings enough, that the defensively assaultive processes can indeed be rerouted toward health. Micro-trauma that is compounding can be a juggernaut toward emotional disaster, unless and until the participants reach that pivotal moment and things change. An important aim of this chapter and of the book in general is to help the analytic therapist become more attuned to the kinds of momentary, seemingly minor events that are micro-assaultive to someone's sense of self-worth and well-being. These can then be turned into constructive pauses involving shared reflection that catalyzes faster and more intensive growth in the patient—and often in the analyst as well.

Note

1 On the one hand, overstimulating childhood environments may heighten the likelihood of emotional intensity. On the other hand, they can also sometimes heighten suppressive defenses *against* stimulation and excitement. Sometimes the suppression is itself emotionally charged, as it was in a person who habitually responded to his analyst's inquiries with a loud, plaintive groan, trying to shut down further probing of his inner life.

Chapter 9

Toward Repair

We've now delved deeply into the nature of micro-trauma and some of its maneuvers and mechanisms. I've illustrated how many seemingly innocent incidents are worth noticing and looking into in slow motion, since they're often part of a subterranean patterning that blights one's underlying sense of well-being and ends up having major relational consequences. Indeed, accumulated micro-traumatic experience often causes low-level currents of depression and anxiety that result not only in outright neurosis, but also in the garden-variety unhappiness that seems so ubiquitous and hard to vanquish. Undiscovered micro-traumatic influences can explain why a person in psychoanalytic treatment may continue to feel dysphoric and why his or her psychological progress stalls, even after higher profile, more severe psychic issues have been analyzed and moved toward resolution.

This final chapter is devoted to some general considerations about micro-traumatic currents. I'll explore how they affect cross-generational relating, and say more about how they can be dealt with and worked through. Before closing, I'll speak to the sort of analytic attitude that, in my estimation, offers the most promise for repairing micro-traumatic injury. But first I'd like to make explicit something the reader has probably gleaned implicitly all along: nothing essentially new or specific needs to be added to our treatment toolkit to address micro-traumatic issues. We can approach them much as we would the dynamics caused by major traumatic events. As I've said, we do well to give special weight to the current manifestations of micro-trauma, both extra-therapeutically and in the analytic relationship. And we need to be careful not to underplay issues that first emerge during the adolescent and adult years, because small psychic injuries so often arise and begin accumulating then rather than earlier. This doesn't mean we should ignore potential historic roots, just that we should respect how impactful the later-occurring, smaller hurts can be.

"The devil is in the details," and once these are identified and addressed, the person can revisit the earlier unconscious factors that contribute to the negative impact those details may have on one's psychological development. Mapping this terrain can, I believe, go a long way toward eradicating recondite sources of lowered self-esteem and anxiety, which are hidden in plain sight because they're either too subtle or overly familiar. Appreciating the power these events develop in the aggregate can set the stage for the constructive reshaping of a person's characteristic self-defeating behavior and relational style.

So now let's move on to some general observations about cumulative psychic injury and how it is experienced over time. After one or more micro-traumatic experiences, a person is likely to be more vulnerable to any sort of rough treatment coming his or her way for some time. One's faith that others are well-intentioned (or at least not markedly malicious) is shaken, which in turn subverts one's emotional balance. The person may wonder if he or she can still trust an injuring loved one at all, if that loved one has proven capable of surreptitiously damaging behavior—What *other* harm may have been done, at present unbeknownst to the victim, that might only become apparent later on? What *further* harm could still newly occur?

Without a dogged, intensive effort to process the bruising experiences, it is rarely possible to render them harmless enough to be no longer consequential. Sometimes the injured party identifies with the aggressor, as in the attitude associated with the "Stockholm syndrome" (see Frankel, 2002), which leads him or her to redirect the techniques of micro-traumatic relating—say, cutting back or destructive connoisseurship—back outward and onto still others. Other times, these micro-traumatic techniques are turned back on the original perpetrator, which perpetuates a noxious cycle. Even if the recipient of micro-traumatic handling doesn't reenact the same sort of hurtful experience, the wounds tend to leave the damaged person bereft of the attunement and vitality needed to treat others as well as he or she otherwise would have. This can generate the collateral damage to others I've already talked about in the context of entrenchment.

The main arena for the dominant–submissive micro-traumatic dialectic is, as we've seen, between two parties, but ancillary roles can also arise in which a third party is experienced as an accomplice or enabler of damage, or more favorably, as a neutral witness or even potential rescuer (see Davies & Frawley, 1992). And the involvement can spread to a larger sphere, wherein one's extended family, one's work team or department, or a given circle of friends may become a network in which toxic maneuvers and protective measures become the currency of the realm.

However, sometimes micro-traumatic moments stay quite private, such that the pattern of injury is invisible to those outside the relationship's orbit. The one experiencing threat or harm in private may fear that, were it to come to light, others wouldn't acknowledge it or believe it actually happened. That is, the cutting back, uneasy intimacy, or unbridled indignation (for instance) won't be recognized by others as being as nasty and destructive as it truly was. The hurt person may have an intense reaction to the injury on the spot and may become self-consciously concerned that others will second-guess and criticize that reaction, which taken out of context may seem unrealistic, overblown, or even "crazy."

Victims of micro-trauma are of course themselves not always conscious of it, given how inconspicuous its machinations can be. But those who *are* aware are often compelled to convince others of the unseen harm done to them. The one plagued by micro-traumatic treatment may narrate the distressing experience over and over to clarify the nature of the injury and also as a form of catharsis. He or she may also need to denounce the perpetrator and then justify this denunciation at length, especially if the perpetrator is to all outward appearances well-meaning. Yet repeating the stories of the offensive treatment may fail to quell the inner dread that one's feelings aren't valid, that one is overreacting, that one's own badness or weakness is somehow to blame. The repetition compulsion involved here is an effort to master the interaction and dull its sting. Derek, who made an appearance earlier in Chapter 8's discussion of emotional coercion, found himself describing in great detail to anyone willing to listen how monstrously controlling his brother had been in the last stages of their cousin's illness. Pinioned by internal conflict, Derek had to revisit his experience and perceptions of the brother again and again, to see yet another listener's understanding nod, in order to reassure himself that his refusal to engage his brother was justifiable, even as it thwarted his wish to be involved in the care of his ailing cousin.

Drawing again from Ogden's (2010) slant on Fairbairn's theory, I would say that re-narrating is an effort to harness the good will of an external good object as a way of potentially overriding the internal saboteur and its bond with the inner rejecting object. One hopes that the untainted new good object will become convinced (and in a way that becomes internalizable), to finally prove to the inner enemy that one was indeed "aggressed against," that one's complaint has merit, and that the ill-treatment does not mean one isn't worthy or good. This is generally to no avail.

There is also the question of how we retrospectively view and metabolize having been micro-traumatized in previous years by someone we currently experience in a more favorable light. A figure who was once quick to tease or sling put-downs may mature and become kinder and gentler, perhaps owing to salutary developments in his or her own life over time. The earlier harmful dynamic still affects the former victim, perhaps having etched its way into his or her character, though the perpetrator's erstwhile destructiveness is not still operative. That past-to-present discrepancy can undermine the victim's conviction about what happened before, causing him or her to lose touch with what initially eroded his or her sense of well-being.

In a sense then, a previously damaging other is an "indefinite bad object," a troublesome figure, whether external or internalized, who eludes articulation and won't hold still, so to speak. Thinking back on their wedding day from the vantage point of a later anniversary, one spouse will turn to the other and ask whether their best friend's toast at the reception really *was* snide, or did he just imagine it having that nasty tone? The micro-traumatic memory of the little murder can get buried amid the inclination to dissociate the meanness that marred a significant moment.

So having a concept such as micro-trauma or cumulative psychic injury helps us attend to the ways in which others have indeed been *partially* malignant, *situationally* destructive, or *previously* toxic to us. As an example of a figure who was only situationally destructive (and therefore confusingly so), consider an intern in a research laboratory who'd counted herself fortunate at how reasonable and understanding her supervisor was and what a great working relationship they'd had for the first eight months of her tenure in his lab. The intern had built up trust in the supervisor's belief in her, which supported her growing confidence in herself as a budding research scientist. Then all of a sudden, as the deadline for reporting their results approached, the supervisor turned harsh and almost dictatorial toward the student. So many revisions were demanded, based on increasingly trivial-seeming criticisms, that the intern began to question whether she was up to the demands of being in this field. Having started to internalize his heretofore approving view of her, the intern had gotten drawn into the supervisor's psychic constellation and now overidentified with his hyper-perfectionistic connoisseurship tendencies. If she'd been alerted to the doings of micro-trauma, the intern might have been able to reflect on the possibility that the supervisor himself had a harsh, self-critical inner voice, now becoming externalized and enacted in destructive connoisseurship within their working relationship. She could thereby have avoided being so swayed by the supervisor's hyper-stringency, which could have allayed her own mounting self-criticalness. Of course, stepping out of an interpsychic bind such as that with a powerful other is notoriously hard to do, especially without the aid of a psychoanalytic clinician occupying a "third" position (whether in the flesh or as an internalized presence) in the psychic force-field.

On the one hand, some degree of micro-traumatic experience in one's relationships is inevitable, given the human need to feel worthy and the human propensity to feel anxious, guilty, and depressed when one doesn't. Society's pressures on us to function in a socially acceptable fashion require us to mask our aggressive urges, but the conflict between pursuing our own goals and seeking social approval sets the stage for many a subtle enactment. We are loath to court the other's disagreement or anger, and hoping to avert these (should we be forthright about our self-interested motivations), we let our needs and wishes emerge indirectly instead. This devious self-assertion itself can generate veiled psychic injury that begets more of the same.

On the other hand, and in the spirit of the truism that "what doesn't kill us makes us stronger," it could be argued that micro-traumatic interactions help us build up the capacity to withstand hostility without crumbling. These experiences when they occur in manageable doses spur the development of adequate defenses. (Perhaps this is the function of teasing, which can be so damnably ubiquitous in childhood and beyond.) And some individuals actually appear to be fortified internally against being damaged by micro-traumatic interaction. They let micro-assaults roll off their back or they turn the other cheek, seemly unscathed by them. If we could understand just what constitutional givens or socialization patterns led to this hearty resilience, the knowledge would be worth bottling and selling worldwide! And actually, we do have one very good idea, in general terms. That is, we have plenty of data (e.g., Beebe & Lachmann, 2014; Cassidy & Shaver, 1999; Mikulincer & Shaver, 2012) that suggest that when the child comes from a secure attachment background, where both needs for attachment and self–object functions were met, the child will develop a greater degree of psychological heartiness than otherwise. Such resilience hardly confers blanket immunity to psychic injury that might occur in later years, but it should make it easier to process the wounds earlier and thereby escape their worst effects. (Later in this chapter, I will discuss this issue in terms of developing an "inner witness.") Conversely, insecure attachment in early childhood is associated with various patterns of aggressive and/or immature relating—just the sort of features that can qualify one as a micro traumatic aggressor or victim. But connecting the dots, so to speak, from the present relationship back to the early formative ones is not always easy. And regardless, the first order of business is to become clear as to what is going on in the present.

Though I haven't emphasized this heretofore for the sake of simplicity, let me also say that micro-traumatic functioning is rarely, if ever, unidirectional, with one party in the relationship always the victim and the other the perpetrator. Each person is likely to be hurtful toward the other from time to time, in any one relationship and in the sum total of the relationships he or she has over the life span. And as the author of this book and therefore a self-styled "curator" of micro-traumatic mechanisms, I must admit (in case the reader hasn't yet surmised it) that where I myself was personally involved in an injurious interchange, I was not necessarily always the one in the sympathetic position. On the contrary, I've unfortunately sometimes been the perpetrator. To the degree that this has been so, I nurse the hope that all the practice this book has given me in naming micro-traumatic mechanisms has further sensitized me to my own aggressive tendencies and lessened my propensity to inflict wounds—unless they were entirely called for! But joking aside, at the very least I'm more realistic about my being as capable of hurtful intentions as of praiseworthy ones, which is a step in the right direction. And becoming franker with oneself about one's own injurious proclivities helps reduce the resentment one might feel toward others for peddling similar wares.

Vagaries of the Working-through Process

The fact that micro-traumatic bruises are by their very nature often minor makes it easy for a person to entertain the possibility that they are not worthy of complaint or exploration. It's easy to second-guess this kind of seemingly detrimental exchange. Questions come up in therapy as to whether the troubling interchange really happened at all, or if it was as bad as it seemed at the time, or whether one is making a mountain out of a molehill. The patient wonders if he or she is being hypersensitive, a charge the offending party may have leveled on the spot in an attempt to deflect responsibility for being hurtful. The analyst may need to keep supporting the patient's exploration once the outlines of the pattern have been firmly established. At some point, she or he will need to tell the vacillating patient something like: "Really, the case is closed. We have every reason to believe that these things did happen and that they did mount up to become quite injurious. Now it's time to put aside your doubts so we can help you do the work to process and overcome the damage."

But it's not so easy. The troublesome patterning has, after all, become etched into the person's character structure, and it therefore pulls on him or her like quicksand. It is quite a challenge to fight the re-enactment of patterns that were originally shaped by similar kinds of negative interactions, especially since these are interlaced with elements that are actually gratifying and constructive. For instance, if you're taught to prove your worth via a toxic kind of connoisseurship, how do you soften or let those attitudes go without losing what was also stimulating and rewarding about them? If you've learned to look for injustices and express yourself indignantly, and this brings a certain degree of strength and meaning to your life, what can substitute for this? For that matter, it's also a challenge to withstand the loss of the (paradoxically) protective function sometimes offered by being in the underdog role. If you're used to being entrenched in self-diminishment, how can you tolerate allowing yourself to feel worthy without running the risk of coming across as "conceited"? Or if you're entrenched in self-contentment, how to tolerate admitting some self-doubt without collapsing? How does one acknowledge having wrought collateral damage without unbearable shame, and what does it mean to make reparations? There is also the problem of how one can belatedly build structures and capacities that one was debarred from building to begin with. So in airbrushing (for example), if you allow the scales to fall from your eyes and see what's inferior, bad, or wrong, how do you now bear the unvarnished truth, when you'd never learned how to do that before? An element of underdevelopment has to be compensated and corrected for. In the case of unkind cutting back, for instance, one must learn to stay present and figure out how to convey to the other that one feels like removing oneself because one is feeling hurt, demoralized, or what have you. Clearly, in many of these instances, there are social skills that will need to be worked on and newly acquired.

Micro-traumatic Relating at the Generational Divide

The generational divide is a frequent site of the inconspicuous wounding that can destructively accumulate. Psychosexual theories once explained intergenerational friction as a function of intrapsychic Oedipal dynamics wherein the child longed for one parent and developed jealous hostility toward the other parent for having an exclusive sexual and emotional relationship with the first, longed-for one. The child felt deprived of a favored role vis-à-vis the desired parent and sought to rectify the situation by competing with the other parent as a rival. In the classical paradigm, resolving the Oedipal constellation leads to renunciation and psychological growth. Micro-traumatic sparring across the generations would be understood in these psychosexual terms as involving the instigation and playing-out of sexual and aggressive dynamics. And in truth, one sometimes encounters an interchange that appears to fit and could be well-described in these very terms. I think here of the sexualized-sounding incident described in Chapter 1, involving the provocative grandmother who insisted that the borrowed jacket worn by her grandson fit him "so much better" than it had fit his father, while the father himself was within earshot and potentially listening.

While still viewing it as an Oedipal-type struggle, Loewald (1980; see also Ogden, 2006) recast the generational feud, transforming it from a dynamic based on sexual desire and aggression into one based on establishing a sense of self-worth, efficacy, and viability as a separate individual. The child must necessarily battle the parents in order to become "emancipated" from their authority, a portion of which the child nonetheless internalizes as part of becoming his or her own sovereign, separate adult. My own thinking, grounded as it is in relational and interpersonalist theory, more readily harmonizes with Loewald's than with the classical psychosexual account in this regard. What is at stake in most moments of intergenerational friction, it seems to me, is each party's longing for narcissistic affirmation and continued attachment along with his or her desire to individuate. Yet to remain attached and at the same time be one's own person can often feel (and in certain unhealthy situations, can actually be) mutually incompatible. Pursuing one aim at the expense of the other can lay the groundwork for child or parent to feel micro-traumatized, especially if there is too much psychological insecurity in one or the other (or both) from the start.

Oftentimes, the damage ends up being especially problematic for just one of the two individuals, and quite often it's the younger person, whose life direction is at an especially formative stage. Loewald (1980) offers the clinical example of a young man who was badly stalled in his work on a graduate thesis, which happened to be in the same field as that of his deceased father. The student insisted that he alone bore responsibility for his lack of progress, yet he also actively sought support from the analyst and others, which Loewald viewed as reflecting ambivalence about his continued dependency on authorities. The young man's paralysis was interpreted as a delay that was unconsciously meant to stave off the "crime" of outdoing his dead father. Reflecting on the case, Loewald sees it as *normative* that there would be intensity and high stakes in the dynamic between the parent and an offspring emerging into adulthood. Insofar as Loewald's picture is apt, this developmental moment is ripe for micro-traumatic experience:

The clinical example puts into bold relief the ambiguity of adult responsibility and autonomy as considered in the light of the Oedipus complex and its vicissitudes in the course of life. In the process of becoming and being an adult significant emotional ties with parents are severed. They are not simply renounced by force of circumstances, castration threats, etc.—although these play an instrumental role—but they are also actively rejected, fought against, and destroyed to varying degrees. Perhaps this active rejection represents a "change of function," a form of taking over actively what had to be endured passively in the beginning. Be that as it may, in the course of what we consider as healthy development this active urge for emancipation comes to the fore (already in early phases of the separation-individuation process).

In the Oedipal struggle between the generations, the descendant's assuming or asserting responsibility and authority that belonged to the ascendants arouses guilt in the descendant (although not only guilt). It looks as if opponents are required with whom the drama of gaining power, authority, autonomy, and the distributing of guilt can be played out. In analytic work, and particularly as revived in the transference, we see this in magnified form.

(pp. 388–389)

Even more bluntly, Loewald adds:

In an important sense, by evolving our own autonomy, our own superego, and by engaging in non-incestuous object relations, we are killing our parents. We are usurping their power, their competence, their responsibility for us, and we are abnegating, rejecting them as libidinal objects. In short, we destroy them in regard to some of their qualities hitherto most vital to us. *Parents resist as well as promote such destruction no less ambivalently than children carry it out.* What will be left if things go well, is tenderness, mutual trust, and respect, the signs of equality. This depends, more than on anything else, on the predominant form of mastery of the Oedipus complex.

(p. 390, italics added)

Each participant in the dyad—the parent as well as the child—both wants and dreads having the power transfer occur, as there are both losses and gains for each in the transition. Any situation that is as full of ambivalence as the struggle for mutual separation and individuation between parent and child may well engender the anxiety and aggression that can end up being expressed micro-traumatically. And part of the reason that there is such ambivalence is the presence within each person of conflicting needs—namely, the need for continued appreciative involvement with the other and for greater independence from the other (with the parent needing independence from the child as well as vice versa).

We've been looking so far at the general, historic patterns that seem to describe Loewald's young man and his difficulty in completing a project that would ensure his progression into his father's area of expertise. If we flesh out some imaginary specifics for this case, we can posit other patterns of a micro-traumatic nature that might have contributed in the here and now to the man's blockage. Perhaps the young man had a thesis advisor who, though supposedly enthusiastic about the project, engaged unconsciously in unkind cutting back. The advisor could have failed to review the student's research drafts promptly, could have delayed responding to email updates on the project, could have been late for advisory meetings, and so forth. It is easy to envision the student getting quite tangled up in and hurt by that relationship, and this in turn could have contributed to eroding his motivation for doing the work itself. We would certainly want to look at such a situation along Loewald's lines for the historic influences, but it would be important as well to examine the contemporary impact of the advisor's unkind cutting back (and any other potentially obstructive factor) on this man's problematic functioning. What role might the current authority figure have played in the blockage of the young man's graduate progression, on top of any residual issues vis-à-vis the young man's dead father? In other words, we'd need to ask, along Levenson's (1991) lines: "What is going on around here?"

Coming back to a point I made a moment ago about conflicted wishes in relation to the parent–child bond, it is also true more generally (and not just at the generational divide) that a micro-traumatic state often arises when there are several interwoven, mutually conflicting needs within the same individual. Let's say that a middle-level employee, Ursula, wants to move up a particular progression ladder within the corporation for which she works. Continuing the imagined scenario, perhaps this involves working with certain co-workers who happen to be overly competitive and back-biting, while also being highly competent and having a lot to teach. Ursula prefers a nurturant and cooperative environment, but she also wishes to progress along that specific pathway and to develop the expertise these other employees already have and can impart to her (intentionally or not). In a situation like this, the employee in question would have to learn to tolerate the overcompetitive environment—and to bear the slights and insecurity that come with it—in order to get the benefit of being on that team, learning from those peers, and ultimately progressing in the desired way. But doing so could create a chronic state of low-level micro-trauma. Looking at this from a different angle, a person will sometimes be inclined to make a choice that inevitably (either predictably or by surprise) sticks him or her in the situation of having to keep relating to an injurious other. (Certain people unfortunately find themselves in this predicament vis-à-vis their in-laws, for example.) Psychic injury of some kind will likely be unavoidable in this scenario. In addition, where an erstwhile victim has indeed been able to pull away from a toxic relational situation, he or she may eventually end up getting drawn back into it, in reality or in his or her imagination, as a means of meeting *another* need whose pursuit was provisionally forfeited in forsaking the maladaptive pattern. (This relates to the oft-observed phenomenon that an abused child tends to remain quite attached to the abusing parent, notwithstanding that bond's damaging elements.) Micro-traumatic interaction can be quite sticky, making it hard for the person to escape unconflictedly and with peace of mind intact.

Bridging the Generational Divide

How can enactments across the generational divide be parsed more closely and reworked healthfully? In an elegant paper, "As generations speak," psychoanalyst Dodi Goldman (2010) describes a 22-year-old man who begins to share a dream with his therapist, only to interrupt it to answer his cell phone. Upon finishing his animated conversation, the patient is invited by the therapist to return to the dream. He responds (and I paraphrase): "Oh, are you still interested in *that*?—Whatever!" Goldman reports having felt in response that his analytic values were being summarily dismissed. From the standpoint of the thesis of this book, we could understand this as a reaction to the patient's micro-traumatic handling of him—that is, the young man's cutting back (answering the phone call), as well as engaging in a non-recognition, a little murder, or both. In return, Goldman catches himself falling into the trap of being critical of the young man. He stops short and queries his own motives for this, leading to some profound reflections on both his own and the patient's psychological positions:

> I am annoyed with him—prefer to think of him as "degraded," impoverished," "perverse"—because he is, among other things, communicating his disillusionment, not only with his own childhood, but with my generation's promise as well. His presence revives memories of

my own youth left unfulfilled and forces me to become more aware of what I prefer to dissociate: the abandoned imagination of my adolescence.

And what is more: I envy the young man's amplified shape shifting because it is better suited to the restlessness and flux of our time than anything I can possibly muster. He is comfortable with simultaneity while my mind is primed for the sequential. He has developed, far better than I, what Robert J. Lifton (1993) calls a "protean self."

(p. 486)

This "protean self," Goldman goes on to explain, is not something wishy-washy, but is in Lifton's view "an expression of human resilience in an age of fragmentation." So the young man's way of being, far more "adjusted to accelerated distractions" than his therapist's, makes him readier for the future than is the therapist himself (Goldman, 2010, p. 486). Goldman's rueful diagnosis of this particular patient–therapist disjunction is that there is a shallowness in what he calls the "generational dialogue" between them. This breakdown in self- and mutual understanding between the therapist and patient reflects something more fundamental in the patient— namely, the glaring absence of psychic dialogue between the patient and his *father*, who had died when the patient was young. By engaging in this sort of empathic/introspective reflection on the longings, anxieties, frustrations, and enviousness of each of them as they are revealed in the micro-traumatic moment, Goldman is able to deepen immeasurably the generational dialogue between himself and the young man. Neither person's set of strengths is ignored, neither is discredited, and both sets are plumbed for all the richness they can offer the other.

I would add to all this that often the members of both generations mistakenly share a problematic fantasy that there is a binary, zero-sum split between the two age groups. The child's life (or substitute psyche, worldview, or value set) cannot be good without casting aspersions on that of the parent, so that one person's goodness, rightness, or strength becomes the other's badness, wrongness, or weakness; one's aggrandizement becomes the other's belittlement. This goes both ways, with the child's goodness "ruining" the parent's as much as vice versa. Looking and listening for this kind of binary thinking is a standard feature of contemporary analytic work within the relational or interpersonalist traditions.

It complicates matters further that whichever generation we belong to, our positions in time and lineage may make us feel inadequate as part of it. If we're younger, we can feel unconsciously ashamed of the concomitants

of our youth, and if older, of the concomitants of being old. These dissociated negative feelings can leak out in seemingly minor attacks on the other.
Unchecked, micro-traumas reverberate interpsychically across the generations. Goldman's vignette and his psychosocial analysis of it illustrate how
the potential for intergenerational micro-traumatic relating is heightened in
subcultures where the new and progressive is prized at the expense of the
old and traditional. Under these circumstances, members of the younger
generation may by their very existence carry more cachet and seem more
worthy than their forerunners. The younger person has the opportunity for
greater exposure to "new and improved" ways of psychosocial functioning, while the older generation holds the fort (in part on the younger one's
behalf) using older modes. The valuation of youth in today's world brings to
mind for me Erich Fromm's (1947) work on a character type he called the
"marketing orientation," which he describes as "rooted in the experience of
oneself as a commodity and of one's value as exchange value" (p. 68). He
notes further that one can feel oneself to be simultaneously the seller *and* the
commodity being sold. No commodity is as hot as youth, and no seller as
automatically persuasive, in today's culture.

If the younger person internalizes these cultural attitudes reflexively, it can lead to an appearance of self-absorbed narcissism and self-
overvaluation. But I'd agree with Goldman that this would be an unfair
judgment and an incorrect understanding of the younger person's true
psychic situation. After all, society itself sets up this sort of self-regard
in our 20- and 30-year olds. The young are encouraged at every turn to
think of their youth as both defining themselves and as the thing they
have to "sell." The younger generation for its part shoulders a double
burden—anxiety over the expectation to be a new and improved self, and
shame at the lack of experiential knowledge (and the wisdom that could
accrue from it) that would substantiate one's supposedly elevated status.
They may therefore *need* the cachet associated with youth to compensate
for the burden.

So there may be a strong element of self-defense involved when the
younger generation trumpets its assumed superiority via micro-traumatic
mechanisms such as the sarcastic little murder. But whatever the reason
behind them—whether it's that little murder, or a devaluing "I know better" connoisseurship, or a spiteful, periodic cutting back from the family
circle—the young can very definitely be micro-traumatic to their elders.
These hurtful modes of relating may etch into the parents' sense of self in
somewhat the same way that, years ago, the parents' attitudes once etched
into their children's (and may still do). Some depressions in a middle-aged

parent's life may be triggered or exacerbated by an erosion in their self-esteem caused by their children's direct or covert attacks on them.

There is also the problem that our self is not a single, coherent entity but a multiplicity (Crastnopol, 2007; Mitchell, 1993). As a result, members of different generations may have different subjective impressions of any one family member. Thus, the flippant, moralistic, or sadistic undertones of a given individual's micro-traumatic relating are differently available to, or registered differently by, a grandchild, say, than by his or her adult parent. The parents' memories or reportage may airbrush, or more broadly, whitewash the grandparents' failings and weaknesses, leaving the child "mystified" (see Laing, [1961] 1971, p. 140) as to the sources of the family's conflicts. In part this happens because we are prone to seek consistency and also to split the other into being all good or all bad. Even the mature, healthy individual sometimes finds ambivalence challenging.

The child may thus at times have a different—perhaps even *clearer*—perception of their forebears' qualities than the parent can have. Registering this discrepancy can generate feelings of disloyalty and guilt within the child, in turn making the child feel bad. Of course, a "blackening" or besmirching of the memory of the deceased other may also occur. Each individual must come to terms with discrepancies between his or her own memory of a family member—especially the undesirable aspects—and the differing images others have of that same person.

Now, the picture of micro-traumatic influences across generations becomes infinitely more complex when we take into account, following Laplanche, that any one individual's psychic message to the other is partially unknowable and mysterious, or "enigmatic." As Hinton (2009, pp. 640–641) explains:

> Laplanche adopts the term "enigmatic signifier" from Lacan, but redefines it to mean the gestures, actions or words of the other—the enigmatic messages of the other . . . The presence of an enigmatic, destabilizing nucleus of experience provokes the development of an ego that seeks to 'bind' the over-stimulating inputs . . .
>
> Following Freud, Laplanche often employs a German word for the "other," *das Andere*, emphasizing the neutral article, the *"thing-ness"* that is inserted into the background of our experience (Laplanche 1999, p. 17). It is always already there in its otherness, "something that eludes phenomenal manifestation," and yet it is the opaque core around which our descriptions circulate (Critchley & Schürmann 2008, p. 135 ff.). Our ego, our thought and character, all emerge around it. The ego is

born to "manage" it (Caruth 2001, pp. 27–38). And yet we can never grasp it. It plagues us like an ongoing riddle, or as Lacan says, it is like finding a "hieroglyph in the desert" (Lacan 1977, p. 194). Our subjectivity and what we call "the unconscious" is indeed formed out of relation to this inevitable "otherness" (Laplanche 1999, pp. 84–116).

Hinton indicates that the enigmatic signifier points toward our own unconscious "otherness," which in itself is like a black hole, unknowable but yet capable of influencing all we are and all we do. In her work on the telescoping of generations, Faimberg (1988) shows us that the ghostly presence of a predecessor's unconscious life can prompt psychic disturbance in members of succeeding generations seemingly out of the blue as part of a hidden intergenerational legacy. Thus, when we try to sort out the origins of our parents' and grandparents' way of being, we are always to some degree working in the dark of their ungraspable otherness.

A Game that Helps Youngsters Stave off Micro-trauma

It's been a major premise of this book that in order to see a micro-traumatic moment coming down the pike and to learn eventually how to stave it off in good time, it helps to have rubrics or applicable categories that capture toxic maneuvers. A theoretical approach to this like the one I've taken here is suitable for adults, especially for those clinicians trained in the ways of psychoanalytic treatment—or so I hope! But how valuable it would be for children also to have some such tool, and one that fits their sensibility and interests. Along these lines, there is actually a rather ingenious board game called "The Land of Psymon," designed by Eric B. Vogel, Psy.D., to be used as part of a cognitive behavioral approach to working with troubled youngsters aged 8 through 14. A "Psymon," for those unfamiliar with this game, is a sort of either malevolent or benevolent psychological entity—a monster, though not the toothy, gnarled creature of the video game variety. The game operationalizes and distills a great deal of cognitive-psychological wisdom, making it a user-friendly learning tool about our own psychic functioning and the other's. The Creative Therapy Store (2010) website summarizes the game's structure this way:

Each of the 10 "bad" Psymon ("psychological monsters") represents a negative thinking pattern and common cognitive distortion. Players learn about their modes of attack and strategies for defending against them. The 6 "good" Psymon exhibit the positive cognitive-behavioral skills that defeat negative thinking habits. Players earn points by identifying the good and bad Psymon at work in the situations described on *Think* cards.

The game thus identifies certain types of hurtful characters one must be on the lookout for, whose ill-intent one must prepare to foil. These catchy figures include the inflator (who exaggerates bad things), extremist (who insists that if something isn't all good, it's all bad), predictor (who warns of the worst happening), negasaurus (who minimizes the value of others' good qualities), overgeneral (one who implies that everything will go badly), mind reader (who threatens that others think ill of oneself), blamer (who foists blame on others), labeler (who calls people insulting names based on their supposed weaknesses), emoticon (who implies one's momentary upset means his or her whole life is bad), and the ought-a-crat (who implies the person is faulty and must improve). The game materials note a particular "method of attack" each type has and offers protective attitudes appropriate for each mode. If, for example, the negasaurus attacks by trying to undercut the "good stuff" in the child, he or she can mount an inner defense by remembering that being in a bad mood causes us to forget our special good qualities, and we should therefore try to focus on our strengths.

Though necessarily oversimplified and formulaic, a game like this has the virtue of offering the child a way to apply articulated understandings of another's toxicity. It therefore helps the child mentalize how the "real" external object—or the internalized object now part of oneself—may undermine one's self-regard. The game's strategies for dealing with this in the context of one's inner relationship with oneself are essentially sound and draw usefully on the component skills of reflective functioning. A productive starting point for a child, this frame of reference could help slow down or avoid the potential for being drawn into a micro-traumatic exchange.

Witnessing Micro-trauma

It's comparatively easier to fend off injury if one comes equipped with insight or a cognitive strategy to protect oneself from psychic assault. If someone lacks that readiness, the first order of therapeutic business is to help the person build it. I'd like to backtrack a little to consider what inner capacity needs to exist for an individual to be able to establish a psychic position from which to catch one's own and the other's destructive tendencies.

Building on precursors in the trauma literature, Dana Amir (2012) speaks about the critical role of the "inner witness" in registering and working through traumatic experience. In her view, the witnessing capacity develops within the infant as a response to his or her helplessness in the face of the "primary violence" of the failures of a good-enough mother's ministrations. The child who develops such an inner witness is able to believe that he or she will be "seen" from the position of a benign "third" (presumably the parents' well-meaning, healthier sides). Amir elaborates:

> An optimal measure of helplessness will orient the child towards a concrete or imaginary third and will allow them to transcend the victim-like situation by adopting and internalizing the "function of the witness" configured by this third. The function of the witness may be seen as the experience of the "observer within the observed." It represents the freedom to transcend the limits posed by the body and the constraints of reality into the ability to create an inner narrative.
>
> (p. 885)

Clearly, the capacity to transcend an interaction and observe it from a certain distance only comes about gradually, and I would hesitate to put a developmental age on it. To some extent, one can see certain forms of dissociation, some of which emerge quite early, as a stop-gap measure in this direction. (I have in mind instances where the child can "see" him- or herself and the hurtful other as though from afar.) More generally, most children and parents develop various strategies for recovering from the inevitable hurts through what Tronick (2007) calls "interactive repair." It is evident, however, that when the mothering has not modulated or been able to modulate the level of emotional "violence" (in Amir's terms) that occurs, this leads to an excessive helplessness and an inability to "witness." Amir goes on to explicate the psychic functioning of the inner witness by building on Britton's (1998) idea that being part of the Oedipal triangular constellation teaches the child to observe him- or herself (presumably by identifying with the vantage point of the "other" parent in the "third" position) while at the same time "preserving" his or her own point of view:

> The function of the inner witness can actually be seen as a derivate of Britton's "third position," which concerns the specific capacity to cope with trauma and traumatization: The inner witness (which constitutes an inner function rather than an inner object) is not merely the

mechanism that enables the shift between the experiencing I and the reflective I, but the one in charge of the shift between the position of the victim and the position of the witness. In that sense, the inner witness is associated not only with the ability to observe oneself, but also with the ability to bear witness to what is observed, namely to validate one's subjective experience. In courtrooms, the witnesses are often those who tip the scales. Their testimony is what determines the sentence. Therefore, the absence of the inner witness means the absence of the sentencing or determining function, which either negates or confirms the subjective experience.

(p. 885)

So the child who is reasonably well-adjusted internally, and is "well enough" raised by "good-enough" parents, eventually develops the inner cognitive and emotional capacities to be able to perceive his or her distressed reaction to psychic assaults and to validate that reaction as meaningful. She or he also acquires the ability to identify the injury, if only generally, and the direction from which it came.

But what about the child who was not helped to develop an inner witnessing? What Amir's work suggests is that in the face of such a developmental lack, therapy can act as a corrective by fostering this self-observing and self-validating function in the adult patient, both in general and, I would add, vis-à-vis micro-trauma. To the degree that analysts become attuned to micro-traumatic functioning and its signs, they empower themselves to become witnesses to the disruption of their patients' adult development. They thereby enable their patients to follow suit on their own behalf. Insofar as the patient is deficient in having a self-witnessing capacity, he or she as a grown individual will need help to overcome the barrier of anxiety (or its reverse, stoicism) that raises the threshold too high for him or her to perceive hurts. He or she will need to be helped to identify what hurts and to discriminate shadings among attitudes or comments that do represent an attack on his or her self-worth from those that don't. And the person will need therapeutic support to take the necessary action to prevent its recurrence, by giving voice to his or her perceptions, and possibly by using his or her influence to evoke healthier, more considerate and respecting behavior in the other.

Facilitating Repair

In a close exploration of rupture and the capacity to catalyze repair, the psychoanalyst Robert Karen (2012) writes about the pull to engage the

other in one's psychically painful scenarios via projection, projective identification, and externalization. When these draw on an individual's early
trauma, they are what he calls "aggravated enactments," seemingly akin
to micro-traumatic relating, though Karen speaks of these generically
rather than as the specific, distinguishable patternings I've examined here.
Wherever they occur—in a marital relationship, in an intimate friendship,
between parent and child, or between analyst and patient—unwinding these
enactments requires the productive "implicit relational knowing" two people
can achieve with one another. (We saw this constructive influence begin to
evolve in the reparative last phase of the interactions between Bromberg and
Martha in the last chapter, and between Goldman and his young adult patient
earlier in the present one.) For this shift to occur, it is important that the individual affected by the hurtful encounter (or sometimes a third party outside but
privy to it) be able to hold onto him- or herself, to resist the pull of a poisonous
exchange, to maintain a position of greater maturity and groundedness from
which one can potentially woo the other into a more healthy psychic space as
well. Karen calls this wooing process "beckoning," defining it as "a process
of unconscious mutual regulation wherein one person is able to bring another
to a more enriched place by inhabiting it her- or himself." He explains further:

> The enriched place is one of integration. Integration implies less
> regression, less dissociation, a greater ease with contradictory aspects
> of self. But integration is never complete and is always in flux. Thus,
> growth and maturity depends on not just achieved integration but also
> on an attitude that seeks integration, particularly in relating; so that
> despite the pull of one's own psychology and the projections coming
> from others, one resists tendencies to split, to idealize or demonize,
> to live through victimization or grandiosity or behind the dissociative
> comfort of a particular self state or role. To retain one's integration in
> moments when one is seized by urgent feelings and pulled toward a
> transferentially defined self is to grow. But, it is not only to grow. It
> is also to have impact. Because it beckons the other to do the same.
>
> (pp. 301–302)

Individuals who can stay in or keep returning to a place of spacious, centered trust in themselves are likely to evoke in others the ability to become
emotionally healthier as well. An invitation is implicitly extended:

> "Come, be this larger self to whom I'm now speaking." That larger
> self can be understood in various ways: as a little more trusting, a little

more forgiving; a self that dwells more in the realm of attachment security; a self that is a bit better able to bear, manage, enjoy its own complexity, and welcome that of the other.

(p. 304)

This is what the good-enough parent does to stimulate the child's growth, and of course what the good-enough analyst or therapist does in the analytic relationship. The clinician in a sense entices the patient to inhabit a less defended self, to be willing to acknowledge micro-traumatic influence, and to take off the blindfold as to the lineaments of what happened.

Nudging oneself in the direction of being one's own "larger self" is in fact what we can each do for the other, at least hypothetically, when we find ourselves in any sort of micro-traumatic interaction. Beckoning reflects generosity toward oneself and the other, an invitation to work from an "authentic position of a reoriented self" (p. 313). But Karen takes pains to mention that this state of integration is rarely rock-solid. Rather, it is better thought of as a guiding light to which one returns when drawn away from it. He also acknowledges how difficult it is to retain such a centered position in the hothouse of everyday relating:

I suspect, however, that a great deal of beckoning gets lost or rejected and goes nowhere. In civilian life (except for the parenting of small children), there is not the kind of role-support the analyst has, the inherent power that goes with it, and certainly no equivalent of the analytic community lending fortitude and supporting creativity. Attachment relationships may open us to growth, but they also worsen our anxieties, sharpen our disappointments, reactivate our wounds. There's no hurt like family hurt, no hatred like family hatred, no enactments as ingrained as family enactments.

(pp. 324–325)

In the context of this book's views on micro-trauma, I can only second Karen's contention that damaging familial interactions are prone to being especially recurrent, habitual, and hard to avoid; the destructive enactments occurring within familial bounds are much more resistant to the healthful influence of beckoning than those occurring outside them. But where the micro-traumatic experience originates in one's own family, one at least gets repeated opportunities to be one's best self and to influence one's co-actors to do the same. To the degree that one achieves this, one has the opportunity to redo and redress micro-traumatic history, bearding the lion in his den. Armed with a therapeutic experience that highlights micro-traumatic functioning, one can go back to the original family of childhood or newly constituted family of one's adulthood and bring the therapeutic understanding along to reshape the family's micro-traumatic tendencies.

Karen's essay closes with a warming vignette about a father–son trip to Paris in which his 16-year-old son complains of his father being annoyingly repetitive. At first stung and inclined to be defensive, Karen manages to locate his "loved-loving (i.e., secure) self" and responds playfully that, no, his *son* was the repetitive one, given his "nonstop bitching" throughout their stay. The son, holding back a smile, comes back with "Yeah, well, I space out my shit more," which draws laughter from his father. Karen sees himself as having "beckoned" to his son in the playful counterattack about the son's griping. But it seems possible that Karen actually came across as giving "tit for tat," and that it was the son rather than the father who broke the accusatory tenor of the interchange, with the amusingly weak argument that at least he (the son) spaces out his complaints. Karen may not have been expecting the beckoning turnaround to come from the teenager, but perhaps it did. And who knows, maybe the son didn't really want to be in Paris with his father at all, but felt obliged to go along, thinking this would support his father's image of himself as a good provider. (I suspect this is often what plays in the minds of the adolescent traveling *en famille*.) Micro-traumatic pressures on one another are indeed very hard to tease apart, and little murders across the generational divide hard to fend off. It's cause for celebration when the hits or bruises are minor enough to be easily treated by a tension-breaking witticism, whoever does the honors.

But to summarize his contribution, Karen offers a salutary stance—a beckoning attitude—for the psychoanalytic clinician to adopt as he or she works to help the patient overcome the pull toward micro-traumatic functioning. Having been nourished by this stance, and perhaps modeling on it as well, the patient can learn how to embody that position too, and how to potentially evoke more mature functioning from his or her loved ones in turn.

Let's dwell a moment longer on the nature of generosity and its close cousin, "generativity," both being forces that can counter injurious relating. Erik Erikson's (1980) psychosocial model of development identifies generativity, the ability to nourish and foster growth in another, as the main characteristic of healthy functioning in the adult years. A poignant depiction of this capacity can be found in the novel, *The Housekeeper and the Professor* (Ogawa, 2009), in which an aging Japanese mathematical genius and his 10-year-old friend attend a ballgame together. The Asperger's-like professor suffers from severe memory impairment and emotional isolation, but his burgeoning tenderness toward the little boy and the chance to impart the vagaries of quantitative reasoning to him seem to arouse new life in the elderly man. At the game, the professor and the boy sit in seats 714 and 715, respectively. Babe Ruth's 1935 home run record was 714, the professor observes to his young companion, a score that was only topped in 1974 by Hank Aaron's 715. The professor goes on to explain the mathematical properties and specialness of this sequence. He then says that what matters at present for the two of them is that he himself is seated in the lower number and the boy is seated in the higher one. The professor deems this fitting, indicating that in his view, it's up to the younger generation to pick up and carry the torch for the older one. While this might sound like he's imposing a responsibility on the boy, the professor's words actually seem to confer a blessing on him. The boy is worthy to carry the torch, in the professor's eyes, and it's his to carry. The old man gently adds that this is how the world should be. I would second that sentiment—yes, this is just how the world should be. The older generation should encourage and bless the younger one—and in whatever way possible, the younger generation should bless the older one as well. Moreover, each of us should strive to do that for the other, to the best of our ability.

For every micro-traumatic moment that might occur between two individuals, there are multiple opportunities for therapeutic ones too. And if one's vision of what makes one worthy includes the capacity to prompt growth in the other, then this self-expectation will go a long way toward offsetting any potential harm done by one's emotional flaws and weaknesses. Those who see themselves clearly for what they are and at the same time trust in their own skills and gifts—however many or few these may be—will more readily honor the skills and gifts of others. This is a good basis for overcoming any inclination to inflict micro-traumatic damage on another, or for that matter, on oneself.

References

Amir, D. (2012). The inner witness. *International Journal of Psychoanalysis, 93,* 879–896.

Aron, L. (1996). *A meeting of minds: Mutuality in psychoanalysis.* Hillsdale, NJ:Analytic Press.

Austen, J. ([1815] 1971). *Emma.* London: Oxford University Press.

Baron-Cohen, S. (2003). *The essential difference: The truth about the male and female brain.* New York: Basic Books.

Bateson, G., Jackson, D. D., Haley, J., & Weakland, J. (1956). Towards a theory of schizophrenia. *Behavioral Science, 1,* 251–264.

Beebe, B. B., & Lachmann, F. M. (2014). *The origins of attachment: Infant research and adult treatment.* New York: Routledge.

Benedek, T. (1959). Parenthood as a developmental phase: A contribution to the libido theory. *Journal of the American Psychoanalytic Association, 7,* 389–417.

Benjamin, J. (1990). An outline of intersubjectivity: The development of recognition. *Psychoanalytic Psychology, 7*(Suppl.), 33–46.

Benjamin, J. (2004). Beyond doer and done to: An intersubjective view of thirdness. *Psychoanalytic Quarterly, 73,* 5–46.

Berne, E. (1964). *Games people play: The psychology of human relations.* New York: Grove Press.

Blos, P. (1967). The second individuation process of adolescence. *Psychoanalytic Study of the Child, 22,* 162–186.

Boulanger, G. (2007). *Wounded by reality: Understanding and treating adult onset trauma.* New York: Analytic Press.

Brandchaft, B., Doctors, S., & Sorter, D. (2010). *Toward an emancipatory psychoanalysis: Brandchaft's intersubjective vision.* New York: Routledge.

Britton, R. (1998). Subjectivity, objectivity and triangular space. In E. B. Spillius (Ed.), *Belief and imagination* (pp. 41–58). London: Routledge.

Bromberg, P. M. (1983). The mirror and the mask: On narcissism and psychoanalytic growth. *Contemporary Psychoanalysis, 19,* 359–387.

Bromberg, P. M. (1992). The difficult patient or the difficult dyad? Some basic issues. *Contemporary Psychoanalysis, 28,* 495–502.

Bromberg, P. M. (1994). "Speak! That I may see you": Some reflections on dissociation, reality, and psychoanalytic listening. *Psychoanalytic Dialogues*, *4*, 517–547.

Bromberg, P. M. (2006). *Awakening the dreamer: Clinical journeys*. Mahwah, NJ: Analytic Press.

Bromberg, P. M. (2011). *The shadow of the tsunami and the growth of the relational mind*. New York: Routledge.

Buechler, S. (2008). Shaming psychoanalytic candidates. *Psychoanalytic Inquiry*, *28*, 361–372.

Cain, S. (2012, March 20). The most unrecognizable airbrushing jobs in Hollywood history. [Web log comment]. Retrieved from www.stylecaster. com/unrecognizable-airbrushing-jobs-hollywood-demi-moore/.

Calef, V., & Weinshel, E. M. (1981). Some clinical consequences of introjection: Gaslighting. *Psychoanalytic Quarterly*, *50*, 44–66.

Cassidy, J., & Shaver, P. R. (Eds.) (1999). *Handbook of attachment: Theory, research, and clinical applications*. New York: Guilford Press.

Celenza, A. (2007). *Sexual boundary violations: Therapeutic, supervisory, and academic contexts*. Northvale, NJ: Jason Aronson.

Celenza, A. (2014). *Erotic revelations: Clinical applications and perverse scenarios*. New York: Routledge.

Celenza, A., & Gabbard, G. (2003). Analysts and sexual boundary violations. *Journal of the American Psychoanalytic Association*, *51*, 617–636.

Chaplan, R. (2013). How to help get stuck analyses unstuck. *Journal of the American Psychoanalytic Association*, *61*, 591–604.

Chess, S., & Thomas, A. (1987). *Know your child: An authoritative guide for today's parents*. New York: Basic Books.

Choderlos de Laclos, P. ([1782] 2008). *Les liaisons dangereuses* (Douglas Parmée, Trans.) Oxford: Oxford University Press.

Chodorow, N. (1978). *The reproduction of mothering: Psychoanalysis and the sociology of gender*. Berkeley, CA: University of California Press.

Christenson, C. V. (1971). *Kinsey: A biography*. Bloomington, IN: Indiana University Press.

Crastnopol, M. (1980). Separation-individuation in a woman's identity vis-à-vis mother. Unpublished dissertation.

Crastnopol, M. (1999). The analyst's professional self as a "third" influence on the dyad: When the analyst writes about the treatment. *Psychoanalytic Dialogues*, *9*, 445–470.

Crastnopol, M. (2007). The multiplicity of self-worth. *Contemporary Psychoanalysis*, *43*, 1–16.

Creative Therapy Store (2010). Psymon. Retrieved from www.creativetherapy store.com/Behavior/Psymon/W-435.

Davies, J. M., & Frawley, M. G. (1992). Dissociative processes and transference–countertransference paradigms in the psychoanalytically oriented treatment of adult survivors of childhood sexual abuse. *Psychoanalytic Dialogues*, *2*, 5–36.

Davies, J. M., & Frawley, M. G. (1994). *Treating the adult survivor of childhood sexual abuse: A psychoanalytic perspective*. New York: Basic Books.

Dimen, M. (2003). *Sexuality, intimacy, power*. Hillsdale, NJ: Analytic Press.

Dorpat, T. L. (1996). *Gaslighting, the double whammy, interrogation, and other methods of covert control in psychotherapy and analysis*. Northvale, NJ: Jason Aronson.

Downing, B. (2012). Umbrage. *The Atlantic*, July/August, p. 93.

Ehrlich, L. T. (2010). The analyst's ambivalence about continuing and deepening an analysis. *Journal of the American Psychoanalytic Association, 58*, 515–532.

Eigen, M. (1999). *Toxic nourishment*. London: Karnac.

Epstein, A. (2013, June 17). "This is just to say," Twitter, and Kenneth Koch's WCW parody [Web log comment]. Retrieved from http://newyorkschoolpoets. wordpress.com/2013/06/17/this-is-just-to-say-twitter-and-kenneth-kochs-wcw-parody/.

Epstein, L. (1999). The analyst's "bad analyst feelings": A counterpart to the process of resolving implosive defenses. *Contemporary Psychoanalysis, 35*, 311–325.

Erikson, E. H. (1956). The problem of ego identity. *Journal of the American Psychoanalytic Association, 4*, 56–121.

Erikson, E. H. (1980). On the generational cycle: An address. *International Journal of Psychoanalysis, 61*, 213–223.

Faimberg, H. (1988). The telescoping of generations: Genealogy of certain identifications. *Contemporary Psychoanalysis, 24*, 99–117

Fairbairn, W. R. D. (1952). *Psychoanalytic studies of the personality*. London: Tavistock Publications Limited.

Fallows, J. (2014). The sad and infuriating Mike Daisey case. *The Atlantic*. Retrieved from www.theatlantic.com/international/archive/2012/03/the-sad-and-infuriating-mike-daisey-case/254661/.

Feiffer, J. (1968). *Little murders*. New York: Samuel French, Inc.

Fiske, S. T. (2010). Envy up, scorn down: How comparison divides us. *American Psychologist, 43*, 17–36.

Fogel, G. I. (1995). Psychological-mindedness as a defense. *Journal of the American Psychoanalytic Association, 43*, 793–822.

Fraiberg, S., Adelson, E., & Shapiro, V. (1975). Ghosts in the nursery: A psychoanalytic approach to the problem of impaired infant–mother relationships. *Journal of the American Academy of Child Psychiatry, 14*, 387–422.

Frankel, J. (2002). Exploring Ferenczi's concept of identification with the aggressor: Its role in trauma, everyday life, and the therapeutic relationship. *Psychoanalytic Dialogues, 12*, 101–139.

Freud, S. (1909). Analysis of a phobia in a five-year-old boy. In J. Strachey (Ed. and Trans.), *The standard edition of the complete psychological works of Sigmund Freud* (Vol. 10, pp. 1–150). London: Hogarth Press.

Freud, S. (1917). Mourning and melancholia. In J. Strachey (Ed.), *The standard edition of the complete psychological works of Sigmund Freud* (Vol. 14, pp. 243–258). London: Hogarth Press.

Friedman, R. C. (1991). The depressed masochistic patient: Diagnosis and management considerations: A contemporary psychoanalytic perspective. *Journal of the American Academy of Psychoanalysis, 19*, 9–30.

Fromm, E. (1947). *Man for himself.* New York: Rinehart and Co.

Gabbard, G. (1996). *Love and hate in the analytic relationship.* Northvale, NJ: Jason Aronson.

Gabbard, G., & Lester, E. (1995). *Boundaries and boundary violations in psychoanalysis.* New York: Basic Books.

Gathorne-Hardy, J. (2000). *Sex, the measure of all things: A life of Alfred C. Kinsey.* Bloomington, IN: Indiana University Press.

Ghent, E. (1990). Masochism, submission, surrender: Masochism as a perversion of surrender. *Contemporary Psychoanalysis, 26,* 108–136.

Ginsburg, S. A., & Cohn, L. S. (2007). To coerce and be coerced. *Journal of the American Psychoanalytic Association, 55,* 55–79.

Goldberg, J. (2007). Refinding the good old object: Beyond the good analyst/bad parent. *Contemporary Psychoanalysis, 43,* 261–287.

Goldman, D. (2007). Faking it. *Contemporary Psychoanalysis, 43,* 17–36.

Goldman, D. (2010). As generations speak. *Psychoanalytic Psychology, 27,* 475–491.

Gopnik, A. (2011, January 3). Notes of a gastronome: Sweet revolution. *New Yorker,* pp. 48–57.

Gottman, J. (1994). *Why marriages succeed or fail . . . and how you can make yours last.* New York: Simon & Schuster.

Grand, S. (2002). *The reproduction of evil: A clinical and cultural perspective.* Hillsdale, NJ: Analytic Press.

Greenberg, J. (1991). *Oedipus and beyond: A clinical theory.* Cambridge, MA: Harvard University Press.

Guadagnino, L. (Director). (2009). *I am love* [Motion picture]. New York: Magnolia Pictures.

Heraclitus (*c.*500 BCE). Sacred texts: Heraclitus of Ephesus. Retrieved from http://sacred-texts.com/cla/app/app19.htm.

Herman, J. L. (1992). *Trauma and recovery: The aftermath of violence—from domestic abuse to political terror.* New York: Basic Books.

Hicks, D. (2011). *Dignity: The essential role it plays in resolving conflict.* New Haven: Yale University Press.

Hinton, L. (2009). The enigmatic signifier and the decentered subject. *Journal of Analytical Psychology, 54,* 637–657.

Hirsch, I. (2008). *Coasting in the countertransference: Conflicts of self interest between analyst and patient.* New York: Routledge.

Howell, E. F. (2005). *The dissociative mind.* Hillsdale, NJ: Analytic Press.

Hymer, S. M. (2004). The imprisoned self. *Psychoanalytic Review, 91,* 683–697.

Isherwood, C. (2009, March 11). Pratfalling through an eccentric childhood, the son of a clown. *New York Times.* Retrieved from www.nytimes.com/2009/03/11/theater/reviews/11humo.html.

Isherwood, C. (2012, March 18). Speaking less than truth to power. *New York Times.* Retrieved from www.nytimes.com/2012/03/19/theater/defending-this-american-life-and-its-mike-daisey-retraction.html.

James, C. (2013, June 2). Whither the hatchet job? *New York Times,* p. SR8.

Jones, D. F. (1995). Conceptions of diagnosis and character. In M. Lionells, J. Fiscalini, C. H. Mann, & D. B. Stern (Eds.), *Handbook of interpersonal psychoanalysis* (pp. 313–322). Hillsdale, NJ: Analytic Press.

Kahn, E. J. (1939, September 30). Creative Mearns. *The New Yorker*, p. 11.

Kantrowitz, J. L. (1993). Impasses in psychoanalysis: Overcoming resistance in situations of stalemate. *Journal of the American Psychoanalytic Association*, *41*, 1021–1050.

Kaplan, H. A. (1997). Moral outrage: Virtue as a defense. *Psychoanalytic Review*, *84*, 55–71.

Karen, R. (2012). Beckoning: The analyst's growth as a therapeutic agent. *Contemporary Psychoanalysis*, *48*, 301–328.

Kerr, J. (2014). Is there a self, and do we care? Reflections on Kohut and Sullivan. *Contemporary Psychoanalysis*, *50*, 627–658.

Khan, M. R. (1963). The concept of cumulative trauma. *Psychoanalytic Study of the Child*, *18*, 286–306.

Khan, M. R. (1964). Ego distortion, cumulative trauma, and the role of reconstruction in the analytic situation. *International Journal of Psychoanalysis*, *45*, 272–279.

Khan, M. R. (1966). Role of phobic and counterphobic mechanisms and separation anxiety in schizoid character formation. *International Journal of Psychoanalysis*, *47*, 306–312.

Khan, M. R. (1979). *Alienation in perversions*. New York: International Universities Press.

Klein, M. (1958). On the development of mental functioning. *International Journal of Psychoanalysis*, *39*, 84–90.

Klein, M. (1975). Envy and gratitude and other works 1946–1963. In M. R. Khan (Ed.), *The international psychoanalytic library* (Vol. 104, pp. 1–346). London: Hogarth Press and the Institute for Psychoanalysis.

Koch, K. (2005). *The collected poems of Kenneth Koch*. New York: Knopf.

Kohon, G. (1986). *The British school of psychoanalysis: The independent tradition*. New Haven: Yale University Press.

Kohut, H. (1971). *The analysis of the self*. New York: International Universities Press.

Kohut, H. (1972). Thoughts on narcissism and narcissistic rage. *Psychoanalytic Study of the Child*, *27*, 360–400.

Kohut, H. (1977). *The restoration of the self*. Madison, CT: International Universities Press.

Kohut, H., & Wolf, E. S. (1978). The disorders of the self and their treatment: An outline. *International Journal of Psychoanalysis*, *59*, 413–425.

Kris, E. (1956). The recovery of childhood memories in psychoanalysis. *Psychoanalytic Study of the Child*, *11*, 54–88.

Krystal, H. (1968). *Massive psychic trauma*. New York: International Universities Press.

Krystal, H. (1971). Trauma. In H. Krystal & W. G. Niederland (Eds.), *Psychic traumatization. Aftereffects in individuals and communities* (pp. 11–28). Boston: Little, Brown.

Krystal, H. (1985). Trauma and the stimulus barrier. *Psychoanalytic Inquiry, 5*, 131–161.

Krystal, H. (1991). Integration and self-healing in post-traumatic states: A two-year retrospective. *American Imago, 48*, 93–118.

Krystal, H. (1994). *Integration and self-healing: Affect, trauma, alexithymia.* Hillsdale, NJ: Analytic Press.

Krystal, H. (1997). Desomatization and the consequences of infantile psychic trauma. *Psychoanalytic Inquiry, 17*, 126–150.

Lachkar, J. (1992). *The narcissistic/borderline couple: A psychoanalytic perspective on marital treatment.* New York: Brunner/Mazel.

Laing, R. D. ([1961] 1971). *Self and others.* London: Pelican Books.

Laplanche, J., & Pontalis, J.-B. (1973). *The language of psychoanalysis.* New York: Norton.

Lax, R. F. (1975). Some comments on the narcissistic aspects of self-righteousness: Defensive and structural considerations. *International Journal of Psychoanalysis, 56*, 283–292.

Lerner, A. J., & Loewe, F. (1956). *My fair lady: A musical play in two acts.* New York: Doward-McCann, Inc.

Levenson, E. A. (1991). *The purloined self: Interpersonal perspectives in psychoanalysis.* New York: Contemporary Psychoanalysis Books.

Levenson, E. A. (2012). Psychoanalysis and the rite of refusal. *Psychoanalytic Dialogues, 22*, 2–6.

Levinas, E. (1998). *Otherwise than being: Or beyond essence.* Pittsburgh: Duquesne University Press.

Levy, S. T. (2004). Splendid isolation. *Journal of the American Psychoanalytic Association, 52*, 971–973.

Lionells, M. (1986). A reevaluation of hysterical relatedness. *Contemporary Psychoanalysis, 22*, 570–597.

Lionells, M. (1995). Hysteria. In M. Lionells, J. Fiscalini, C. H. Mann, & D. B. Stern (Eds.), *Handbook of interpersonal psychoanalysis* (pp. 491–515). Hillsdale, NJ: Analytic Press.

Little, M. I. (1985). Winnicott working in areas where psychotic anxieties predominate: A personal record. *Free Associations, 1*, 9–42.

Loewald, H. W. (1980). *Papers on psychoanalysis.* New Haven: Yale University Press.

McCord, D. T. W. (1955). *What cheer: An anthology of American and British humorous and witty verse.* New York: Modern Library.

McKechnie, J. L. (Ed.) (1983). *Webster's new universal unabridged dictionary* (2nd ed.). New York: Dorset and Baber.

McLaughlin, J. T. (1991). Clinical and theoretical aspects of enactment. *Journal of the American Psychoanalytic Association, 39*, 595–614.

McWilliams, N., & Lependorf, S. (1990). Narcissistic pathology of everyday life: The denial of remorse and gratitude. *Contemporary Psychoanalysis, 26*, 430–451.

Mahler, M., Pine, F., & Bergman, A. (1975). *The psychological birth of the human infant.* New York: Basic Books.

Masterson, J. (1976). *Psychotherapy of the borderline adult: A developmental approach*. New York: Brunner/Mazel.

Mesman, J., Van Ijzendoorn, M. H., & Bakermans-Kranenburg, J. (2009). The many faces of the still-face paradigm: A review. *Developmental Review, 29*, 120–162.

Mikulincer, M., & Shaver, P. R. (2012). An attachment perspective on psychopathology. *World Psychiatry, 11*, 1–15.

Miller, A. ([1949] 1998). *Death of a salesman*. New York: Penguin Books.

Miller, A. (1981). *The drama of the gifted child: How narcissistic parents form and deform the emotional lives of their talented children*. New York: Basic Books.

Miller, S. (2011). My father the clown: In a new solo work, a "circus kid" embraces his colorful past. *Encore: Seattle Repertory Theatre*, 11/12, pp. 6–7.

Minuchin, S. (1974). *Families and family therapy*. Cambridge, MA: Harvard University Press.

Mitchell, S. A. (1988). *Relational concepts in psychoanalysis: An integration*. Cambridge, MA: Harvard University Press.

Mitchell, S. A. (1993). *Hope and dread in psychoanalysis*. New York: Basic Books.

Mitchell, S. A. (2000). *Relationality: From attachment to intersubjectivity*. Hillsdale, NJ: Analytic Press.

Mitchell, S. A., & Aron, L. (Eds.) (1999). *Relational psychoanalysis: The emergence of a tradition*. Hillsdale, NJ: Analytic Press.

Morrison, N. K., & Severino, S. K. (1997). Moral values: Development and gender influences. *Journal of the American Academy of Psychoanalysis, 25*, 255–275.

Ogawa, Y. (2009). *The housekeeper and the professor* (S. Snyder, Trans.). New York: Picador.

Ogden, B. H., & Ogden, T. H. (2012). How the analyst thinks as clinician and as literary reader. *Psychoanalytic Perspectives, 9*, 243–273.

Ogden, T. H. (2006). Reading Loewald: Oedipus reconceived. *International Journal of Psychoanalysis, 87*, 651–666.

Ogden, T. H. (2010). Why read Fairbairn? *International Journal of Psychoanalysis, 91*, 101–118.

O'Shaughnessy, E. (1992). Enclaves and excursions. *International Journal of Psychoanalysis, 73*, 603-611.

Patchett, A. (2002). *Bel canto*. New York: Perennial (Harper Collins).

Phillips, A. (1988). *Winnicott*. Cambridge, MA: Harvard University Press.

Poland, W. S. (2009). Problems of collegial learning in psychoanalysis: Narcissism and curiosity. *International Journal of Psychoanalysis, 90*, 249–262.

Rich, S. (2008, August 4). Play nice. *The New Yorker*. Retrieved from www.newyorker.com/humor/2008/08/04/080804sh_shouts_rich.

Rosenthal, R. (2014). UC Riverside faculty page for Robert Rosenthal. Retrieved from www.psychology.ucr.edu/faculty/rosenthal/index.html.

Rosenthal, R., & Jacobson, L. (1968). *Pygmalion in the classroom*. New York: Holt, Rinehart & Winston. (Rev. ed. 1992. New York: Irvington.)

Roth, P. (2008). *Indignation*. New York: Vintage International.

Rucker, N. (1993). Cupid's misses: Relational vicissitudes in the analyses of single women. *Psychoanalytic Psychology, 10*, 377–391.

Rush, S. (2000). Gaslighting, the Double Whammy, Interrogation, and other Methods of Covert Control in Psychotherapy and Analysis: Theo L. Dorpat, Northvale, NJ/London: Aronson, 1996, 278 pp. [Book review]. *Psychoanalytic Quarterly*, *69*, 811–816.

Sampson, H. (1992). The role of "real" experience in psychopathology and treatment. *Psychoanalytic Dialogues*, *2*, 509–528.

Schafer, R. (1983). *The analytic attitude*. New York: Basic Books.

Schafer, R. (2006). Taking/including pleasure in the experienced self. *Psychoanalytic Psychology*, *23*, 609–618.

Schmalhausen, S. D. (1921). On our tainted ethics. *Psychoanalytic Review*, *8*, 382–406.

Secunda, V. (1990). *When you and your mother can't be friends: Resolving the most complicated relationship of your life*. New York: Delta Trade Paperbacks (Dell).

Semple, M. (2008). *This one is mine*. New York: Back Bay Books.

Shabad, P. (1993). Resentment, indignation, entitlement: The transformation of unconscious wish into need. *Psychoanalytic Dialogues*, *3*, 481–494.

Shakespeare, W. (1938). *The complete works of William Shakespeare*. New York: Oxford University Press.

Shaw, B. (1912). *Pygmalion* (D. H. Laurence, Ed.). London: Penguin.

Shengold, L. (1991). A variety of narcissistic pathology stemming from parental weakness. *Psychoanalytic Quarterly*, *60*, 86–92.

Sherby, L. B. (2007). Rediscovering Fairbairn. *Contemporary Psychoanalysis*, *43*, 185–203.

Shipstead, M. (2012). *Seating arrangements*. New York: Knopf.

Skolnick, N., & Scharff, D. (1998). *Fairbairn, then and now*. Hillsdale, NJ: Analytic Press.

Sommerfeld, J. (2005, February 13). Seattle (n)ice. *Seattle Times*. Retrieved from http://seattletimes.com/pacificnw/2005/0213/cover.html.

Stein, R. (1998). Two principles of functioning of the affects. *American Journal of Psychoanalysis*, *58*, 211–230.

Steiner, J. (2006). Seeing and being seen: Narcissistic pride and narcissistic humiliation. *International Journal of Psychoanalysis*, *87*, 939–951.

Stern, D. B. (1990). Courting surprise: Unbidden perceptions in clinical practice. *Contemporary Psychoanalysis*, *26*, 452–478.

Stern, D. B. (1997). *Unformulated experience: From dissociation to imagination in psychoanalysis*. Hillsdale, NJ: Analytic Press.

Stern, D. B. (2010). *Partners in thought: Working with unformulated experience, dissociation, and enactment*. New York: Routledge.

Stolorow, R. D. (2008). The contextuality and existentiality of emotional trauma. *Psychoanalytic Dialogues*, *18*, 113–123.

Stolorow, R. D., & Atwood, G. E. (1992). *Contexts of being: The intersubjective foundations of psychological life*. Hillsdale, NJ: Analytic Press.

Sue, D. W. (2010). *Microaggressions in everyday life: Race, gender, and sexual orientation*. Hoboken, NJ: John Wiley & Sons.

Sullivan, H. S. (1953). *The interpersonal theory of psychiatry*. New York: Norton.

Sullivan, H. S. (1954). *The psychiatric interview*. New York: Norton.

Sullivan, H. S. (1956). *Clinical studies in psychiatry*. New York: Norton.

Symington, N. (1983). The analyst's act of freedom as agent of therapeutic change. *International Review of Psychoanalysis, 10*, 283–291.

Taylor, G. J., & Bagby, R. M. (2013). Psychoanalysis and empirical research: An example of alexithymia. *Journal of the American Psychoanalytic Association, 61*, 99–133.

Thomas, A., & Chess, S. (1980). *The dynamics of psychological development*. New York: Brunner/Mazel.

Tronick, E. (2007). *The neurobehavioral and social-emotional development of infants and children*. New York: Norton.

Tronick, E., & Beeghley, M. (2011). Infants' meaning-making and the development of mental health problems. *American Psychologist, 66*, 107–119.

Tuch, R. H. (2008). Unraveling the riddle of exhibitionism: A lesson in the power tactics of perverse interpersonal relationships. *International Journal of Psychoanalysis, 89*, 143–160.

Tuch, R. H. (2011). Thinking outside the box: A metacognitive/theory of mind perspective on concrete thinking. *Journal of the American Psychoanalytic Association, 59*, 765–789.

Van der Hart, O., Nijenhuis, E., & Steele, K. (2006). *The haunted self: Structural dissociation and the treatment of chronic traumatization*. New York: Norton.

Van der Kolk, B. A. (1987). *Psychological trauma*. Washington, DC: American Psychiatric Press.

Van der Kolk, B. A., McFarlane, A. C., & Weisaeth, L. (Eds.) (1996). *Traumatic stress: The effects of overwhelming experience on mind, body, and society*. New York: Guilford Press.

Wachtel, P. L. (1980). Transference, schema, and assimilation: The relevance of Piaget to the psychoanalytic theory of transference. *The Annual of Psychoanalysis, 8*, 59–76.

Wachtel, P. L. (2014). *Cyclical psychodynamics and the contextual self: The inner world, the intimate world, and the world of culture and society*. London: Routledge.

Weiss, J., & Sampson, H. (1986). *The psychoanalytic process: Theory, clinical observations, and empirical research*. New York: Guilford.

Williams, W. C. (1968). *The selected poems of William Carlos Williams*. New York: New Directions.

Winnicott, D. W. (1965). *The maturational processes and the facilitating environment: Studies in the theory of emotional development*. London: Hogarth Press and the Institute of Psychoanalysis.

Wolf, E. S. (1995). Psychic trauma: A view from self psychology. *Canadian Journal of Psychoanalysis, 3*, 203–222.

Wolstein, B. (1987). Anxiety and the psychic center of the psychoanalytic self. *Contemporary Psychoanalysis, 23*, 631–658.

Woolf, V. (1927). The new dress. In S. M. Gilbert & S. Gubar (Eds.), *The Norton anthology of literature by women* (pp. 1364–1370). New York: Norton.

Zane, J. P. (2013, February 12). In pursuit of taste, en masse. *New York Times*, p. F1.

Index